Robin Pohl
Transboundary Cooperations in Rwanda

Culture and Social Practice

Robin Pohl (Dr. phil.), anthropologist, specialises on the practice of cooperation across social boundaries, and on doing field research in organisations and technical environments.

Robin Pohl

Transboundary Cooperations in Rwanda
Organisation Patterns of Companies, Projects,
and Foreign Aid Compared

[transcript]

Bibliographic information published by the Deutsche Nationalbibliothek
The Deutsche Nationalbibliothek lists this publication in the Deutsche Nationalbibliografie; detailed bibliographic data are available in the Internet at http://dnb.d-nb.de

© 2016 transcript Verlag, Bielefeld

All rights reserved. No part of this book may be reprinted or reproduced or utilized in any form or by any electronic, mechanical, or other means, now known or hereafter invented, including photocopying and recording, or in any information storage or retrieval system, without permission in writing from the publisher.

Cover layout: Kordula Röckenhaus, Bielefeld
Printed and bound in Great Britain by Marston Book Services Ltd, Oxfordshire
Print-ISBN 978-3-8376-3312-2
PDF-ISBN 978-3-8394-3312-6

Table of Contents

Foreword | 7

Thanks | 9

1. **Introduction | 11**

2. **Transboundary Cooperations in Sub-Saharan Africa | 19**
   2.1 The Context of European and Asian Actors | 21
   2.2 Comparing Foreign Aid and Private Business | 22
   2.3 Transboundary Cooperations – A Working Concept | 27
   2.4 Actors, Institutions and Organisations Toolbox | 34

3. **Processing Social and Cultural Heterogeneity | 39**
   3.1 Heterogeneity and Epistemology: Africa from a Western Viewpoint | 40
   3.2 The Substructures of Difference and Diversity | 50

4. **Field Studies in Companies, Agencies and Projects | 59**
   4.1 Project Experts and a Bilateral Development Agency | 59
   4.2 Brewery – Multinational Beverage Corporation | 71
   4.3 German Media Technology Contractors | 89
   4.4 Rwandan Construction Enterprise | 95
   4.5 German Catering and Hotel Enterprises | 103
   4.6 A Mixed Arena: Energy Crisis and Millennium Development Goals | 114
   4.7 Indian Traders | 130

5. **Analytical Framework: Three Aspects of Transboundary Cooperations | 147**
   5.1 Local Embeddedness | 148
   5.2 Institutionalisation vs. Technical Orientation | 158
   5.3 Management of Heterogeneity | 167

6. **Synthesis: Most Important Patterns and Types in the Field** | 177
    6.1 Institutionalisation and Local Embeddedness | 178
    6.2 Heterogeneity – Structural Inconsistencies in the Aid Sector | 182
    6.3 Four Types of Transboundary Cooperations | 188
    6.4 Different Kinds of Transboundary Capitalism in Africa | 193
    6.5 Comparing Development Aid and Private Business | 198

7. **Conclusion** | 203

8. **Appendix** | 213
    8.1 The Institutionalisation Test | 213
    8.2 Theories for Organisation Field Research | 216
    8.3 Fieldwork and Qualitative Methodology | 221

9. **References** | 229
    List of Abbreviations | 245
    List of Figures | 246
    List of Tables | 246

Foreword

The present study seeks to address the question of how cooperation between international actors and their local partners is conducted in the East African country of Rwanda. Since my first visit in the field I realised the unspoken relevance of this topic and attempted to understand the structures of collaboration and the exchange of ideas. One of the initial guesses was that the settings in which the involved individuals meet and work are playing a major role in the creation of mutual approximation. Following up on that idea I also wanted to know more about the structural differences between the worlds of development aid and private business. I was subsequently presented with opportunities to conduct more in-depth research. The focus lay above all on the organisational behaviour of cooperations between Rwandan, European and Indian protagonists. This account should, therefore, not be understood as a depiction of the country of Rwanda or the culture of its inhabitants. It rather is a study of different organisational patterns which are in use by transnational actors of small and large scale. The research builds on anthropological approaches to otherness and concepts from organisation sociology. The presentation has retained the character of an ethnographic field study in which the development of insight follows a set of transparent steps. The ostensibly immediate derivation of the analytical model from the empirical material was, for the most part, left unaltered. In this manner, the present manuscript fulfils the purpose of both depicting research results and illustrating the methods developed. Helpful analytical tools are explained and several approaches arise for practical use.

Thanks

This study is the outcome of a doctoral research at the University of Mainz. The present book is based on a thoroughly revised version of the original dissertation manuscript. For the completion of this project I am deeply indebted to many people, and first of all to the hosts and interview partners of my fieldwork. It lies in the nature of the matter that the individuals who shared their workplace and thoughts will remain unnamed for the sake of privacy. If any of you ever read this: thank you. Beyond the scope of research I am grateful to many people in Kigali and throughout the country where I found open doors and Rwandan hospitality. Quite some have shared their wit and wisdom with me and provided invaluable help or input. Unfortunately it is impossible to name them all. At the University of Mainz I am especially thankful to my former professor who supervised the original research and was an academic teacher for quite some years; and to the coordinator of the academic partnership between the Universities of Mainz and Butare for her scholarly guidance, and for directing me to Rwanda in the first instance. Research grants were gratefully received from Sulzmann Foundation and German Academic Exchange Service. Earlier versions of the manuscript were read by a friend of the family, a friend from studies and a competent lady from Canada. Without them there wouldn't be a book now. My greatest thanks go my wife, my parents and family for making all of this possible.

1. Introduction

This study examines cooperation structures of organisations and enterprises from Europe and South Asia with actors from East Africa, specifically Rwanda. At first I found the international presence in Rwanda to be astonishingly high for a country of such a small size. Like other African societies, it seemed to experience a high input of foreign activities customised to African environments, and of domestic ones tailored to interaction with external interests. In line with this observation, I aim to provide an in-depth comparison of some of the underlying organisational patterns that shape transnational cooperations between foreign and domestic actors in a dynamic but challenged East African social environment.

As an introduction to the topic, imagine a world in which there were no differences between African and European societies: some transnational actors would benefit from this situation, while others would certainly suffer. Some types of activity would almost become impossible, while others would just be different or hardly be affected at all. In other words, potential divisions on the global scale turn into assets or liabilities on the operative level of transnational cooperations, depending on their individual settings and paradigms.

I have taken a look at various types of organisations and some important forms of activity that sustain foreign-domestic cooperations in Rwanda. A first glance at the country calls to attention the massive challenges it is facing, as well as a number of distinctive potentials at its disposal. The domestic situation and the regional political development have been the focus of attention for quite some time, yet mostly for reasons other than research on organisation and cooperation structures. However, the present book is concerned with the question of which empirically observable elements play a role in the constitution of the implicit organisation patterns on top of which trans-continental actors enfold their businesses, projects and aid agencies. In Sub-Saharan Africa, several types of actors can be found where strikingly different models of how one's own activity relates to the local context are in place. Furthermore, these forms of interaction are rooted in implicit understandings of how the inherent transcontinental boundaries are to be perceived and crossed.

Three practical reasons demand the development of additional expertise in this field: First, civil society actors play an increasingly important role in African[1] globalisation while the diversity of their types and objectives seems to be largely unresearched. Second, the daily affairs of cooperations are usually managed through projects, companies, agencies, subsidiaries, NGOs or joint-ventures, thus through organisations of various kinds that are maintained according to the priorities of their stakeholders. And third, the actual in-depth knowledge of how much the structural settings of such international cooperations really matter is still inadequate, both on the side of foreigners and domestic actors. Most of the publicly available expertise in the field has been acquired within the foreign aid sector, which therefore assumes an important role as a starting point for further comparisons.

Taken together, these three points constitute a backdrop before which a fresh comparative approach to the activities of companies, foreign aid and projects seemed both mandatory and manageable. It is the goal of this book to lay the foundation for the assessment of transnational cooperation structures in the micro-environments of developing Rwanda. The reader may adapt these findings to other countries and circumstances, which certainly is useful. I strongly encourage the application in post-conflict, poorly developed and weakly institutionalised countries, or any other place with a high density of international orgnisations and a strong local dependency on external resources.

Cooperation substructures

Countries classified as 'least developed'[2] and 'post-conflict societies' form a special field of international cooperation. Transnational organisations or ventures, much to the same extent as the so called international community as a whole, often have a great impact and gain a high standing within these countries; institutional weaknesses and an undifferentiated openness of the socio-economic environment render the activities of foreign stakeholders both visible and influential. At the same time, this leaves foreign stakes comparatively vulnerable and exposed. Countries falling under this characterisation, as Rwanda does in several aspects, might benefit from the direct inflow of global expertise. That being said, they often serve as theatres in which transnational actors are able to pursue their own interests with less formal restraint than in industrialised countries.

---

1 In this book I speak about Sub-Saharan Africa when 'Africa' is used.
2 The term 'least developed country' (LDC) is used for countries that are scoring low according to the common development indicators.

For organisations that cross the boundaries of the social spaces between Europe (and Asia) and the developing parts of Africa, certain elements in their operative 'substructures' can be identified that demand a new empirical and theoretical approach. In the course of their operation, these trans-boundary activities frequently display elements of an organisational behaviour, which might go unnoticed at first, but in fact demands a closer look. What makes the subject so interesting is that these transnationally connecting organisations are partially driven by factors that cannot simply be explained by recourse to their tasks or goals, by the effects of globalisation or by any specific conditions in African environments. During the research process it was of interest to uncover some of the parameters that are fundamental to organisational practice in such circumstances. The issues under examination are almost entirely remote from the self-appraisal of the organisations involved and their members. Once consciously appraised, however, they appear to be self-evident.

The background idea

This study introduces for the first time an analytical framework that provides a language for the assessment of transnational activities in African civil societies. The idea was inspired by the notion of "transboundary formations" developed by Callaghy, Kassimir and Latham (2001). My study revealed that their concept is effective in its aim – assessing global-local networks of power in African environments of political crisis. However, it falls short in the face of formally legitimated transnational organisations and companies, which is the field I attempted to cover.

At this point it is necessary to undertake an important fine-tuning to the conceptual baseline of the book. In order to describe the common nature of the examined structures, I am going to speak of them as 'transboundary' cooperations, in place of 'transnational'. The major gain of this shift is that we can ask questions about the boundary itself, instead of taking for granted the common assumptions about its properties. For the East African, European and South Asian actors described below it turned out that they all had their particular ways of dealing with the divergences and separations in the field. Among this set of actor types each of them developed their very own, specific assurance of the boundaries they are crossing. These assurances are then enacted through the organisations themselves.

The present study is based on qualitative fieldwork conducted in various organisations and companies of different size, ranging from small to large scale. In line with the comparative nature of the analysis the focus is directed at the underlying patterns of collaboration rather than the actual content of the activities.

Combined these issues lead to questions:

- In what way are the objectives and purposes of foreign activities in African countries influenced by the fact they are taking place in Africa?
- How do different kinds of foreign activities in African countries tend to behave in terms of their organisational structure, goals and internal control? Can we compare different types of companies, foreign aid and projects?
- In what kinds of local settings do they operate?

Points of departure

There are two central concepts in this book. The first one is *Transboundary Co-operation*. For my purpose, the term refers to organisational forms of any kind that carry out activities of foreign actors in Rwanda in collaboration with local counterparts. It begins with the notion that European and Asian actors in Sub-Saharan Africa are intentionally crossing continental and social boundaries and are shaped by this circumstance (Chapter 2). The second central concept is the notion of *global and organisational heterogeneity*. Divergences within Transboundary Co-operations and between their protagonists become implicitly manifest on sociocultural, societal, mental and also strategic levels. They tend to become embodied in the organisation structure in the form of underlying differences and diversities. The ways in which a given organisation 'understands' the nature of globalisation, and of globalisation's heterogeneity, has a significant impact on the outcomes of its local affairs. Some types of transboundary activities take for granted the existence of marked differences between the participating social spaces, where others seek or imply a more universal communality in the cooperation. The epistemology and practice of transcontinental cooperation are deeply affected by these issues (Chapter 3).

Empirical approach and overview of case studies

The findings presented here are based on anthropological fieldwork. According to the focus on commonplace cooperations the research took place in formalised and legalised organisations that work for defined purposes. Furthermore, I compare European-Rwandan activities with the habits of traders from the Indian diaspora. The reason for this selection is the symbolical and historical importance of European actors for African globalisation and the high relevance of Indian migrant communities in Eastern Africa. Seven case studies were thus conducted in organisational settings where external actors either became inserted into local settings or created their own agenda within the domestic socio-economic environment.

Each case study, and thus each of the observed organisations, agencies or companies, represents a distinctive type of activity. These different types are subject to their own organisational self-concept and specific local interactions, corresponding to their particular modes of activity.

The field sites were mainly approached from the viewpoint of their transboundary character. As a multi-sited ethnography, the cases are treated individually, then subsequently combined into a concise picture of the field as a whole. We cast a first glance at the cases involved in the following:

- Case 1: *Project experts and a bilateral development agency.* A German agency as an example of a mid-sized project organisation with a focus on the local secondment of expatriate personnel. Development assistants, technical experts and local counterparts at their workplace and in cooperation projects.
- Case 2: *Multinational beverage corporation.* A local subsidiary of one of the world's large beer producers. Management and work relations are entirely characterised by a multinational enterprise setting. At the time of research, the organisational culture was undergoing a period of adjustment, as former relationships between domestic, social and cultural demands, as well as the strategies of the corporation were in a long-term process of rearrangement.
- Case 3: *German contractors for media systems.* Short term projects for the installation and implementation of technical equipment for Rwandan customers. The contractor's regular activities are predominantly situated in their own German markets, and there has therefore been no previous business contact with Rwanda or Africa.
- Case 4: *Rwandan construction enterprise.* In several ways a typical local company, but with a special client focus on European organisations and an outstanding ability to cater to foreign customers.
- Case 5: *German food and catering enterprises.* Operated by Germans who became residents in Rwanda. The owners follow their own standards but are nevertheless subject to the conditions of the local environment. In legal terms, they are normal Rwandan companies but in practice many aspects of transnational actors are relevant.
- Case 6: *A mixed arena: energy crisis and Millennium Development Goals.* A complex setting that involved various actors with different backgrounds and strategies. They were connected through their involvement in a Public Private Partnership (PPP) programme dealing with rural electrification and the situation of the Rwandan energy crisis from the years 2005 – 2006. This case study describes in detail (1) the donor agency that promotes a PPP programme, (2) a potential private small-scale investor consisting of a Rwandan-German group,

and (3) the public power and water utility under a foreign management contract in a privatisation framework.
- Case 7: *Indian traders*. South Asian entrepreneurs have a long history in East Africa and play a vital role in local trade. They are embedded in diaspora networks, and follow life strategies that encompass commercial activities to the same extent as individual and cultural affiliations. This case study highlights the situation of a successful trader.

Analytical framework

The seven case studies are presented one by one (Chapter 4), and then subsequently taken up for comparison. The analytical framework was derived from the ethnographic material itself. Three main aspects were found to be most relevant for explaining the structural patterns of Transboundary Cooperations:

(1) *Local embeddedness*. The depth and nature of the intersections between a transboundary organisation and the surrounding social environment. The extremes are to be wholly assimilated or locally disconnected.

(2) *Institutional vs. technical orientation*. Organisational objectives and their operative orientations can be derived either from the technical environment (task fulfilment, technical effectiveness, commercial gain) or from the institutional environment (seeking legitimation, compliance to institutional demands).

(3) *Management of heterogeneity*. Implicit concept of transboundary relations in structural and epistemic ways. Here, the extremes are a universalistic approach or an assumption of relativism that builds on bilateral differences between actors. (The analytical framework is dealt with in Chapter 5.)

In the final step a synthesis of parts reveals several conclusions (Chapter 6). The identified types of transboundary actors are summarised. Then, relationships between local embeddedness and institutional dependencies are demonstrated. A deep-seeded mismanagement of heterogeneity is highlighted that renders development aid less efficient than desired. Finally, the 'colourblind' and the ethnic form of transboundary capitalism are discussed.

Outcomes

The most important achievements of the study can be summarised as follows:

- An empirically founded concept of Transboundary Cooperations was developed.
- Several important types of transboundary actors were discovered and described.
- The 'processing' of social and cultural heterogeneity could be empirically observed in organisational contexts. It can further be related to epistemic foundations that are rooted in the organisational substructures.
- A terminology of transboundary activities from the viewpoint of organisations, actors and institutions could be created and applied.
- Insight into a variety of case studies spanning a wide area of activities.
- A deep comparison of development aid and private business from the viewpoint of their transoundary nature.
- Empirical differentiation between 'colourless' and 'ethnic' forms of capitalism.
- Contribution to the question of which type of Transboundary Cooperation generates favourable outcomes for its stakeholders and local society.
- The overall concept and the practical considerations described should be sufficiently independent of the Rwandan context to be applicable to similar environments as well.

2. Transboundary Cooperations in Sub-Saharan Africa

Besides the large players of the globalised age such as the multinational corporations and bodies of governance, many transnational cooperations are rather small and approaching something like a micro format. They appear as commonplace activities, do 'normal' things and yet are true acts of globalisation. This fieldwork aims to cover some of those commonplace activities and shed light on the underlying modus operandi in their daily operations. We regard small to medium cases situated in Rwanda, conducted by individuals and locally based organisations. Each of the activities described has a foreign origin with a local execution, relating to a globalised concept. In the following I will outline a research model that allows a structural assessment of such civil society enactments of transnational cooperation to be made.

As a point of departure, we are looking for basic factors of how and why certain transnational cooperations behave the way they do in their Rwandan settings, while vivid examples of differently behaving organisations exist in the same location. To meet these ends it becomes essential to understand African-European and African-Asian cooperations on a level deeper than usual. We have to go beyond the lines of country factors and local folklore, statistical trends or cultural management styles, even if such perceptions are quite regularly endorsed by international cooperation experts. Accordingly, for African observers the way to understand foreign cooperations might often times lead out of familiar appraisals of those expatriate organisations solely by the traits of their national origins (Germans typically do X while Indians usually want Y). Although I would not question the distinctive impact of a host country's situation on any transnational arrangement taking place in that country, and neither a distinctive influence of the foreign partner's home country, *the way a given Transboundary Cooperation corresponds with that local-global situation is noteworthy and type specific.*

The issue of Transboundary Cooperations

In order to get started conceptually, I strongly build on the notion of *potential* divergences among the actors involved. Such divergences may be based on social, structural, cultural or just geo-spatial possibilities for disjunctions of practical relevance. This potential for divergence should at best be understood in a neutral, even technical sense. Such boundaries are somehow, but frequently, apparent in the realm of cooperation between African and foreign actors. The type of activity bridging these divergences shall be called "interactions across the boundaries of social spaces", an expression borrowed from Latham (2001:71). The case studies in this book take place in settings where crossing the boundaries of social spaces plays an integral part in these activities, and where the purpose of the observed activities is *implicitly related to* the very act of boundary-crossing. Hence, the introduction of the key term *Transboundary Cooperation*. We will get to a working concept of what exactly a Transboundary Cooperation is in Chapter 2.3.

Search for organisational patterns and substructures

The basic understanding of how an organisation in a certain domain should be built and run can be seen as an expression of a world view. In a sense, organisation patterns act as representations of their inventor's assumptions about the structure of reality in the chosen field of activity (of what they would call reality, to be precise). By an organisation pattern, I would understand a general template according to which formal and informal organisations are likely to be set up in order to comply with certain priorities relevant in that domain. An official development aid agency will most likely have some organisational properties, regardless of its location. A family-owned trading enterprise anywhere in Africa might display certain organisational traits that can be found in many businesses of that kind, simply because it makes them viable; it makes them viable according to their owner's priorities set along personal expectations and boundaries.

All this is especially true for Transboundary Cooperations. Crossing boundaries always implies an *inherent definition* of the nature of that boundary. This study asks for the epistemological background of organisational priorities, and through this aims to uncover how the implicit understandings of transcontinental boundaries impact the observable organisation structures. World views on the nature of the relational quality of a Transboundary Cooperation are embedded in some of its organisational structures. Hence they are hardly visible, as they virtually form the basic level of operation. I therefore call them *substructures*. As transboundary actors evolve and operate in repeatable settings over time, certain substructures and organisational patterns can be observed. This shall be explained in Chapters 5 and 6.

2.1 THE CONTEXT OF EUROPEAN AND ASIAN ACTORS

There exists a long history of African protagonists corresponding with counterparts on a regional and transcontinental scale. As is widely regarded now, the continent has never been the closed-off native ground for which it has long been taken by European explorers. Many examples of outward-oriented ventures and interactions have had their place in African societies over the centuries (examples are the Swahili coast, cf Pearson 1998, or medieval contacts in the Mediterranean, cf Orrells et. al. 2011). While in some of these early contacts political will and forceful outreach were clearly involved, it can be assumed that others may be considered precursors of our contemporary transnational exchange. In part, these interactions may have been arranged along similar lines as some types of Transboundary Cooperations. The developments of previous epochs can be taken as a sign of the fact that exchange and the local action of foreigners are nothing exclusively new. Yet it is not the aim of this study to pursue those historical aspects; instead I shall focus on contemporary forms of local cooperation structures in which African, European and Asian actors meet, work and live. It should be taken into account that the global era and the spread of possibilities regarding how and where to cooperate have brought about a new quality and possibly also quantity of local-global interactions. The scope is, thus, set for old and new forms of transnational involvement that take place within the framework of civil society or similar non state-governed activities.

'North-South' and 'South-South' in transnational activities
In order to look into different kinds of cooperation, activities from Western protagonists are the compared with those of South Asian origin.

European-Rwandan: The notion of 'European' is employed as several case studies with protagonists from European countries were observed in Rwanda. Additionally, I would argue that European involvement in many African countries still has a symbolic relevance of its own due to the colonial past as well as present aspects of the dependency discourse, and should therefore be regarded cautiously against this background. Being European myself, I found this general type of cooperation both important to research and accessible.

Asian-Rwandan: The view on Asian actors serves the function of a comparative counterpart to European forms of cooperation. The major scope of this study still rests on cases of European origin. We will take a look at one exemplary candidate of Asian cooperation forms, namely the activity pattern of traders from the Indian diaspora. These individuals belong to migrant communities with a long history in Eastern Africa. Living dispersed across major cities of the region, these diaspora groups share the upholding of their cultural links to India and, through their commercial activities, exercise a considerable impact on national economies. Rwanda is a comparatively minor destination for Indian networks, which nevertheless maintain a characteristic and vital presence. Far from being a new phenomenon, these ethnic migrant networks lie at the foundation of the so called 'South-South' relations trend. As a counterpart to the 'North-South' relations they are of increasing interest as new ways of establishing interconnections between southern developing countries. In this respect, Chinese activities in Africa are generating a great deal of attention since the first decade of this century (on Chinese business networks in Africa: Bräutigam 2003, Broadman 2007, comparing Indian and Chinese activities, and van Dijk 2009, which is an edited volume that presents a broad overview. Media coverage: Lorenz/Thielke, 2007, Blenford 2007, Blume/Grill, 2008). 'Southern' protagonists, Indians and Chinese alike, follow their objectives with a different set of priorities than many Western actors. This becomes apparent in the higher importance ascribed to material and political interests in opposition to political and developmental discourses. Another difference is the tendency of commercial relations from Asia to frequently have roots in ethnic affiliation, migration and kin-based business links (Chapter 4.7 and 6).

2.2 COMPARING FOREIGN AID AND PRIVATE BUSINESS

This category of comparison is directed at the two principal forms of cooperation between African and Western actors. For many years it has been all but self-evident to the majority of observers that foreign activities other than political ones were to be directed at aid-giving, humanitarian involvement and charity, even more so when Europeans were involved. Usually there was no other kind of business to be expected for small or medium sized European organisations working in African countries. On the receiving end, Rwandan society as a whole as well as individual local protagonists have, in part, accustomed themselves to the inflow of aid in various forms, calculable or incalculable as it might have been (the above statement is based on the personal experience of the author, general reference in Chabal/Daloz 1999). Until recently, private business has been meagre and in parts almost non-existent in both Rwanda and the wider region.

The principal differences in the mode of operation between an enterprise and an aid agency are analytically easy to assert. However, in addition to their formal distinctions both cooperation forms also build on different sets of foundational assumptions and success factors. I consider it important to distinguish between the working patterns of foreign aid and private business as a contribution to the understanding of how different modes of cooperations lead to different conceptual substructures. Organisations are built on these substructures. And as previously mentioned, I suggest that an organisation can be regarded as a manifestation of a world view.

Foreign development aid: All foreign non-profit activities that take part in the practices and discourses of 'development', ranging from official bilateral budget aid to small agencies. The name 'foreign aid' can be used as well, as I did in the book title. However, for analytical purposes the term 'development aid' shall be applied here. It covers all sorts of related activities and is synonymous with other terms such as 'development assistance' or 'development cooperation'. Development aid, according to this terminology, is a set of formally organised long-term operations that are funded, and often initiated, by foreign agencies in donor countries. The international system of development aid is called the 'development sector'. What is not addressed here are humanitarian aid, crisis intervention and disaster relief, which are separated from the notion of 'development aid' for the purpose of this study.

Private business: Formally organised activities with the aim of generating private profits by means of entrepreneurship, investment, joint-ventures or any other legally registered form of commercial activity. It can be conducted by individuals, small enterprises or multinational corporations. Here, the definition applies to European, Indian or Rwandan owned and operated companies in Rwanda.

Excluded from the study are religious organisations, public and private churches,[3] as well as those activities that are often seen as 'notorious' forms of African transnationalism: international clientelism in politics (e.g. for France and Africa, Gregory 2000), arms and resources dealers[4] or the activities of military companies, as described by Shearer (1998).

---

3 The Catholic Church certainly is one of the most important transnational actors in Rwanda, and additionally one of the country's strongest economic powers. The Vatican itself is acting globally as it carries out its own diplomatic missions on behalf of its interests and clearly resembles a condition of successful local-transnational networking (Kallscheuer 2005:14). However, as indicated, the present study does not include religious organisations.

4 A typical example is shown in the documentary film "Darwin's Nightmare". Besides showing grotesque effects of local fish farming, it introduces the viewer to the world of clandestine arms dealers, cargo planes and shadowy aspects of African-European trade.

The omnipresent development discourse and a precarious private sector in Africa

As is the case in most African countries, the foreign aid sector is well established in Rwanda. The country is an important destination for many bilateral agencies, aid organisations, private foundations and private initiatives and equally for a greater proportion of the multilateral donor community, including the UN and the World Bank. Thus, a majority of those organisations that together form the global development sector are present. The country is a continuous recipient of official development assistance (ODA) and during the time of research foreign aid constituted approximately 50% of its national budgets (OECD 2006). Over extended periods it possessed an excellent reputation throughout the donor community. Despite doubts related to political and humanitarian issues, Rwanda's involvement in the Congo wars and forms of political authoritarianism, the country again enjoys a strong standing as an aid recipient that can demonstrate successes in the implementation of key developmental concepts such as good governance, decentralisation, female empowerment, and others (see also Chapter 2.4).

The development aid sector might be considered one of the most important transnational regimes on the continent, and consequently exercises a great influence on Rwandan society, including national policy making and local strategies.

Nevertheless, the country's steep restrengthening has led to an increase in publicly made rejections of the necessity and outright legitimation of the mainstream international development discourse by its political leaders. The Rwandan government questioned the legitimacy of external interference that is usually connected to aid disbursements. In this context, foreign aid is pejoratively labelled as 'charity', whereby its character is lamented as being asymmetrical and structurally non-constructive. Aid, understood like this, is set in opposition to the benefits of commercial investments. The Rwandan president was one of the first African country leaders to elaborate on this matter (THISDAY, October 5, 2007). These acts of self-confident proclamation seek to place the country among the ranks of emerging markets ready for profitable business while trying to weaken the image of a totally dependent, least developed and crisis-torn country.

Private business, as one of the main sectors of interest in this study, has long been a problematic and virtually non-existent topic in the African context. Abstracting from the Rwandan situation, the continent's unstable institutional environments combined with poor economic prospects made it widely unattractive for commercial actors from abroad, with exceptions in primary resources, certain areas of trading and special types of consulting and services. The continent has largely followed other modes of managing its economies over the past several decades. In many cases entrepreneurial success instead is attained through strategies of rent extraction and profits gained from the forceful exploitation of asymmetries. Africa's dependency proved to be a valuable resource for many of its own elites who are still able to extract large amounts of 'development rent' without being productive themselves. These practices were described by Bayart (1993, 2000) who used the term 'extraversion' for this type of transnational linkages. The idea was to turn oneself into a suitable junior partner of a global-scale power and extract as many benefits from this relationship as possible. This type of activity is not what I have in mind when speaking of civil society Transboundary Cooperations. For many decades, doing 'normal' business in Africa has, for domestic entrepreneurs, been a cumbersome but potentially very profitable venture, and for foreigners a topic bordering on the exotic.

Doing business in Rwanda is slowly becoming a possibility, as in Africa

However, this overly complicated situation has been subject to recent improvements. The initial, lasting effects of a profound change in the economic potential of several African countries have been measured repeatedly. The World Bank's report series on Global Economic Prospects (2014, 2011, 2009) documented a long-term trend according to which a rise in the GDP of a number of key economies and important sectors was observable since the first decade of the new century. Some caution is appropriate when applying these figures to the everyday life of populations, and thus to the practical conditions of most Transboundary Cooperations. As the AfricaFocus Bulletin (2011) put it, "growth in GDP is hardly an adequate measure of sustainable economic advance and even less of equitable human development. Nor does the growth trend extend to all countries. But, the World Bank report notes, the growth trend extends to quite a few countries".

The international press on economic affairs has identified Rwanda as one of the paragons of development in Sub-Saharan Africa and shifted its focus from coverage of the genocide to reports of the business-friendly environment (example: The Economist, Africa's Singapore? Feb 25th 2012). The new perception of the country in large parts is to be seen as an effect of the government's efforts to build up a new and positive image. However, it may as well be regarded as a true sign that some conditions are changing indeed. Reports from the World Bank and the International Finance Corporation on "Doing Business" in 2011 and 2012 indicated Rwanda to be of the countries with the greatest improvements in that domain.

First decade of the new millennium: emergence of a new private sector

Being in a practically undeveloped economy for many decades – in terms of international comparison – Rwandan business life had a difficult start after the war period of the 1990s. Governmental initiatives in favour of the private sector were rudimentary at first, and the local situation has largely been out of scope for most foreign observers. However, a small number of international enterprises were present in the country long before the war, next to the smaller but well-established branches of South-Asian business networks. During the first decade of the new century, individual investors from various countries were attracted by the unexplored market. Many of these early post-war ventures were merely extensions of regional trade networks or acts of local import business. Other, highly ambitious initiatives collided with the complex domestic conditions or unsuitable foreign partners. One of the more prestigious projects, which nearly ended in failure, was the implementation of large scale internet access and mobile network services by an American entrepreneur. The topographical complications of a mountain landscape were multiplied by factors related to the infant stage of the economy – its lack of skilled personnel, unclear regulations, high dependency on a few key players and the frequent power cuts. After several years, public pressure mounted, and the original investor sold his venture to a large corporation already operating similar networks in other African countries.[5] As these examples demonstrate, an undeveloped market is inevitably connected to an undeveloped work environment. Enabling civil institutions are hardly in place and technical means often times not available locally. Most of the enterprises, of both foreign and local origin, that worked successfully were thus comparatively small and isolated or backed by large but highly specialised corporations. The first real waves of international interest in conducting business with Rwanda were initiated through positive news and media incidents, such as the movie "Hotel Rwanda".[6] Such progress notwithstanding, Rwanda still had to be regarded as one of the frontiers of contemporary

---

5   Examples: Zachary/CNN Money.com, August 1, 2007; The New Times, April 26, 2008. A headline story on an American-Rwandan IT and telecom venture nearly turned failure: Schmundt (2006) and Nixon (2007).

6   As an example, in 2007 public awareness around the motion picture "Hotel Rwanda" initially supported the promotion of Rwandan interests. According to CNN, a considerable number of US American investors gained interest in the country after seeing it (Zachary, 2007). However, the film, along with competing historical interpretations, at a later stage led to inner-Rwandan political frictions which stopped its official endorsement by the government (The Nation, 28 March 2008).

capitalism. Experience with a liberal market economy has been gradual, as was the case during the time of research.

Over the years a number of larger foreign investments have been made, especially in the energy sector. It can be assumed that an increasing number of enterprises are developing the capability to move beyond the structural confinements that characterised the Rwandan economy for a long period of time. Such fundamental changes in the socio-economic field notwithstanding, the greater part of the formal business sector together with the related infrastructure are rather small while the majority of the population is still confronted with the same living conditions as before. It is therefore important to note that the transboundary business spheres discussed in this book are not directly touching the life world of many ordinary Rwandan citizens. Their influence is nevertheless to be regarded as high due to their role as socio-economical connection hubs.

2.3 TRANSBOUNDARY COOPERATIONS – A WORKING CONCEPT

Now that the regional and comparative aspects of the research subject have been introduced, it is time to focus on the research design. This chapter describes a working concept where the notions of 'boundary' and 'Transboundary Cooperation' are laid out. The *scope* of this working concept encompasses structural patterns of cooperation between Africa, Europe and Asia. It is centred on formally and legally legitimated acts of civil society in a broad sense: foreign and local actors in their explicit or implicit cooperation for the sake of maintaining their activities and making their business, agency or project work. The goal here was not to look at transnational or foreign interests with an immediate link to the catastrophic, violent or illegal, or to the exploitation of unjust benefits in problematic environments with which foreign affairs in Africa are so often associated.

Practical epistemology: When considering an encompassing yet ambiguous research subject, the need arises to gain a conceptual grasp on the empirical domain in a way that clarifies exactly what the research is concerned with. At the same time, it is decidedly useful that the concept leaves space for 'surprises' that empirical observation might reveal or an open interpretation of the data might offer. Such an approach has the potential to uncover something that previous accounts of this research domain may have overlooked. Organisation anthropology, as a research form, frequently takes this course, and is therefore different from a mere field test of preformulated hypotheses. I believe that this approach is sufficiently open to fresh input from grounded theory and fieldwork, and at the same time analytical, coherent and systematic.

At the beginning of this chapter, the starting point of Transboundary Cooperations as a research concept was paraphrased as 'activities across the boundaries of social spaces'. What is the nature of these boundaries that the actors involved have to cross? Interactions across which spaces? In a certain sense, the definition of these terms has to remain somewhat technical as long as we aim for an epistemologically clean and, at the same time, feasibly workable understanding of the matter. Therefore, here the blunt assumption of a blurred geographical-sociocultural distinction 'out in the field' serves as a starting point for an initial heuristic of 'the transboundary'. The sum of all distinctions between Africa and Europe, or Africa and South Asia, is great enough to justify the notion of a boundary-heuristic in itself. In other words, the common sense observations of social and cultural distinctions between these parts of the world is taken as a substantiation that boundaries exist and should be conceptualised. Such a distinction-as-heuristic is already the reason for the existence of many approaches to interculturalism and diversity management (which is not really wrong) but a real explanation of what it is that actually marks a social boundary in the globalised environment of organisations should delve deeper. The question thus remains: what makes a social boundary work as a boundary in transnational cooperations?

Awareness of two key factors is of crucial importance for the working concept. First, boundaries are at least partially socially constructed. Second, methodological openness is required in order to access the level of implicit world views and resulting organisational substructures. At this point social boundaries are gaining empirical relevance, and, as will be shown in the case study analysis, the most important discoveries about the organisational patterns of Transboundary Cooperations are to be found beneath the hum of their daily business.

Organisations across the boundaries of social spaces

I continue the elaboration of a transboundary concept with the basic notion of what I understand by 'boundary': the general assumption of 'something being simply different' between the social space of the continents. Let us regard this step as being safeguarded by the personal experiences of everyone who has spent time on the other continent (e.g. Europeans in Africa, Africans in Europe). Nevertheless, an illustrative heuristic does not yet constitute a real empirical category. It should not be taken as a fixed concept of what is to be divided and how.

The relevance emerges on the operative level of a concrete transnational organisation between external/foreign/European/Asian and local/domestic/Rwandan/African actors. The nature and relevance of the boundary between the social spaces of Africa, Europe and Asia is left open to empirical verification in each of the case studies. At this point, the heuristic does not yet tell us whether the distinctions are rooted in geographical-sociocultural backgrounds or simply in divergent interests. Note that we are not yet ready to take differences for granted, nor do we relativise them at this point. It is hard to grasp the boundary in a thorough manner without entering a constructivist-positivist dilemma; either we treat sociocultural differences as primordially given and definite and thus become unreflectively positivist, or we treat them as being open, as mere acts of social construction, and risk becoming pointless. I chose to make use of an integrative approach: an operational 'truth' of social boundaries most likely lies somewhere in the middle, at least for the purpose of this research. Chapter three will deal with the matters of difference and diversity in greater depth.

Global, trans- and 'glocal'

Acting locally is a central issue in the transnational organisations and companies I observed, although the actual execution depends on the organisational settings and structures which are not generalisable at this point.

It is a speciality of the anthropological approach to see things from the local viewpoint rather than from statistical or regional aggregations. Ethnography is a suitable means for assessing the empirical reality of transnational actors on their immediate ground of action as being embedded in the domestic setting. This is the *local*. But what ethnography does not always do easily by itself is generate the more abstract 'bigger pictures' of a regional or global scale. "The descriptive space of ethnographies itself has not seemed an appropriate context for working through conceptual problems of this larger order. The world of larger systems and events has thus often been seen as externally impinging on and bounding little worlds, but not as integral to them" (Marcus 1986:166).

A pragmatic methodological solution can be found in observing the ability of these transnational operations to act locally in a way that makes sense in a global perspective. To fit transnational and boundary spanning organisational activities, the *global* can become one size too big for fieldwork. And on the other hand, even multi-sited ethnography would ultimately deal with local entities. In fact, Transboundary Cooperations are global and local at the same time, a state for which Robertson (1998) has coined the term *glocalisation*. A simultaneity of spatial reference is inherent to this concept, as any global formation depends on local events for its very manifestation, and local events or places are essentially part of global contexts. What makes 'glocalisation' an interesting notion for this fieldwork is the manifestation of global affairs on the local level. The 'global' itself can be seen as a multi-contextual entanglement across the world. It emerges from the sum of its 'glocal' enactments, which become locally relevant.

Transboundary formations and Transboundary Cooperations

In order to arrive at a working concept of Transboundary Cooperations I have built upon previous research with a similar background. Investigating the complexities of transnational intervention in African arenas, Callaghy, Latham and Kassimir's (2001) work on transboundary formations has been a great inspiration for my own research on 'Transboundary Cooperations'. They edited a volume that, in my opinion, formed a true foundation for the analysis of global-local intersections in African contexts. In a variety of cases the book illustrates increasingly diverse types of transnational intervention, which have occurred within the context of contemporary African politics during the last decade of the 20th century. "[I]nternational interveners of all sorts, by their presence, are caught up in dynamic intersections involving international, national, and local forces. We have labelled these intersections 'transboundary formations' because they often have lasting and deep impact on the political and social terrain within which they operate. The problem is that we do not yet have a language to describe and analyze these formations" (Kassimir/Latham 2001:269).

These transboundary formations emerge in a considerable range of diversity.

"They link global, regional, national, and local forces through structures, networks, and discourses that have wide ranging impact, both benign and malign, on Africa, as well as on the international community itself. Above all, they play a major role in creating, transforming, and destroying forms of order and authority." (Latham/Kassimir/Callaghy 2001:5)

The authors attempt to explain the fundamental dynamics of international intervention, of what happens when the global interacts with the local, and how that interaction redefines concrete local formations of political, economic and social life.

"One starting point for thinking about structure is to focus on the ways in which intersecting fields of international, global, or transnational forces directly collide with seemingly concrete political and social life 'on the ground'. This life can include [...] the ethnic group, social movement, militia, political party, town, and village." (Latham 2001:69)

My own approach, as previously mentioned, adds civil society and formally legitimated types of organisations and companies.

What is 'transboundary'?

In the most common sense the term 'transboundary' usually expresses the fact that certain affairs concern actors from more than one nationality, origin or background. Policy issues such as cross-national disputes or regional natural resources management, for example, are referred to as 'transboundary' (Scheumann/Neubert 2006, Lowi 1993). The theoretical considerations and case studies in Callagy, Latham and Kassimir (2001) render it more precisely: transnational regimes in which economic and political formations that are fuelled by global affairs take hold, and subsequently weave themselves into the fabric of a local scenery. Overall, the general idea draws attention to the dynamics of transnational networks of power, organisations, and policies. It also provides indications for a research perspective that encompasses several levels of analysis at the same time and reaches beyond the scope of 'hybridity' (although the authors do not provide a clear cut local/global concept such as Robertson's glocalisation).

"Transboundary formations are a widespread phenomenon in the developing world. And while the range of forces associated with them is very broad, not all relationships across international, state, and local realms constitute transboundary formations. As we have defined them, transboundary relationships become formations when they produce and/or sustain forms of authority and order. Development aid, for example, can in one context be part of an effort to refashion socio-economic relations in a country (which otherwise could not occur without the aid program). In this case not only are international development experts likely to be deployed directly to one locale or another, but models and norms of development would be as well [...]. In other contexts, aid might simply flow to state coffers without directly changing the nature of authority and order in the 'targeted' country (however much it might be a resource exploited by existing elites to maintain power or a means of increasing donor influence in the receiving country). In the former instance we have a transboundary formation, while in the latter we do not." (Kassimir/Latham 2001:276)

While transboundary formations can principally emerge everywhere, they have a particular significance in Sub-Saharan Africa where the confinements that apply to formal order and state structures facilitate their emergence, making them particularly consequential. Applications of this concept can be found in the literature on the Central African political scene, describing political-military rebel factions (Vlassenroot/Raeymaekers 2005), or regional-global shadow networks (Taylor 2003). The reception of the idea of the 'transboundary' mostly evolves around political problems and crises (cf book review by Cannon 2005). Out of the group of original authors only Kassimir (2007) pursues this direction further, stressing the potential problems that transboundary formations bring with them.

I propose that transboundary processes in general are not necessarily harmful to the regions or settings in which they take place. Also, peaceful and constructive undertakings such as a legal private business exercise a form of local order and authority. When, for example, in the middle of the crisis-torn DRC some few commercial enterprises uphold a sphere of minimal structure and predictability by way of conducting business, this may be a new type of transboundary formation that operates differently from warlordism and exploitative politics. One such example is a Congolese brewery that belongs to the same multinational corporation which also operates the Rwandan brewery from my second case study (Frankfurter Rundschau, March 11, 2005). Similar but less dramatic are the structuring effects of international enterprises and organisations in Rwanda.

Conclusively, Callaghy, Latham and Kassimir's general concept can also be used for the purpose of observing comparatively well-ordered arenas on a smaller scale. What is easily forgotten between failing states, migrants, development rents and global capitalism is the assessment of small and medium sized African transboundary settings which quite often try to operate peacefully outside the headlines of IRIN.[7] Such situations can be found where actors link social spaces under globalised conditions and where they exercise social, political or economic order in local settings.

Working definition for empirical research

Aside from their individual objectives, for instance conducting business or running projects, organisations operating across the boundaries of social spaces are determined by characteristics that do not originate in their official purpose but rather in their implicit transboundary figuration.

In my understanding, the term 'transboundary' in the context of organisations and companies applies to the involvement of protagonists from different sociogeographical origins. Such activities generate 'glocal' formations, regardless of their actual size. In this sense the observed organisations where glocal actors, linking Rwandan and external/foreign frames of reference. They are called 'Transboundary Cooperations' here. This definition is aimed at activities from civil society, private business and development aid. Transboundary Cooperations have

---

7   IRIN (Integrated Regional Information Networks) provides news and analysis about Sub-Saharan Africa, the Middle East and parts of Asia for the humanitarian community. In crisis-torn regions it takes the role of a neutral news agency. It was founded as part of the UN and later became independent.

the ability to exercise forms of social order and authority in their spheres of activity, even when this occurs in a micro-environment. Glocality does not have a downward limitation of magnitude as long as the situations are marked by an entanglement of the local and the global. In contrast to transboundary formations in general, Transboundary Cooperations are characterised by clear-cut arrangements as well as more clearly defined actors, protagonists and stakeholders. In the context of this study, the main characteristics of Transboundary Cooperations are:

- *Purpose or objective:* Actors follow objectives or purposes that are related to a local Rwandan context. Affairs are conducted with an intention of durability, as is the case in a long-term development project or corporate subsidiary.
- *Glocal setting:* In the course of interaction, global or external issues intersect with local ones and generate a state of glocality. The TBC can be an independent entity or a local subsidiary of a transnational organisation. But a Rwandan enterprise that successfully connects with European discourses also embodies certain aspects of glocality.
- *Implicit or explicit cooperative element:* The notion of cooperation is a strictly formal one. I apply a rather abstract concept of 'cooperation' which does not imply a sense of affective togetherness. It does not necessarily entail a common vision, intercultural empathy or shared personal interests among all actors involved. From this perspective, interactions are cooperations when they are structured by patterns of mutually facilitating actor interests. Explicitly or implicitly the involved actors agree on terms of interaction on which they can build their own strategies. With this definition I follow Gambetta's concept: "'cooperation' is meant in the broad sense of agents, such as individuals, firms, and governments, agreeing on any set of rules – a 'contract' – which is then to be observed in the course of their interaction [...]. Agreements need not be the result of previous communication but can emerge implicitly in the course of interaction itself, and rules need not be written but can be established as a result of habit, previous successful experience, trial and error, and so on" (Gambetta 2000:213, Footnote 2). To sum up, in the above sense, a predictable, reliable way to interact can be called a cooperation.
- *Operational core:* Transboundary Cooperations tend towards durability, routine and formal structures, which together form an operational core. This is the centre from which activities are chiefly initiated or controlled and which disposes resources. For the most part, but not necessarily, this operational core rests within a formal organisation.
- *Definable actors and stakeholders:* In contrast to wider and more ambiguous transboundary 'formations', 'arenas' and 'networks' (see Kassimir 2001),

Transboundary Cooperations possess more precise regulations regarding who belongs to them. In most cases it is rather simple to determine the main actors (organisations and individuals) as well as the most important stakeholders. The glocal constellations around enterprises and agencies are often more straightforward than those of shadow networks or failing states.

To summarise, Transboundary Cooperations are 'glocal' formations which possess a formal operational core and have, as the term indicates, cooperative elements. The main actors and objectives are clearly definable. Now the question remains of how Transboundary Cooperations actually work, and what their orientations are in relation to their organisation schemes.

2.4 ACTORS, INSTITUTIONS AND ORGANISATIONS TOOLBOX

The technical roots of the current study, being directed at the search for organisational patterns and substructures, lie in organisation sociology. The focus was set on three major concepts from this field: *actors,* the active social agents; *institutions,* which provide guidelining frameworks for actors; and *organisations,* a form of corporate actor. In the following I introduce these three terms as they are used throughout this book. These basic concepts are subsequently broadened by incorporating aspects from three bodies of theory found in the field of organisation research: (1) *rational actors* and *New Institutional Economics*, (2) *Sociological Neo-Institutionalism*, and (3) *Actor-Centred Institutionalism*. For the sake of clarity and theoretical differentiation, the discussion is completed in appendix 8.2. In the following section, the aforementioned three basic terms are explained.

Actors
The term 'actor' encompasses individuals and aggregated social entities such as organisations, agencies and enterprises, which are referred to as 'corporate actors' (Gabriel 2004). For research purposes, individuals and organisations are conceptualised as actors in the form of social entities that follow their own interests. They are guided by their orientations and capabilities, but remain simultaneously subjected to the limits of their own perceptions and capabilities. In addition, they are facilitated and limited by their social environments (Scharpf 1997). The notion of 'actors' applied in this study is condensed, and concentrates on the concept's key element from a viewpoint of organisational analysis: 'how people get to do things'. Actors develop their preferences and perceptions under the influence of

institutional contexts, which shape their interests and define the possibilities and constrains of the social environment. A 'corporate actor' is an aggregation of individuals, while 'organisations' are a form of corporate actor.[8]

Institutions

Institutions are defined as the formal or informal 'rules of the game' that govern the behaviour of people and organisations, as well as social life in a more general sense. Organisations, along with individuals, are considered 'players in the game' (North 1990). Institutions thus become manifested as norms, laws, social rules, behavioural patterns and conventions. They are durable and embody characteristics of social order and regulation perceived as legitimate. On top of conventional legitimation, their existence is also accomplished by the threat of sanctions. Institutions enhance the predictability of social events, thereby enabling actors to make assumptions about the likelihood of each other's decisions and preferences. Institutions provide guidelines, and as a result contribute to the preservation of social contracts. While the majority of institutions are not embodied in material objects they nevertheless directly or implicitly fortify the order of social life. On the other hand, they act to confine the freedom of actors, making them dependent upon institutional legitimation. This is the controlling aspect of institutions. Activities that are negatively sanctioned may have to be abandoned. Behaviour not appropriate in a social situation due to institutional constraint is, thus, mostly refrained from, or only performed by actors willing to take the risk of punishment. Nevertheless, despite their authority and durability, institutions are not completely static and can be subjected to evolutionary and, with greater effort, intentional modifications (Mayntz/Scharpf 1995:45). Additional important characteristics of institutions are:

- Facilitation and constraint of actors in pursuit of their interests. They define juridical, political and symbolic resources, and point to legitimate interests.
- Frequently, institutions have a longer durability than the 'life situations' of individual actors. As a product of historical constellations at a given moment in time, they do not necessarily conform to social evolution, and may 'freeze'.

---

8   Not all sociological theories operate with a concept of "actors". The theoretical importance given to intended action, decision and independent will of social entities distinguishes actor centred approaches from others, i.e. systems theory or structuralism. Prominent in German social theory, Luhmann totally rejects the theoretical viability of actors and action, concentrating on autopoietic communicative events instead (1988:132, quoted after Scharpf 2000:96).

- They carry greater weight in the decision making process than individual inclinations. This makes it possible to form a collective decision out of contradictory and divergent individual preferences via a common frame of reference.

This working definition is based on references to Mayntz/Scharpf (1995), Scharpf (1997), North (1990) and Williamson (1985, 1990).

Rising incomes and/or expansions in formal economic activities increase the importance of formal institutions. Adverse effects occur when enabling and stabilising institutions are, on the whole, absent. In unstable environments capable people may find it more lucrative and viable to commit their efforts to strategies that exploit social power and asymmetry than to productive activities that depend on stable institutions (Auty 2003:11f). Rent-seeking practices, political entrepreneurship, corruption, exploitation of dependencies and similar occupations go hand in hand with weak institutional regimes and low degrees of formal legitimation in political elites. In terms of formal and legal aspects, Rwandan society and economy are marked by a comparatively low level of institutionalisation in the eyes of a Western observer. This should, to a great extent, be considered as one of the long term liabilities arising from the destruction of Rwandan society during events related to civil war and genocide in the first half of the 1990s. New, stabilising 'rules of the game' in the economy, politics and society as a whole are still weak, but their re-establishment forms an important part of post-war recovery. Over time, the prevailing high commercial and individual risks attributed to a 'low trust environment' may gradually decline. For example, institutional and civil volatility has been (visibly) reduced since Rwanda's introduction into the COMESA group of countries.

Organisations

While the research subject poses questions about transboundary issues and glocal relations, the immediate points of interest are situated inside localised organisations or their immediate surroundings. In order to come to a practicable understanding of what an organisation is in analytical terms, I follow Bea and Göbel (1999:3-7). They propose a set of three different possible perspectives on organisations, each with a distinctive focus:

- First: 'Organisation' can be considered an act, or a goal oriented execution of principles aimed at creating order.
- Second: An 'organisation' can be seen as a durable set of rules applied by corporate actors (enterprises etc.) to achieve goals and execute management.

- Third: An 'organisation' can be seen as a specific type of institution with certain characteristics. These include definitions of who is a member and what the defined rules of the game are (North 1990), setting the boundaries between organisation and environment or between members and non-members (Schreyögg 1996:10), which goals are to be achieved and how they are created (North 1990).

Here I principally endorse the third concept of organisations as a type of institution. Reasons for establishing and maintaining an organisation are numerous; their basic purpose, however, is typically to ensure that objectives are shared, and that assets are allocated in a controlled manner in order to reach certain goals. Bea/Göbel (1999:12) delineate these requirements by proposing that organisations have to manage several key issues:

- Composition, distribution and direction of tasks
- Distribution, legitimation and safeguarding of power
- Control, discipline, and motivation of organisation members
- Determination of the organisation's borders
- Facilitation and management of self-organisation
- Safeguarding of potential for future development

One important feature of organisations is their ability to operate and deal with environments and situations that are too insecure or unpredictable, and too complex or ambiguous for other types of actors. This capacity to manage complexity distinguishes organisations from other actors with lower degrees of aggregation (Williamson 1985, 1990). It makes them predestined for tasks where the likelihood of complications is high and where an active coordination of people and assets in turbulent environments is needed. Market structures, by contrast, are veritable and efficient optimisers, but they do not actively aggregate or coordinate. They are, therefore, ineffective in situations where complicated arrangements among involved parties must be reached.

Organisations are potentially inefficient, but often work in difficult situations

Often times, the inefficiencies and pathologies of organisations are lamented. These problems, however, can also be seen as indicators of the complexity of the tasks for which organisations are set up. This complexity is often much greater than what can efficiently be coordinated through market exchange. Yet, despite the relative effectiveness of organisations in situations with difficult transactions (compared to markets), they remain quite inefficient in absolute terms, and carry inherent high costs (Preisendörfer 2005:44, on "permanently failing organisations," Meyer/Zucker 1989).

The principle of formal-rational organisations as it is currently spreading over the world primarily emerged during colonial times as a culture-bound export model from Western societies. In some parts of the developing world and especially in Africa, formal-rational organisations still represent an embodiment of their Western origin. In this context, social scientists point to unfinished, hybrid or even malfunctional adaptations of the formal-rational principle in African contexts. Von Oppen and Rottenburg (1995) presented a volume of case studies dealing with a variety of organisational practice in Africa. Rottenburg (2002, 2009) points out that the apparent cultural neutrality and universality of formal organisations is part of a specific discourse that emerged in Western modernity. In this light the rational-formal principles of organisation can only be regarded as superficially 'context-free'.

However, the historical boundedness of formal-rational organisation to Western modernity should be no excuse for questioning the relevance of modern organisations in Africa. On the contrary, every attempt should be made to foster their efficiency. Hüsken (2004:322) correctly mentions that organisational practices should not be seen as exclusively belonging to the Western world or as being incompatible with social structures in developing countries. Such an opinion seems almost self-evident, while also pointing to the responsibility of rulers and managers in poor countries.

3. Processing Social and Cultural Heterogeneity

I have proposed an understanding of Transboundary Cooperations as 'activities across the boundaries of social spaces'. In the previous chapter the general meaning of social boundaries was explained, according to the heuristic way in which they are understood in this book. We left this consideration with the preliminary conclusion that boundaries do exist in a practical sense and that social entities or social spaces potentially diverge from one another. This perspective consequently implies the notion of *heterogeneity*, in the sense of social and cultural distinctiveness. Boundaries emerge between distinctive entities, where they mark and constitute this distinctiveness. In this regard it makes no difference whether two different observers describe the nature of these distinctions in a similar way or not, or whether the location and relevance of the boundaries are commonly acknowledged. As I have previously stated, the incipient notion of social spaces, boundaries and divergences in daily life long ago established many starting points for heterogeneity.

We have seen that it can be rewarding to enter the research with a heuristic of the 'transboundary', as long as it does not presuppose a premature interpretation of the nature of the differences themselves. The trick lies in allowing the meaning of the differences to be dictated by the output of fieldwork itself. This chapter is devoted to the development of a procedure that allows for this.

A social world of boundaries is inherently heterogeneous

We can say that the worldwide variations among people, societies, economies, and life in general, are important for the constitution of the domains in which Transboundary Cooperations work. Perhaps these variations will gain increasing importance in the future, as transcultural human differentiation enters additional areas of organisations and work environments. At the same time, it seems that the nature of these variations is being questioned more cautiously throughout society.

Is someone or something culturally different? What does that mean? Can't we work over there just like we work over here? Are these differences somewhat entrenched, deep-seated, or even incomprehensibly profound? Can we just leave our mutual otherness behind for a second? Does human variation contribute to innovation and positive results, or does it inhibit them? How do transboundary actors deal with the meaning of the social and cultural heterogeneity they encounter within their operations? Answers to these questions have been attempted many times before, and they are increasingly entering public discourses in the media (Eriksen 2006). The approach I attempt to enfold aims not so much at solving these issues as more at demonstrating how various types of Transboundary Cooperation have built their own working patterns on top of particular ways in which these issues can be regarded.

What we do in this chapter
In this chapter I will initially outline two distinct thoughts which will subsequently come together. At the beginning I will discuss how scientific epistemology can take different approaches to the study of cultural and social heterogeneity in general, and to African issues in particular. I then ask the same question in the context of transboundary actors and organisations: how do they take on global heterogeneity within their own settings? To make these insights workable for empirical research, I combine the two directions into an effective scheme that simultaneously deals with social and cultural heterogeneity on the epistemic and operative level.

3.1 Heterogeneity and Epistemology: Africa from a Western Viewpoint

The issue of heterogeneity is significant for Africa in its relations with the Western world. Historical excesses, political asymmetries, quests for equality and cultural esteem, or the new link to Asia, are just some ways in which this field can be circumscribed. Also, questions of development, the nature of progress, and ways to work and organise fall under this large umbrella. Closely connected to these is the topic of transcontinental cooperation. Items and ideas must be transferred across boundaries whose nature is far from clear. Many prolonged disputes populate discussions in this field. I dare to simplify them here for the sake of the ongoing argument as a situation of two extremes. If we follow this simplification for demonstrative purposes, it mainly depends on the observer to determine whether the social worlds on the African continent and the so called industrialised Western countries are to be perceived as basically being of a common fabric, thus a 'nearly the same' [first] ; or whether Africa has to be seen as possessing its own distinct social, historical, cultural and intellectual fabric where genuine explanations are needed, and the mere transfer of external ideas must fail [second]. There are good reasons for both these perspectives:

- [first] In the end we are speaking of a single humanity which is endowed with similar attributes all over the globe. From this point of view, why should there be principal distinctions between Africa and the Western industrialised world in organisational, socio-political and rational terms?
- [second] Even though humans are just humans all over the world, social life has its own distinctive sense and value everywhere. The excessive neglect of this simple fact has caused massive problems and human loss in Africa and elsewhere. Should Africa therefore be regarded as different from the West, as possessing its indigenous value sphere? Is allowing for the possibility of this position a humanistic and epistemic requirement for the sake of correctness, and even political fairness?

Beyond scientific reasoning, such thoughts arouse questions of cross-cultural respect, social evolution, value hierarchies and so forth. For that reason this topic also plays an important role in the discourse of African identity, philosophy, and politics (Sosoe 2006). The Nigerian author Soyinka (2006) argues that the dialogue between civilisations becomes an unequal practice as long as the African world is judged merely by seeing the mutilated and modernised remains of its former holistic autonomy instead of acknowledging its distinctive intellectual and cultural values.

Heterogeneity – a drawback for African development?

When observations of social and cultural heterogeneity are made in order to explain important issues within or across societies, the observers implicitly reify an underlying paradigm upon which the marks of distinction are built. Easterly/Levine (1997) and Ziltener (2006) state that high levels of heterogeneity within societies hinders development. In their report, Easterly and Levine stress the highly fractionated state of African societies, as this continent contains the world's most disparate countries. Ziltener analyses statistical data on developing countries and proposes that ethnic and linguistic divergences are negatively correlated with economic growth and life expectancy. In addition, indicators for effective governance throughout Asia and Africa were found to be affected by it. Heterogeneity in these contexts is perceived as the totality of ethnic, linguistic and religious divisions in a society (Ziltener 2006:296ff). Yet, Rwanda, as a very poor country with a history of ethnic hostilities and civil war, is among the African countries with the highest ethnic homogeneity according to these categories, despite the descriptive evidence of statistical data. It is characterised by a strong Christian religious majority, no significant religious fundamentalism, and is ultimately one of the African countries with the biggest population speaking a single native language. In fact, Kinyarwanda is the biggest Bantu mother tongue and one of the bigger African languages (Ntihabose 2003). The formerly violent ethnic distinction was not fragmented but expressly dualistic. These characteristics make Rwanda one of Africa's most homogeneous countries according to Easterly/Levine's and Ziltener's definition. Consequently, it must be noted that low scores on formal scales of differentiation are not necessarily reliable predictors of 'development', and explanations may also be found elsewhere.

Two perceptions of the unknown in social science

How can this matter be presented in a workable form for research on Transboundary Cooperations? Social and cultural heterogeneity is an essential factor in activities that cross social boundaries, although its relevance cannot simply be ascribed to the occurrence of 'otherness'. Speaking of the 'unknown other' in the humanities opens up a vast field of possible interpretations. How do we examine human expressions that are strange, or outright alien to us? What is an appropriate way to approach them scientifically? How do we do this on the operative level? In order to avoid a discussion of positivist/essentialist versus constructivist views, I endorse the elaborated criticisms of positivist culture theories, and the well-informed arguments against essentialist approaches to the social sciences, as presented by Chabal/Daloz (2006) and Hüsken (2006). I further endorse Hüsken's rejection of the opposite approach, namely a 'borderless' constructivism circling around infinite notions of cultural createdness, which leads to a volatility of meaning without grounding.[1]

In order to explain why it is important to have a close look at the concept of heterogeneity as it is applied by transboundary actors, I intend to illustrate a subtle but far reaching epistemic opposition. For the purpose of my approach, I distinguish two principal positions in the social sciences by the way in which they treat the 'unknown other'. This opposition becomes relevant in organisational anthropology, as well as in the hands-on work of transboundary actors themselves.

---

1   There is no possibility of entering into a discussion of this topic here. I follow the position of the above quoted authors.

(1) In the first position I refer to the social anthropologist Hüsken (2004, 2006), who laments a 'culture obsession' in the official rhetoric of the development aid sector. Culture, he explains, disguises the existence of solid conflicts of interests. A recourse to indigenous cultures often merely serves as a camouflage for strategic interests on the part of the recipients, and development experts. Gallon (1991) presents an illustrative case where an indigenous group acted out a fictive and romanticised cultural tradition in order to fit into a specific project design that made them eligible for foreign support. Comparable incidents still take place today. Hüsken maintains that intercultural negotiations are indeed more often affected by acts of rational choice than many culture scientists would prefer (2006:165f), even if this happens in the guise of cultural expression. The dominance of both overreaching positivist *and* constructivist cultural explanations is questioned, both of which are said to have remained naïve in the face of material interests. Hüsken's methodological project could be paraphrased as re-emancipating social science from the excesses of the cultural turn.[2] Culture is 'out there' and it does have its own influences, but it cannot explain everything, especially when hard facts are evoked by material interests. Or, as Trouillot has critically put it: "Culture now explains everything from political instability in Haiti to [...] the difficulties of New York's welfare recipients in the job market" (2002:37f).

Hüsken maintains that power, political governance, institutions of conflict management and formal or informal organisation are not only symbolic orders but also possess factual relevance. Hüsken attempts to explain social structures and political-economic agency as not derived simply from constructed meanings and symbolic evocations of culture. He introduces the idea of a 'sceptical social anthropology' which starts with the assumption that the productive handling of social heterogeneity confronts all societies with similar challenges. In this sense he advances the position of a pragmatic universalism, together with a normative commitment to democratically legitimated institutions, and a civil integration of different ideas and interests (Hüsken 2004:318ff). Critical social science is effective when it works with clear and generalisable categories of analysis and explication (ibid:323). This is what Hüsken seeks to (re-)establish with his recourse to the scientifically grounded universalism of general concepts and values. In fact, this position also provides the backdrop for important parts of the conceptual and theoretical background of my own research approach, which I have introduced throughout Chapter 2.

(2) In treating the social 'unknown', the second position starts with the notion that "universal models [...] continuously reproduce and discover their own assumptions in the exotic materials" (Gudeman 1986:34). This viewpoint is not

---

2   On the cultural turn in the social and cultural sciences, Bachmann-Medick (2007).

simply another effort in cultural relativism but rather the insight that the 'strange other' (in cultural or epistemic terms) cannot be understood in one's own terminology. When the 'strange other' is explained, that which is strange may get lost in the very process of explication. Explanation means translating the unknown into a form that is accessible through one's own cognitive map, scientific terminology or organisational processes. This act runs the risk of losing the 'otherness' during the approach of the heterogeneous. In this sense, Rottenburg (2006) identifies the epistemic challenge of translating inaccessible, alien strangeness into comprehensible, familiar strangeness without losing that which 'really makes the difference' between the distinct contexts. Seen from this angle, the goal is not to seek universally proven ways of basic truth behind the acts of the strange. Here, the goal is to preserve the potential of the inexplicable and unapproachable in the 'other' in order to save it from reductionist categorisation. Only through this process can real newness be discovered and other forms of existence be treated with profound respect. The potential of the *inexplicable* is a residual risk attached to the act of preserving the *other* in its otherness. Rottenburg argues that the gains from this act are indispensable elements for the science of anthropology and similar fields of research. On the level of transnational development practice, as the same author notes, hidden processes have become established which render invisible the deep contextual distinctions between the social spaces of the donor countries and the receivers of aid. As a result, the 'other' is valued, while simultaneously being treated as self-explicating by the donor. The pragmatism of a universal meta-code is thus established to stabilise the fiction of a common rationality (ibid. 2009, 2002, 2005).

To complete the picture of the 'strange other', however, the dark aspects of the relativist option must be acknowledged as well. When the experience of social otherness and mental distinctiveness among humans is guided by the notion of radical strangeness, this possibly opens up gates of separation, outright discrimination or even the denial of human mutuality. In extreme situations, perceived strangeness is a likely cause for the withdrawal of human commonality, for which the Central-African region bears a richness in contemporary examples. Ethnicity has gained a relevance far beyond cultural stimulation. 'Othering' can, and did, lead to a dehumanisation of the other, which has also led to the intellectual preparation of mass killings. For this reason, discussions pertaining to social difference are a delicate topic in contemporary Rwanda. The social structure in this country does not (yet? not yet again?) seem to allow explicit displays of social boundaries, because racial, political or direct economic separations threaten to erupt into new violence. Emerging from this, political discourse on the denial of 'divisionism' spans both reconciliation and coercion.

For the remainder of this section, I will first outline the relevance of keeping the potential for inexplicable strangeness alive. This becomes particularly relevant when interpreting sociocultural heterogeneity (position 2 above). Based on this step, the pragmatic need to overcome the separation between both epistemic positions (1 and 2) will lead me to a working concept, which can be used to assess the case studies with a dual view.[3]

Examining different kinds of Transboundary Cooperations, I wanted to find out on which of the two basic epistemic views they are oriented. This prospect can be turned into a *practical* question faced by them: how to apply universal procedures and (assumed) universal principles that constitute the field of rational organisation, when at the same time the notion of contextual differences becomes allowed?

Familiar strangeness and alien strangeness

Sociocultural strangeness occurs in many kinds of relations where heterogeneity is a characterising element (i.e. national or ethnic culture, worldviews, age, religion, gender, political orientations, income, taste, etc.). Heterogeneity becomes manifested in cultural, intellectual, and social otherness. The occurrence of such otherness leads to experiences of strangeness, which, considered formally, is the very cause of and reason for interpretative science. Hermeneutic sciences such as anthropology owe their existence to it. In all these approaches the concept of the 'strange' is not a property of social entities themselves but a relational matter, as is well known.

I open the next step of the discussion with a quote that quite directly demonstrates the tension my empirical approach seeks to bridge: "There are two broad approaches to the relevance of culture. The first considers that, however marked, cultural differences between societies are superficial and merely mask similarities between all human beings. The second asserts that such cleavages are so deep they put into question the very concept of 'human nature'" (Chabal/Daloz 2006:58). Heterogeneity, standing here for the sum of differences and cleavages, can thus be seen as an open term that signifies both deeper and more superficial incidents of social divergence. In their work on comparative politics, Chabal and Daloz highlight the importance of cultural meaning in the political sphere. They state that, for example, the very notions of political legitimacy and justice are distinctive between many societies, for which reason common comparative terminologies of political science may run the risk of losing their relevance (these authors gained their insights during comparative work in African and European societies).

---

3 Dualism in itself is not the solution to philosophy, but is, however, a workable foundation for an empirical tool-set.

Pointing in quite another direction, postmodern culture theory of industrial societies tends to build on freely floating notions of symbolic reflexivity, mediatisation and aesthetics, including the dynamics of popular culture and sub-cultures (e.g. Fornäs 1995, Hansen 2000). These approaches are highly sophisticated in analysing the current state of Western societies but share the tendency of levelling out certain modes of cultural differentiation that are perhaps not as free and negotiable, especially in relation to other parts of the world. Important in the context of social and cultural heterogeneity is the awareness that culture theories which are designed for the explanation of (post-)modern industrial societies are often highly specialised approaches. They may be too lenient on the 'otherness' of social relations in non-capitalist societies or cultures unrelated to postmodern media societies and the West. They might also not always adequately explain the great structural gaps between the 'home societies' where these theories come from and countries that are not, not yet, or not going to be formed or 'developed' in the Western sense of the word.

'Anthropology beyond culture?' is a question asked by Fox/King (2002) in their volume on the state of the art of the anthropological culture concept. They argue that anthropology can continue with or without a common concept of culture. This depends on the research questions being posed, and that when culture is retained no single definition is practically necessary or even feasible.

Together, these arguments point to the scientific necessity of leaving a possibility for the 'incomprehensively strange' and unfamiliar across cultures and societies that cannot be aligned with universalistic models (Rottenburg 2006). However, the price to pay for this epistemic sincerity is that the powerful tools of universalistic science and organisation do not work in such settings. In his effort to re-establish the epistemic possibility of treating the 'other' as 'strange' beyond explication, Rottenburg asks: "How can we talk comprehensively about something that is incomprehensible? How can we approach something radically different without at the same time subsuming that difference and thereby eliminating it?" (2006a:10).

Socio-cultural heterogeneity can be conceptualised as 'shallow' or 'deep', where the shallow is still explicable from the outside and at least partially open to a universal terminology, but the deep is not. Despite the availability of universal analytical concepts and the theoretical desire to leave no open epistemic spaces, the possibility for that which is 'definitely different' should be left open. Note: this allowance of 'realities' beyond the actor's own frame of reference is linked to the necessity for a deep hermeneutic approach and should not be confused with simple explanations of other people's lives in the terms of culture essentialism![4]

Trivialisation of heterogeneity

Rottenburg identifies a 'trivialisation of difference' in the arguments of constructivist theories even though his own work is based on that background. He states that overly constructivist models implicitly presume that most social and cultural divergences are the result of 'performative acts'. These can ultimately be regarded as avoidable and also as potentially malicious. While making cultural science much easier and probably more fun, the assumption that differences can be easily constructed and equally un-constructed has the unfortunate potential of seriously trivialising the implications of social and cultural distinctiveness.

From a bird's eye perspective, we have to state that the sophisticated constructivist-postmodern view regarding the nature of social and human distinctiveness has mainly taken into account the bridgeable and thereby harmless differences (implicit in multiculturalism and the hybridization of identities). In principle, this position partially excluded the possibility of unbridgeable, radical difference that allows for epistemological inaccessibility and thus for the unpredictable. Such a domestication of radical difference functions as an immunization strategy that protects one's own (universalistic?) claims from influences that might be too alien to be incorporated.[5] It is nevertheless a question central to interpretative reasoning whether it might be possible to translate inaccessible alien strangeness into comprehensible familiar strangeness without losing the 'real' difference in the process.

---

[4] Unfortunately it is beyond the scope of this text to go into the foundations of hermeneutics and the philosophical backgrounds of alterity and difference. Further reviews and critical remarks in Rottenburg (2006).

[5] The notion of multiculturalism has come under severe criticism throughout the years. As Eriksen (2006) demonstrates, the perceptions and moral predispositions of European societies towards immigrants from Muslim countries have changed. The peaceful integration of cultures in Western societies is increasingly perceived as having failed and, conclusively, becoming even undesirable (this also becomes a driver of election campaigns). It has become apparent that multiculturalism based on postmodern culture optimism is not a viable basis in scientific analysis and perhaps neither a practical solution in politics and society. Nevertheless, I strongly and vehemently propose the philosophical and ethical values of multiculturalism as an abstract ideal of human civilisation. Despite all the practical and theoretical complexity attached to heterogeneity: who can seriously hope for the best in globalisation and at the same time demand the multicultural idea to be abandoned?

The solution to this issue is most likely not a theoretical one, but one found in individual pragmatism.

Strangeness in familiar and alien terms

We see that the notion of cultural strangeness is blurred between the two possible forms of (1) familiar strangeness, and (2) alien (or radical) strangeness (Rottenburg 2006). In this sense it is unlikely that it will be possible to thoroughly approach the absolutely strange, or strictly heterogeneous, not to mention comprehending something totally alien. On the other hand, it also becomes clear that if we can only speak of that which is strange in our own terminology, its strangeness will probably become lost in this process (Rottenburg 2006:27).[6] Even when the notion of a fundamental human unity is not questioned, it is a worthwhile aim to preserve the possibility of the 'alien' in perceptions of sociocultural heterogeneity. Efforts may then be devoted to gradual approximations of an understanding of the strange subject in its own terms (which is basically a hermeneutic approach). *Radically different social events or entities cannot be expressed logically within the observer's own framework, and thus they cannot easily become part of predicative procedures*. This is particularly problematic when the events involve formal organisations. To make them manageable they must not be radically different, otherwise they pose a challenge of alienity to the observer (and even more so to the practitioner!). "Wittgenstein expressed this point well: 'Unless you can show that a puzzle is not a puzzle you are left with what really puzzles: a puzzle is something with no solution' [Wittgenstein 1988:348]. If Wittgenstein is correct here then we must continue to insist on the possibility of alienity" (Rottenburg 2006:30).

An abated version of this issue takes place in the form of 'shallow differences', which are encounters of 'familiar strangeness' as a variety of one's own frame of reference. Such familiar strangeness can be seen as an accessible variety of oneself.[7] Familiar strangeness is bridgeable and actors are able to make sense of the heterogeneous experience. They can find satisfying ways of explaining it in their terminology and with their logic. An example of bridgeable sociocultural divergences are the "cross-cutting cleavages" in democratic societies. Rae/Taylor

---

6 The Africanist Jungraithmayr elaborates on the 'unresearchable' and opts for the possibility of alienity: "Would it not be a pretension to expect that one could lift the veil on all the complex processes of language? Following Goethe's advice, one should do one's research in a mood of consideration and respect. Humans and things – here languages – possess their very own inner self which we should not violate. Rather, one should stand before it and honour the untouchable other." (Jungraithmayr 2002:12-13, own translation)

7 Rottenburg calls this 'alterity' (2006:28).

(1970) asked the question of why and how pluralist democracies, consisting of opposed parties, contrary ideals and competing policies can exist and prosper peacefully without slumping into permanent civil war. They found that prevailing cross-cutting cleavages and social factions are a trademark of successful democracies. Generally, most individuals in these societies are involved in clusters of overlapping and uncoordinated commonalities and disparities, which together make up multiple societal subdivisions. No single cleavage can dominate the whole society, and this empirical fact explains the stability of democratic pluralism. It is nevertheless vital for such democratic societies to safeguard their pluralistic arrangements and protect themselves. This task demands sophisticated self-observation and sound ethical foundations together with a minimum of political predictability. What is important is that although they are open to internal criticism, such pluralistic arrangements are not made to allow for the unknown. Allowing for alien strangeness in both its evil and harmless forms relies on a different principle.

Pluralistic societies and similar modern arrangements of higher complexity are open to foreign influences, yet their readiness to incorporate outer influences that go beyond their own frame of reference is naturally limited. At this point, some of the basic criticism is rooted that comes from parts of the world that are not included in the aforementioned model of modern societies. The discourse on African identity has one of its origins here too.[8]

"The fact that collective identities are always plural social constructions that are hybrid, relational, and situationally fluctuating does not exclude the possibility of alienity. Trying to take into account radical strangeness does not necessarily imply naïve realism or some other form of essentialism. Rather the opposite is the case: Only those who believe that they possess a universally valid explanatory schema will regard everything that eludes that schema not merely as irreconcilably strange, but as something that cannot even exist. From this perspective, there can only be [...] familiar strangeness [...], but not alienity (radical strangeness). [And, in the context of interpretative and, more importantly, normative questions, R.P.], could it be that the methodological abolition of alienity is ultimately the most arrogant position we could take toward strange cultures or life-forms? [...] Does it implicitly assert our own familiar image of the world as the only one possible?" (Rottenburg 2006:30-31)

Some Rwandan criticism on European behaviour, which I encountered during my fieldwork, settled on this issue. A frequently expressed source of annoyance arose

---

8   Here I don't discuss to what extent the claims of actors from non-pluralistic/democratic societies should be acknowledged by actors from pluralistic democracies.

from the impression that (Western) foreigners made when they were seen as neglecting the possibility of different worldviews. When snappy foreigners after an initial period of adaptation to the local context are shifting their own perception from a mental state of radical strangeness to one of familiar strangeness in the midst of action, their local conversation partners do not necessarily follow. Appearances of arrogant expatriates with an apparent master plan to save Africa are common. Often times, African settings are judged in terms of familiar strangeness after the initial impacts of radical strangeness have been digested.

A Friendly joke from a Rwandan while introducing an anthropologist to another German: *"Here you have another Rwanda expert."* Anthropologist: *"Rwanda expert?"* Rwandan (laughing): *"Yeah, all the Germans who have been here turn themselves into Rwanda experts immediately afterwards. Suddenly they know everything and have the best ideas how to solve things here. You know, we get angry often, and so we make our jokes about it."*

These nuisances, however, can also be turned upside down. The propagated self-advertisement of Rwanda as an 'investment hub' connects rhetorically with Western notions and terms of economic institutions. The presentation of local conditions takes a form that has an active potential of obscuring the African background behind the phrases. In speeches, presentations and brochures, which introduce the country to potential investors in a lively way, a neutral language is employed devoid of situational specifics which might make the Rwandan market appear deviant from Western expectations. Thus, Rwanda's self-presentation as an investment hub attempts to evoke the notion of familiarity rather than of strangeness.[9]

3.2 THE SUBSTRUCTURES OF DIFFERENCE AND DIVERSITY

As has become apparent throughout the course of this chapter, social and cultural heterogeneity can either be seen as accessible to scientific analysis and terminology, leading to universalistic approaches (as exemplified by Hüsken's sceptical social anthropology). Or, it can be conceived that sociocultural divergences are potentially so profound that any real representation of the 'other' in one's own terminology (including science) inevitably reduces the specific identity of that

---

9   More information on Rwanda as an investment destination at www.rwandainvest.com. Besides the comment on the applied rhetoric: the existence of investment opportunities is definitely unquestioned.

which is strange (here Rottenburg's valuation of 'difference' finds its starting point). The question remains of how to make the concept of heterogeneity useful in practice when dealing with the field of organisation research. Here I chose a way which starts with a translation of the theoretical gains from the notion of heterogeneity and strangeness into a simpler and more accessible form.

To begin with, I transform the distinction of radical versus familiar strangeness into a more pragmatic separation between 'deep' and 'shallow' differences. Then, concerning the relationships between social entities in Transboundary Cooperations, my working concept introduces the opposition between *difference* (approx. deep differences and radical strangeness) and *diversity* (approx. shallow differences and familiar strangeness). Here I follow Eriksen (2006), who explained intercultural and political tensions between contemporary Western society and oriental immigrants in the terminology of difference versus diversity. Central to his idea is the contrast of these two terms as the appearance of two fundamentally distinctive ways of identifying and dealing with social and cultural heterogeneity. "This seeming contradiction indicates that cultural difference is not just one thing. [...] A non-technical but potentially useful distinction could be made between 'shallow' and 'deep' cultural differences" (Eriksen 2006:15). For the reminer of this text these terms shall be understood as follows.

Diversity refers to the shallow distinctions that characterise plural societies, and provide the basis of productive and stimulating intercultural relations. Most prominently, the idea of multiculturalism as a state where all cultures and human backgrounds live together without disturbing the common goal of peacefulness and respect is also subsumed under this point. In the appearance of diversity, cultural aspects are conceptualised as socially constructed and of more of an aesthetic nature connected to heritage, customs and identity creation. Diversity thus refers to acceptable distinctions that are politically and morally neutral. Example: political governance systems are easily accepted internationally when they subscribe to general understandings such as, for instance, human rights. On top of this basis, colourful cultural variation is often welcomed rather than condemned. To achieve this state of cohesion, diversity and its management depend on a shared and accountable foundation. When this foundation is in place it disappears from sight and silently works as a communicative substructure. In this sense the concept of 'diversity management' implies that the covered variations are still manageable and that they are all part of a common ground. "Diversity is [...] largely associated with phenomena such as rituals, food, folktales, arts and crafts, as well as a few traditional economic adaptations which are either threatened by modernity or proven to be consistent with it (and should, by that token, be given a chance). The social organisation of society, including its political structure and voting rights, human rights, its kinship structure and rules of inheritance, its gender roles and educational system, its labour market and its health service are kept separate from the notion of 'creative diversity'... [or should one, R.P.] regard child marriages, political despotism or religious intolerance as expressions of creative forms of diversity [?]" (Eriksen 2006:14). In operative terms, heterogeneous settings covered by diversity are not a critical issue for sophisticated actors, institutions and organisations. Works and logics do reach the 'other', and accountability is usually not really at stake in diversity management. Performance is measured against policies and standards, which renders variation acceptable within the 'business logic' of a common frame of reference. However, any variation that lies outside the 'business logic' is by definition no longer accountable.

Difference, in contrast, refers to observations of incomprehensible otherness in social and cultural relations. Human backgrounds, deeds and beliefs between counterparts can be perceived as being incommensurable or outright incompatible. Here, demarcations of belonging become more fundamental and insurmountable, as the definitions of what is reasonable are found to be unequal. Such deeper differences are not necessarily negative, but they are generally endowed with a higher potential of confrontation. Heterogeneity in this context is at first an epistemic and practical experience. The gap between the 'own' and the 'other can no longer be bridged by one's own established methods, which consequently leaves open spaces of indetermination and insecurity.

Mutually objectionable or at least non-alignable notions and practices betweencounterparts become likely when differences cannot be discussed openly and without outside pressure. Then a notion of radical difference can also become ascribed as a group feature. In such circumstances a particular social group is identified with a deviant set of characteristics, which makes them just different. This topic is described further by Eriksen (2006), who mentions the changing perception of Muslim immigrants' cultural separation in Scandinavia as an example. It could be added that such deviant characteristics often are stressed when settled societies are confronted with migrants and refugees.

Indeterminated strangeness poses a serious challenge to actors and institutions, especially collective ones. In cross-cultural relationships, a pejorative undertone or the appearance of exoticism are common reactions (exoticism being a state of projections of the own within the other, as happened with the 'noble savage'). Both alternatives, the pejorative or the exotic view of the other, stand for common ways of dealing with encounters of the different on the practical side. Their applications are an often condemned issue in the Western world's relation to Africa. However, in the event of an open-ended interaction being guided by 'real difference', the 'other' is not appropriated by such rationalisations. Rather, it remains logically inaccessible, and the relation of the own to the other is unspecific at first. These events can create real newness, but are often limited to individual action in the fields of science, humanities, arts and personal interaction. A practical solution for organisational activity in unspecified situations may be the application of a double measurement that covers each side differently, and consequently leads to a relativism of values. In operational terms, difference means that one side has assumptions and ambitions about the heterogeneous relationship that no longer correspond with those of the other side, which bears the likeliness that the situation is not commonly accountable.

Characteristics of diversity and difference

Diversity lies within the observer's own scope of reference. It can be explained in one's own terms as it covers 'shallow' divergences and describes positions of others which are commensurable to the observer's own principles. Diversity is accountable and a transfer of basic items is possible. It can be perceived as a potentially creative enrichment or only a minor problem as diverging contexts usually can be covered by one 'business logic'.

Difference is beyond the observer's own scope of reference. It cannot be explained with one's own terms as it covers 'deep' divergences and describes positions of others which are incommensurable with the observer's own principles. Difference is unaccountable and a translation even of basic subjects is necessary. In a positive context, difference provides the way to surprise and radically new and input. In a negative context the related perceptions potentially are pejorative or perceived as threatening. The diverging contexts cannot be covered by one 'business logic'. Hermeneutic approximation is required instead.

Essential note: the question of whether a relationship is structured by difference or diversity is always seen from the actor's point of view. There is no 'correct' or 'real' external view on heterogeneity. It is, after all, individually or socially experienced.

Operative universalism and operative relativism

It matters how social, political and economic structures on the global scale are reflected in the objectives, paradigms and operations of Transboundary Cooperations. In this respect, the impact of global-scale heterogeneity on organisation patterns can be assessed through a basic guideline: how do the actors and/or organisations define heterogeneity within their own structures? How do they perceive the nature of the boundaries they cross, and what is their own reflection on these boundaries? These questions were asked at the operative level of a Transboundary Cooperation, where things are actually done and handled.

I subsume the matter of crossed boundaries into two main modes of how actors perceive them. By perceiving global-scale boundaries in a certain way they also reproduce a certain kind of heterogeneity within their own transboundary activities. The point is laid out in the following two opposing positions:

- *Operative universalism:* Despite worldwide variation, humanity is regarded as one entity and as having common fundamental principles. This logic is the underlying assumption that serves as the powerful foundation of modern Western civilisation, rational science, and the capitalist expansion. It means that everything complies with the same fundamental structures. These structures understand themselves as a grasp of all human experience, where all inherent diversities (cultures, meanings, colours, habits, materials) are still part of a single logic of truth.
Operations that are based upon universalism, nevertheless, have to fine-tune their activities to local environments. They devote efforts to the establishment of universalist logic in new places in order to make its expansion possible. Particularly in places where the conditions are not optimal (i.e. developing countries) they are willing to take 'sociocultural factors' into consideration. It can be expected that with sufficient reason and patience real work on the ground will follow these common principles all over the world.
- *Operative relativism:* This perception leads to assumptions of epistemic and functional distinctions between geographical or mental spaces. Other places work with other principles. These positions may come in the form of respectful relativism, but often they also provide the background for transboundary arrangements that are built on unequal relationships. These operations allow for, and simultaneously depend on basic differences between connected social worlds in order to sustain themselves.

Operative relativism in transboundary relations

According to the opinion of relativists, no universal standard exists by which to assess the absolute truth of any intellectual or cultural proposition. At this point I spare a discussion on the philosophical backgrounds of this term. However, it is my aim to make the notion of relativism useful for the description of distinctive types of Transboundary Cooperations.

The very reason for the emergence of a Transboundary Cooperation is sometimes attributed to its symbiosis with the different contexts within which it is embedded. These contexts are then characterised by vastly different socio-economic worlds. The transboundary actor is equally at home in each of them, even though the actor cannot or will not align them with each other. In other words, in this model several parts of the world are so different from one another in practical-organisational terms that all matters of work and life are affected. To operate between them, some actor types apply more than one distinctive set of operational guidelines (logic, ethics and objectives). This leads to the fact that some kinds of Transboundary Cooperations exist *because* of the necessity or possibility of applying two sets of operative standards.

Example 1: networks of resource exploitation that link African warlords to Eastern European mercenaries and Western resource dealing companies. In these organisational fields, sophisticated product development and recycling standards of industrial societies coexist with shadow markets flourishing in, for example, Congolese crisis communities. Even though not all actors know each other, awareness of the underlying structure exists, and is made use of.

Example 2: Western development agencies are linked to activities in target countries (i.e. projects in Rwanda) to which they attribute their resources. The receivers of these resources are provisioned with aid because the conditions in which they exist justify this allocation in a way that would not be justifiable within the donor countries themselves. The assumption of a universal ethic that demands aid does not contradict relativism on the operative level. In fact, in order to be in a position to receive foreign aid, the receiver must be in a state where non-aid activities would not work. One effect is that development banks must give credits to countries that are not creditworthy according to the standards which commercial banks are bound to follow. Creditworthiness is thus one of the conditions to which commercial banks are bound by law in donor countries, a condition that does not exist in classical development banking.

In technical terms, operative relativism implicitly proposes that some areas and issues must be treated in a different way than others. These asymmetries lead to occurrences of 'double measurement'. In such a case, for example, African and Western issues are seen as set apart from one another. It is not the aim of transboundary arrangements specialised in operative relativism to overcome any potential incomparability of standards underlying the interaction, as these arrangements cannot work when there are no differences.

It is not uncommon that operations exist because they are specialised to exist under a specific heterogeneous condition. In this regard the development sector stands out prominently as it owes its existence to the separation of the world into developed and underdeveloped parts. But also the conditions of Africa's insertion in global relations were classically subsumed under this category. This is not only caused by outer exploitation, but also by domestic African actors knowing how to make use of asymmetry. The common practice of 'extraversion' (Bayart 1993, 2000) can be seen as an attempt to locally exploit Africa's dependency by African actors in the face of the world's willingness to devote some small proportion of its resources to this continent.

Operative universalism in transboundary relations

From the viewpoint of universalism, the complexity that arises from global and cultural interconnections is normal as long as the operational common ground remains secured. Usually no reason arises to doubt this common ground despite occasional problems of adaptation in certain areas of the world, such as in the greater part of Africa. But in the end, after all the chaos has been organised, the 'true' basic facts of science, the economy, technology and human life follow (or should follow) the same patterns everywhere. This is the way scientific and technological modernity is perceived, and perceives itself.

Universalism works as

"a knowledge which has successfully shed all vestiges of its particular origin, place and context, it belongs nowhere and can therefore penetrate everywhere. In a certain sense, mechanistic causality, bureaucratic rationality and the law of supply and demand are rules which are cleansed of any relationship to a particular society or culture. It is because they are disembedded from broader contexts of order and meaning that they are so powerful in remodelling any social reality according to their limited but specific logic." (Sachs 1992:109-110)

Transboundary operations based on operative universalism gain additional effectiveness when the underlying logic on which they are built can be replicated across locations and continents. This replication leads to scale effects and is intended to apply to all contexts, despite local diversities which could become relevant. Regarded from this position, the world's inequalities, although lamentable, are bridgeable through intelligent processes and grand visions. This mode accepts divergences but subsumes the 'basics' behind diverging positions into one common frame of reference. Universalistic examples include the global propagation of the market economy, worldwide standards of all sorts, human rights, and the universalistic tradition in science. These patterns are also expected to be valid in the face of geographic, historical or cultural variation.

In addition, the practical logic of development aid possesses universalistic characteristics in the way that foreign aid can, and should, transfer certain ideas from industrialised societies to developing societies. Such a transfer only makes sense when one can expect that transferred principles are of general value, and that they are also improving the human condition in the target population. The universality of transferred items and ideas is taken for granted. Classic candidates in this respect are the modernisation theories, but contemporary democratisation and civil society efforts evolve along similar lines. In the corporate world, global enterprise management self-evidently builds on the assumption of general validity and the execution of rational capitalist logic. In organisational contexts, the proliferation of financial accounting standards turned out to be one of the most relevant factors for global standardisation processes (Hoffjan/Weide 2006:1). Diverging viewpoints and local variation are allowed as long as they remain on the common ground of diversity and accountability. Everything that is diverging, then, is subject to 'diversity management'.

Is Rwanda a country like any other? Can a worldwide model of civilisation or one corporate logic apply everywhere? Will standard, high-class technology transform its society into a successful life form? Positions guided by operative universalism would answer these questions positively. Transboundary Cooperations based on this approach exist *despite* the occurrence of unique local circumstances that complicate their activities.

A matter of perspective and experience

Where some organisations and enterprises make distinctions that ultimately evoke notions of structural asymmetry and difference, others relate to the same contexts in a spirit of practical universalism or at least practical sameness. This becomes apparent when comparing how international business planners look at the African market. Taking a look at 'North-South' and 'South-South' enterprise activities respectively, it can be seen that company structures are generally somewhat different. While firms from the North are usually of greater financial value and size, firms from the South tend to employ more people, perhaps due to lower capitalisation (Broadman 2007). When engaging in African contexts Southern companies have an advantage over their Northern competitors in that they potentially better understand how to operate in the specific business climate (InWEnt 2006:22). Where many Northern (or Western) actors see the African continent as an object of otherness and even radical strangeness, many Southern (South African, South or East Asian) actors are not faced with this perception of conceptual difference. This little shift can, and does, lead to lucrative investments which would be considered too 'alien' for their Northern competitors. Notably, South African enterprises have become expansionist, aiming at achieving economies of scale in Sub-Saharan Africa. They perceive the continent as a field for 'normal' business where generalised schemes and standards are applicable. African countries are seen as a calculable market instead of an alien space.

"South Africans set themselves apart from other investors in their willingness to invest in areas outside the extractive sector, the sector that traditionally attracts the most investment on the continent. Instead, they have also moved aggressively into retail, telecommunications, tourism, property, franchising and finance alongside mining." (InWEnt 2006:21)

In conclusion, it can be said that some operative patterns in Transboundary Cooperations aim at the achievement of what could be conceived of as scale effects (multiplying the applications of one logic - universalism), where others uphold schemes that are based on the utilisation of contextual differences and structural arbitrage (customising the applied logic for a specific prevalence of differences - relativism). The assessment of the case studies takes these considerations into account.

Intermediary conclusion about transcontinental heterogeneity in Africa

Heterogeneity and social boundaries belong together. Wherever Transboundary Cooperations are concerned with socio-cultural divergences, their epistemic and structural predispositions will invoke a particular management of heterogeneity. The question of how such boundaries are conceptualised is always to be answered at the ground level perception and self-assurance of a given cooperation. From this point onwards the substructures of difference and diversity as much as of operational relativism or universalism are leading into the formal set-up of the cooperation as much as into further expressions of the protagonists. All that which is accessible through direct observation, such as mission statements, project plans, business and trade, stakeholder selection, is based on the underlying model. The protagonists' roles are related to these substructures as well, as much as some of their opinions e.g. about the decision of whom to trust or the overall meaning of their own work. It should be added that a Transboundary Cooperation does not 'choose' whether it wants to be oriented towards difference, diversity, operative universalism or relativism. These assurances are derived from wider discourses in the social and economic spheres from which the actors originate.

4. Field Studies in Companies, Agencies and Projects

In the following chapters seven case studies are presented. Each case focuses on a particular type of organisation or setting where a specific kind of Transboundary Cooperation is in action. While the main purpose of these field accounts is to provide the basis for a comparative approach to the larger research subject, they might also prove fruitful in themselves, providing insights specific to their respective topic. For this reason the seven cases are aligned according to a common guideline directed at their interpretation in a wider framework. At the same time, important issues directly connected to their context are discussed and referenced individually, wherever appropriate. The following ethnography can thus be read as a pre-organised set of raw data for the further steps of elaboration, or as a collection of field expertise in highly specialised areas. For readers interested in the questions of method and approaching the field I refer to the remarks in appendix 2 (Chapter 8.2).

4.1 PROJECT EXPERTS AND A BILATERAL DEVELOPMENT AGENCY

During this first case study I present fieldwork based on several projects of a German personnel secondment agency. The main focus of this development agency is to assign experienced European professionals to partner organisations in partner countries. The overall purpose of this activity is organisation development and knowledge transfer into disadvantaged sectors in developing countries. Such personnel assignments are embedded in cooperation projects that usually connect the German agency to suitable local partners such as public or semi-public organisations, departments or administrations. Typically the partners deliver services in the sectors of public administration, medical treatment, education, academic training, public healthcare, social security, and others where hands-on expertise in combination with profound academic or technical knowledge is required. The relevant organisations of this type in recipient countries are frequently severely understaffed, underequipped, and held back by a lack of access to profound expertise. Within the framework of bilateral development goals between Germany and Rwanda these deficiencies are identified as major hindrances in societal development. The mission of the secondment agency is to improve this situation.

While being a developmental organisation, this agency does not execute its own projects. Its mission is to deploy German professionals to local partner organisations according to the guidelines of official German development priorities and bilateral agreements. Such cooperation projects are often rather small and person-centred rather than overly visible, and are established in close collaboration with the local partner organisations. An essential requirement for local organisations to become candidates for the free deployment of a (usually) German expert is compliance to the agency's policies and its current central focus on development. Prospective local organisations also have to prove and justify a long term need for German expert knowledge. Following a selection procedure, a cooperation contract is signed between the German agency and the local partner organisation. The agency then publishes job offers in the relevant European labour markets to find professionals with relevant competencies. The selection procedure for suitable candidates for these expert positions and the pre-departure training of the new candidates are handled through the agency's German infrastructure. It takes roughly one year for the selected experts to arrive in the target country after an initial partnership agreement has been made. Their assignment usually spans 2 - 4 years and defines specific goals that usually serve the aim of capacity enlargement, training and high-level support, e.g. improving education in a hospital or enhancing communication procedures in a public administration. It is the policy of this agency that the foreign experts work directly with those local professionals who are immediately concerned with the tasks in which the lack of expertise has been identified. Development assistants, as these foreign experts are called, thus become part of the settings and daily routines of their counterparts. By means of this arrangement the transfer of expertise, as well as opportunities for personal communication are expected to be most direct. This directness is also one of the agency's central strategy arguments. Every foreign development expert is assigned to a local colleague from the same professional field and a similar job position in order to facilitate mutual exchange and the transfer of knowledge. It is not the task of the expatriates to do normal operative jobs in their partner organisations. They are formally and explicitly deployed for the sake of knowledge transfer, organisation development, education and training on the job.

There are numerous development organisations active in Rwanda, although not all possess the same objective and organisation structures. In comparison to other bilateral donor agencies, the agency from this case study is by far not one of the biggest. Size notwithstanding, as part of the official bilateral policies and programme agreements it is an 'official' actor in the country.

I am now going to outline several aspects of a cooperation project where technical development assistants were deployed to a project for organisation development in public administration. I then further highlight important issues in similar cooperation projects that could be observed in various fields of the public health and social care sector.

Development assistants in public infrastructure

A cooperation project between the development agency and a Rwandan public infrastructure department provided the opportunity to observe the evolution of personnel secondment into a setting that was characterised by a severe lack of means and capacity on the side of the local partners. The objective of the project was to improve the overall effectiveness of public infrastructure management and urban planning in the responsible administrative department. As with similar projects, the abstract cooperation goal was a general aim of 'improving the population's living conditions'. The more direct objective related to the task level was to improve the administrative performance in this department by means of organisation development, i.e. implementing communication and management structures and a transfer of expertise. Additionally, it was agreed that suitable structures for civic participation in infrastructure planning processes were to be implemented.

Work in the infrastructure department demanded high levels of technical expertise and project management skills. Besides a severe lack of provisioning within the department, a distinct lack of these skills was one of its main challenges, and the reason for calling in the German experts. Once the collaborative goals had been set out between the public administration and the German agency, two engineers were assigned as development assistants. These experts had previously occupied relevant positions in the fields of public infrastructure implementation, participative planning procedures, and so forth. Their decision to apply for this assignment in Rwanda was a combination of personal interest in working abroad, professional motivation and a willingness to contribute to a good cause.

Formal arrangements between the German development agency and the Rwandan public administration had set the position of the development assistants.

The experts formally reported to the departmental head but worked in their own office and had no direct operative responsibilities. Within this framework they were officially expected to act as advisors and facilitators, working closely with Rwandan colleagues to help improve issues brought to their attention. Yet, their primary task was to conduct organisation development in order to improve the administration's internal procedures. Prior to the project's inception, an official meeting was held at which a formally agreed cooperation framework was adopted consisting of schedules and task descriptions. Among the more central points of this plan were the notions that by the project's completion *"The organisation within the department [xyz] is improved"* by the means that *"The planning and execution of all projects of [xyz] are more participative and efficient"* and that *"The public infrastructure in [xyz] and their management are developed and modernized according to the priorities of the population"*. Finally, the technical assistants were expected to work out a practical guideline for improving the department's ability to access the complicated but numerous options for international donor funding, which were available for public infrastructure projects in developing countries. Due to a lack of staff capabilities and inaccessible information, those sources of external funding were only seldom used. In technical terms, everything pertained to implementing models and practices of proven effectiveness in an understaffed and sparsely subsidised public administration. On the whole, the tasks of this technical assistance project resembled the attempt at an in-depth re-organisation of a municipal department with wide ranging responsibilities and severe deficits by two foreign assistants who were operating on a mutual goodwill basis. This department, however, employed too few people tasked with too many projects. Mixed responsibilities, urgent unexpected issues, time spent on administrative 'hot-fixes' along with inadequate means of transportation and communication all worked to hinder the project's success.

In the process, after one year

After one year had passed a comparison of objectives and results revealed that the original project plan had to be modified in several ways, and that the overall progress was slower than scheduled. The experts provided a geographically and technically sound assessment of the current state of the physical infrastructure network under the department's control. In order to gain an overview of their subject they had created a standard map of the urban settlements and infrastructures. Now they disposed of a reliable data basis in form of this map and additional material in a quality that was never available before at this location. While not one of the predefined project objectives, this map was regarded as an important precondition for (any) further work. It was felt that they needed to know exactly what they were talking about when doing an engineer's job. The original prospects for organisational improvement, however, had to be adapted to fit the existing situation.

According to technical guidelines, the department was highly ineffective. One major difficulty the experts encountered was an inability to adhere to medium and long term planning. Interference commonly came in the form of *"urgences"* from the directorate, which frequently rendered regular schedules obsolete. In the department's management the common practice of what could be called 'authoritative situational organisation' in combination with a short term resource allocation became visible. Not uncommon in such departments, this manner of operation stands at odds with the 'German' methods of public infrastructure administration, which were supposed to be introduced through the cooperation project. In line with the official project description the assistants worked on a strategy to implement a concept for civic participation in urban planning. This initiative came from the donor side, based on the argument that involving the residential population could demonstrably enhance administrative effectiveness and planning quality in public infrastructure. Other European agencies at that time were already occupied with promoting or trying to implement similar participative approaches in Rwandan organisations. These changes were not really seen as a feasible option by the departmental authorities, who supported the argument that the population's lack of participative capability would render such efforts fruitless. While the foreign engineers promoted the position that local inhabitants were to be involved, even if this included greater efforts and higher costs during decision making, the Rwandan directors defended a top-down approach explaining that without sufficient literacy and education, civic participation was useless and would not lead to beneficial results. By challenging hierarchy and authority within the administration, the German experts had touched upon a matter embedded much deeper in societal and political roots. The unspoken difference of opinion concerning the right infrastructure strategy was eventually identified as a divergence of approaches to human organisation, which were not easily aligned. Practical questions on the operative and strategic level, such as the incorporation of civic participation or methods of internal project management, were in conflict with values and power structures that went far beyond the scope of this single project.

Meanwhile, in addition to their formal tasks in the field of professional facilitation and organisation development the engineers were frequently called upon to assist in difficult matters during ongoing project implementations. Throughout their employment the experts participated in the execution of ongoing infrastructure projects, and supported their Rwandan colleagues wherever they could. This was much welcomed, especially since the department's core staff had shrunk to 60% of its original size since the Germans' arrival; where the original figure had already been a result of under-staffing. Reductions in public and administrative personnel, as a result of a World Bank reform program, meant that more staff could not be devoted to the department. The lack of planning and engineering capacity in infrastructure rebuilding programmes became a serious liability. Even if an operative involvement in routine work was not part of the original project design, participation in practical activities helped the experts gain an understanding of the local context and facilitate communication between both parties. One engineer became successively involved in operative project management to such an extent that he implicitly assumed the role of project manager with major responsibilities. Demands for capable project management personnel surpassed the capacities of most domestic staff members. One such case involved long-term support in the context of a massive infrastructure project funded by the European Union. As it could not be handled by local experts, this project consumed a great deal of the German expert's time, which had originally been scheduled for organisation development.

Time and effort devoted to operational project management went far beyond the original project objective. Due to the lack of staff, however, it was an appropriate use of the German engineers' competence. In other words, the Rwandan administration could draw upon the foreign experts to soften their critical gaps in providing experienced personnel. As a result, the original goals of the German-Rwandan cooperation project were increasingly lagging behind. Despite these developments, the experts valued their experience and the additional insights they could obtain through their operative work.

Outcomes and obstacles

Although an informal skill transfer formed part of their daily activities, the development assistant's organisation development initiatives suffered multiple delays. All too often, pressing operative problems demanded their engineering expertise in order to prevent urgent work from coming to a standstill. *"In daily work we can only act as a fire service and help where we can in urgencies. We have to help in the ongoing projects because they have no manpower here.... stable project planning is almost impossible."* Consequently the first year's annual plan could not be fulfilled as scheduled; the local counterparts could not and/or did not deliver the basic necessary information required by the Germans for good organisation development. Rather, they continued working in *"urgences"* as a principal method of organisation. For the remainder of the cooperation period, the experts proposed a (possible) modification of the project schedule. This modified framework served more as a self-obligation than as a bilateral guideline for joint efforts, however.

Among the Rwandan staff members, the most pressing issues concerning their work environment included a lack of materials, office equipment, means of transportation and communication. However, organisational difficulties were also stated, such as a rampant disruption of work by frequent and unanticipated *"urgences"* issued by the head office. These critical remarks were in line with the organisational problems identified by the Germans. Members of the department's staff showed a great deal of motivation in learning opportunities and engaged in cooperation at work, even if the unreliability of the organisation in addition to an extensive workload due to understaffing made this difficult. The inadequate transportation and communication facilities reduced the staff's effectiveness and made work possible only when it was conducted by means of constant improvisation and compromise. These conditions also applied to the Germans, who were forced to adapt to this operational model if they wished to collaborate with their Rwandan colleagues. The entire department operated on a de-formalised and poorly equipped basis with informal relations and personal authority in place of predefined guidelines.

Summarising their experiences, the development experts hoped that their presence would elicit positive effects on the future workflow of the administration, but saw little opportunity for a real consultative role. Instead, they came to characterise their efforts as *"emergency action in place of capacity development."* [German development expert]. At the department level, the unpredictable work environment together with a lack of personnel and continuous *urgences* consistently hampered adequate project work in the sense the Germans had intended. In search of reasons, they cited a mixture of cultural orientations and authoritarian leadership.

As an external observer we are inclined to note that in order to achieve their project objectives, the German engineers would have needed to change fundamental aspects of organisational behaviour typical for many Rwandan bureaucracies during the time of research. The paternalistic and person-centred approach to managing people and resources had its own operational logic and was unlikely to be penetrated by two foreigners alone. Such insights notwithstanding, the German engineers had to move forward with their project. Development experts must deliver results, both to their own agency and to the authorities of the local partner organisation. All in all, the most crucial influences on the work of the German engineers, in their function as technical assistants, were not related to complexities of their task environment, but to the conditions and limitations of a public administration in a poor African country. An effective entry point for substantial organisation development would most likely have been a better provisioning of the administration with resources and manpower, as well as a modification of the leadership style within this department. But as the cooperation project was aimed at technical and organisational objectives and was hierarchically dependant on the administration's directors, this option was not part of the process. Consequently, the possibilities for change in the authority structures were limited.

As mentioned by one of the German engineers, the fact that development experts are bound to the strategic focus of their own agency is an occasional if unexpected complication. This was at odds with potentially useful initiatives coming from immediate project work but not in line with key developmental issues. It was difficult, for example, to relate useful technical project ideas to the agency's current major focus on HIV, which had to be implicated in all activities *"even when planning roads. Sometimes our own organisation causes such trouble to us here when we just want to do our own job well and creatively"* [German development expert].

Although their project work turned out to be different from what the engineers had initially expected, and was also more difficult and probably less effective than scheduled, they were still content with their overall situation and their stay in Rwanda. They regarded work and life in the country as a positive enrichment, and valued their unique personal experiences. Between the lines they may have succeeded in passing some of their knowledge to counterparts in a personal and long-lasting way.

Further activities and aspects of interpretation

Cooperation projects in the fields of public health, education and social care belong to the core activities of the agency, and German development assistants from these professions undertook project work in several Rwandan partner organisations. In order to keep up the flow of operations the agency's country coordinator must acquire new opportunities for such cooperations on a regular basis. Maintaining a constant project volume in the respective partner country is one of the coordination office's tasks. Like any other bilateral donor institution, this agency had to deliver a sufficient number of successfully conducted projects in order to justify the allocated resources and the political strategy. In this context, the acquisitions of new local project partners is a precondition for new cooperation projects into which new development experts could be assigned. Naturally, these new projects had to correspond to the donor's official development goals and bilateral agreements between the German and the Rwandan governments. The selection procedure for potential local partner organisations is therefore an important strategic activity of the agency's country office. Prospective cooperation candidates, and thus suitable local organisations, are expected to submit proposals to be evaluated by the agency. In fact, not many potential partner organisations approach the agency of their own volition by the means of a self-developed proposal. Of those that submit an application, many are not in line with the agency's formal requirements and strategic orientations. The desired strategy consists of a development goal (e.g. poverty reduction, female empowerment, education) and a set of activities indicating how this goal can be approached in a given country. Relatively strict definitions of a suitable local partner are in place in order to secure the effectiveness of this form of aid and to ensure compliance with development goals. As a result, the agency frequently has to search for suitable local project partners so as to maintain a sufficient number of organisations within which project work can be conducted.

Among the newly arrived development experts, the personal reasons for becoming development assistants varied. They ranged from the opportunity to go abroad and enhance one's vision to engaging in useful activities and to 'getting something going'. The situation on Europe's labour market also plays a decisive role. Positive first impressions and bursts of motivation are common among experts upon arrival. Frequently, however, this positive introduction phase is followed by a period of pessimism, or what could be called 'pessimistic realism'.

Anthropologist: *"There are these two new arrivals in [the agency] who gave a somewhat desperate impression because they were not sure about the viability of their project and it was rather different from what they expected."* Development assistant: *"I don't have pity with them anymore, everyone has to go through this."* From an observer's point of view, most expatriates tend to develop either an attitude of cautious optimism or one of pragmatic cynicism after an initial period of several weeks or months.

Expectations and translations between the contexts of cooperation

A development assistant in a coordinative position in the fields of social care and public health recalled an offer she made to her Rwandan counterparts: *"I wanted to offer them some on-the-job-training to facilitate their working capabilities, like teaching professional skills, coaching and therapeutic practice. When I asked what they needed, they mostly wanted training for a driver's license."* In this case, grossly diverging expectations and motivations were apparent between the German expert and the Rwandan staff. In such settings one of the most demanding aspects of daily work for both parties was the constant translation between the differences of their personal and work-related backgrounds. Additionally a strong demand was present in the need for a constant parallel reasoning between the project design, which obviously had the donor's stamp on it, and the complex interests of the local partners. After all, the execution of development assistance aims to translate immaterial donor interests into tangible activities within target groups, with the receivers' consent. In practice, events do not always follow expectations or run as smoothly as anticipated at the beginning of an assignment. *"It is really stressing to have this every day, to balance the different backgrounds and requirements"* [German expert in public health].

The necessity for sociocultural translation is inherent in the working environment of development assistance. Nevertheless, not all activities executed by foreign donor agencies are structured in the same way as they are formed by other influences. The agency experts from this study made a distinction when comparing their work with that of another more consultancy oriented German agency that focused on 'technical cooperation', as they themselves called it. This type of aid is more common among donor agencies from other industrial countries. In contrast to the development experts from this case study, those technical assistants often manage projects of considerably larger financial volume and are frequently linked to the higher echelons of the recipient country's administration. While less integrated into the 'real local' domestic affairs and less exposed to the social and cultural backgrounds, the technical assistants and their projects are still subjected to the challenges of sociocultural translation. Yet, the pressing need for active involvement in all the potentially unclear aspects of direct intercultural relationships was only part of their work to a lesser degree. The above quoted development assistant noted: *"I'm behind the coulisses. I'm inside the process while the [technical assistants and consultants on official levels] only see the outcomes."* Another expatriate involved noted: *"Here we see how things evolve because we are really involved in the process of intercultural work and so we can try to understand why and how it worked or not. The people from the more official organisations work on bigger and more official projects that look nice and where they communicate with big officials only. They have no real opportunity to get an impression of the backgrounds that are sometimes hidden to them or to realise things that happen because of misunderstandings"* [development experts in public health]. This statement reveals the importance of the specific transboundary relationship between donors and recipients; but also that the outcome of cooperations is dictated by the exact objective and organisational design of a donor agency and its local counterparts.

Projects, work and troubleshooting

During fieldwork, it became apparent that the development assistants were frequently drawn into the daily troubleshooting of their counterparts' organisations. Rather than following the predefined agenda of structured skill transfer and organisation development, they were deeply involved with the hands-on work and regularly replaced missing staff. From the individual expert's viewpoint work, in these situations, entailed assisting with various difficult situations. Initially, this was a relatively fulfilling experience. The German experts often found themselves taking on the role of a respected foreign co-worker rather than that of a facilitator or teacher. Most expatriate experts within local partner organisations took on intense workloads that were officially intended to be performed by unavailable Rwandan staff.

Relating to this, one German development assistant acknowledged this situation by recognizing an existing difference between the Rwandan and German attitude towards their shared work. Three years later, after completing the greater part of her assignment she adopted an attitude of *"letting things happen"*, and refrained from interfering in the activities of her counterparts and household personnel. A positive pragmatism together with a 'tolerance of the not-understanding' was thus established. This apparent change in attitude helped bridge differences and occasional misunderstandings, while opening up possibilities for positive partnership and mutual trust. Accordingly, a solid base of general cooperation appears vital to the routine work of development assistants as their immediate working environments do not provide effectively applicable guidelines.

The development experts who participated in this study considered it an unfortunate commonality that the formally shared goals and schedules that formed the practical side of the cooperation were frequently disturbed by short-term interferences and improvised modifications from the side of the counterparts. These circumstances created an atmosphere of unpredictability which acted as a barrier to consistent, organised work. One possible interpretation of this problem relates to the often critical shortages of experienced and affordable manpower in the recipient organisations, which may possibly be content with gaining access to foreign professionals for free. Other explanations point to the inherent threat that a strict compliance to the cooperation plans would pose to the autonomy of the recipient organisation. Socio-technical "capacity development" exercises weakening and destabilising effects on patrimonial power structures which are often controlling domestic organisations.

In many cases of collaborative projects, the European protagonists were likely to be the most committed and often the most strained. It was not uncommon to see Western project experts in full action, plagued by stress while local counterparts and target groups were seldom found to be on a similar level of personal engagement. Expatriate development experts often tended to draw many things into their sphere of activity, and tried to manage 'their' projects according to private expectations. These expectations involved personal measurements and professional styles, as well as individual goals of self-achievement. Local counterparts frequently possessed a different outlook. Having potentially encountered several experts from previous assignments or similar projects, they may be familiar with the short-term bursts of activity and motivation that these foreigners generate before their assignments come to an end or are terminated. Such disparities are a common source of ambiguity and stress in bilateral development cooperation.

In the public infrastructure department in the aforementioned case study many of the problems in the ineffective local organisation were the result of an authoritative but unfocused leadership. In accordance with Hüsken (2006), I assume that in the case of this public administration the 'rational' organisation concepts as propagated by the Germans were probably also quite well known or at least within reach of the responsible Rwandans, but that a wish for autonomy and the persisting strength of patriarchal authority sustained defensive behaviour and power-oriented micro strategies in place of opting for a programmatic change for which the means were not really sufficient. Supported by the previous statements, it can be concluded that under the premise of participartory development cooperation it remains impossible for expatriate organisations to reform or even dominate the activities of their local counterparts. To meet their objectives (i.e. conduct projects in order to sustain their organisational legitimation), most donor agencies are dependent on the goodwill of local partners as much as these local partners depend on the inflow of foreign resources in order to sustain their status quo. *"Not only Rwanda needs the Germans, Germany also needs Rwanda"* [German development coordinator]. An additional issue that could be observed in the case studies in line with Spies (2009) is the manifestation a participatory paradox. It becomes apparent that the experts carrying out participative development assistance, as well as their domestic counterparts, are faced with the open question of how to maintain a stable teacher-like relationship (role of the agenda setting donor) and simultaneously remain open for an inclusive negotiation of the actual needs and positions of the ones to be developed (those who should participate). These contradictory demands make it difficult for the experts to engage in deeper intercultural exchange.

As a final point, it must be noted that the different types of bilateral development agencies display crucial differences in the depth of their insertion into local settings. The degree of local embeddedness seems to be connected to the objective and nature of projects conducted. It can be additionally assumed that the experiences of the expatriate experts are directly affected by their own organisation's depth of insertion into the local context. Moreover, within the "donor community" different levels of prestige are implicitly attached to the different types of projects. More consultancy-oriented activities on higher levels of public administrations are conducted in a business-like manner that seeks to resemble corporate management (cf Hüsken 2006, Warnier 1995:102). On a hypothetical scale the agency from this case study would have to be grouped with the less 'business-like' organisations, which execute smaller and less abstract projects. While these organisations often are associated with a lower prestige factor and pay lower salaries to their Western employees, they experience deeper embedding into the background dynamics of the host society.

4.2 BREWERY – MULTINATIONAL BEVERAGE CORPORATION

Rwanda's consumption of beer and soft drinks over several decades was served by a single industrial brewery. Since its foundation under Belgian colonial rule it has operated continuously, and has for a long time been the only producer of bottled drinks in the country. In the 1980s the brewery was acquired by a multinational beverage corporation which owns and manages similar breweries around the world. Aside from this Rwandan facility three other former colonial breweries in the DR Congo and Burundi belong to the same multinational corporation and are operated under similar conditions. In the course of continuous upgrades and increasing integration into the mother company, these central African breweries were slowly transformed from a post-colonial legacy into globally linked corporate subsidiaries.

The brewery looks back on a history of successful operation since its foundation, with the only temporary breakdown during the most crucial months of the genocide in 1994. Between the 1960s and the early 2000s the company held a de facto monopoly as the only industrial beverage producer in Rwanda. Its beers and soft drinks were among the most important consumer goods in the country and became deeply rooted in material culture. During that period it was also the biggest industrial company in the country and one of the few international businesses. After the war it formed a cornerstone of international corporate culture in Rwanda, together with only a very small number of other multinationals. Triggered by the ongoing economic recovery and the first market liberalisations since the early 2000s, the first waves of new competition came from new local producers and rising quantities of imported beer. The time of this study marked the end of a single player market in bottled drinks, even though the brewery's market share continues to be monolithic. Among employees, discussions about the future position of the brewery in society were common, and the need to enter a new stage of marketing and strategy was apparent.

This case study concentrates on organisational and social intersections between the contexts of three units: the multinational corporation, the organisation of the brewery as a corporate subsidiary, and the dynamics of its embedding in Rwandan society.

The workforce, staff and expatriates

Over a long period of time the brewery was one of the country's biggest employers for educated individuals aside from public administration. In recent years this has changed with the expansion of the economy, but it still remains in the top group. Most employees mentioned that they valued the company for a positive working atmosphere. Even though respect for authority and the display of status were seen as very important, the overall climate was more relaxed than in many other organisations throughout the country. When compared to its beginnings in the 1960s, the personnel structure had changed considerably over time. Over the years, it has increasingly offered professional jobs to skilled Rwandans, where during the period between the 1960s and the 1980s most technical jobs were executed and supervised by European experts. Throughout the beginning of the new century this had changed significantly. All technical positions, administration and accounting, almost all marketing and many directive tasks were now executed by trained Rwandan workers and professional managers. European executives were now only assigned to those top positions vital to securing the interests of the mother corporation.

Being in an international company: It was a common dream for many individuals from the Rwandan management staff to gain an opportunity for an international career. Younger professionals and junior managers often came from backgrounds where they had already acquired some international experience. They had partially been living or studying in Western countries, and some were hired from abroad and repatriated in order to work for the brewery in their home country. For multinational corporations (MNC) this is not uncommon as professionals from the diaspora represent an important talent pool when seeking to fill vacancies in Africa (InWEnt 2006:19).

Western management personnel: The general manager and around two or three other European top level directors represented the interests of the mother company, and took control over general strategy and operations. Ideal candidates for these positions were internationally experienced executives with a taste for living abroad. Most of these individuals were recruited from a pool of corporate managers active in the international departments of the corporation, but occasionally expatriate managers were also externally hired. The overall assignment of Western staff has been declining steadily, and aside from the directors, Western expatriates were mostly present in the role of company-internal short-term consultants or technicians flown in from headquarters to implement new procedures and technologies.

Expatriates

Apart from the aspect of control over the subsidiary, the mother corporation also used vacant positions in the African breweries as a training field to broaden the international experience of younger European executives. These individuals stayed for a predefined period and then returned to their original workplace or changed within the international department. As one example, a younger Dutch manager filled the position of commercial director at the brewery. Similar practices were observable within the brewery's sister company in Burundi where an Italian junior controller, who wanted international experience, agreed to a temporary assignment. When inquiring about an opportunity to go abroad he envisioned something like the US or Great Britain but quickly found himself making calculations on bottle lines in Bujumbura. Working in central Africa was as much a burden to him as it was an opportunity. He was coping with different working conditions but technically did the same job he had done in Italy.

Another type of Western corporate staff would continuously lose their former importance. I call this the 'classic expatriate', thus the rough and tough individualist long-term expert or country specialist. Individuals of this kind were often so accustomed to the conditions of the tropics or African countries that they were perfectly capable of maintaining a company (or at least its technical aspects) in the absence of a European 'normality'. They often became deeply involved in local situations and over the years found it difficult to re-adapt to European life. An example of this type was a technical brewery expert, in fact an old hand in his field who knew 'how things work' in Africa. He had lived in various tropical countries together with his wife, being in international service for the corporation for decades. Although the beginning of the internationalisation of the enterprise during the 20th century was managed by people like him, the international cadre now increasingly consisted of other characters. Deployment of Western expatriates was reduced to top positions in management, finance and supervision, holding up ties with head office. Perhaps the change in numbers and characters of expatriates and their tasks was a process similar to the gradual 'decline' in relevance and numbers of the technical experts in development aid (as reported by Zevenbergen 2002).

In their private lives, European managers and their families often only very selectively integrated into the settings of the local society. Most of their social contacts were among the expatriates themselves. The small group of foreign corporate individuals interacted predominantly with similar folks from the Western 'international community'. *"We're lucky to be such a nice group here, because with such few people you come to depend on one another"* [European manager's wife]. In their own perspective these expatriates were managing their daily life under special conditions distinct from a 'normal' and 'ideal' situation as it was seen at home. A Rwandan manager compared their orientation with that of urban African teachers who are sent to rural areas (*"into the bush"*). Nevertheless, these individuals intensely valued their foreign experience and had a high personal identification with their expatriate status. They could *"not imagine to have always stayed at home"* [expatriate manager].

The Rwandan staff, particularly the middle managers, saw the difference in salaries and standards of living between the few expatriates and the local staff. This was a cause of unspoken but constant observation and debate within the group of Rwandan managers. This disparity also led to silent tensions. *"They keep firing people when they have to cut costs but only one of the white directors costs as much as half of the local staff. If we only had to pay for local management all the fired people could have stayed"* [Rwandan middle manager].

Local subsidiary and multinational corporation

The brewery was one of the country's most prominent Rwandan companies and a producer of essential consumer goods. At the same, time its corporate culture became increasingly inserted into the wider structure of the multinational mother corporation. Within this local subsidiary the intensifying demands for control from the corporate centre met with implications arising from its embeddedness in the Rwandan economy and society. The corporation increasingly treated its Rwandan subsidiary as a part of its own bigger whole, expecting it to contribute to the big picture rather than solely to its own local market. The African breweries were managed in a regional cluster and benchmarked like a portfolio.

Manager: *"You see, now [country XYZ] is number one, they are currently our best one in Africa. But this can change. Usually we have some countries going well and they have to make up for the others which are lagging behind."* Anthropologist: *"So you don't expect them [the African subsidiaries] all to be profitable then?"* Manager: "Well, no, sometimes not at the same time [laughing]."

The Rwandan brewery supplied the local market exclusively and depended on the satisfaction of the Rwandan consumers. On the organisational and technical front, however, a direct link to corporate headquarters became increasingly important in daily affairs. The central departments were already responsible for taking control of the technical, commercial and administrative aspects of corporate subsidiaries, and they were gaining more direct access to the local processes and operations through IT-based observation techniques. In this context the process of human resources development took the role of preparing the local brewery for this enhanced global integration. The wider background of the mother company was made present to Rwandan employees and their awareness of trans-local responsibilities was actively facilitated. As a result the organisational culture turned into a mixture of a classical Rwandan company and a foreign corporate unit with international linkages. Conversely, this international awareness in the Rwandan brewery gave rise to claims of corporate-wide equal treatment of staff members, also in terms of wages and career opportunities. *"We want internationality within [the corporation], the same standards to have here like in [the corporate home country]"* [Rwandan junior manager]. *"We want to know about our career [...]. You feel that you are important, do your job responsibly, but you're not taken into consideration"* [Rwandan marketing officer].

Over the years the management had executed initiatives to reduce the necessary amount of bureaucracy in the company in order to enhance efficiency. It is safe to say that the effectiveness of the brewery's bureaucratic and administrative system was high above country average and functioned relatively well. But compared to international corporate standards it appeared fairly slow and old fashioned. Formalised bureaucracy in Rwandan organisations was initially implemented by colonial supervisors as a means of control and discipline, as elsewhere on the continent. Later on the establishment of a stable organisation together with enhanced automatisation made it possible to lower the intensity of bureaucratic measures. To achieve this, the professional capabilities of the Rwandans had to be improved and their independent working capacity enhanced. During the time of research these efforts appeared to have been partially successful.

Professionalisation

As one precondition for self-reliant management, professionalisation is one of the main driving forces behind the corporation's human resources policies for its African subsidiaries. The increase in personal qualifications among Rwandan employees enabled them to perform in an effective and increasingly flexible manner. This allows for a decrease in severe and costly control measures such as discipline, enforcement, subordination and tight bureaucracy.

The corporate training centre carried out special training sessions for African professionals and managers, a matter to which many resources were devoted. Besides hands-on techniques and skills, these training sessions were mainly concerned with the commitment to professional work ethics and corporate standards. Without making this explicit, the normative and ethical aspects of this proposed professionalism (Leonard 1997) work as agents of cultural change. They lie at the foundation of the propagated management orders, reporting techniques and communication procedures. The resulting unification of organisational environments is common in industrialised countries and was now expanding to the African breweries. Personal qualifications of Rwandan managers were intended to become gradually aligned with international skill profiles. Such efforts led to a reduction of divergences between African and other subsidiaries of the corporation. This fact was also noticed by Rwandan employees who had international experience within the corporation: *"Next week I'll go for training to [the corporation's European headquarters]. To colonise my brain a little bit"* [Rwandan professional]. Professionalisation, as DiMaggio and Powell (1991:71) have explained, "may override variations in tradition and control," making individuals working in organisations almost "interchangeable." Viewed from this angle, the staff training appears as an instrument for socialising African executives into the corporate culture. But even more importantly; what is celebrated as the 'corporate way' enfolds its specific properties in Africa only. Much of what is propagated belongs to a standard repertoire of a Western company's management logic. As the societies of industrialised countries have become accustomed to the principles of modern rationalism, the normative impact of professionalism and standardisation is more apparent and crucial in Africa.

Moral economy and modern professionalism

Rwandan managers and professionals had to find an individual balance between the potentially conflicting demands arising from the rational-individualistic world view that was expected from people aspiring to corporate careers, and the well-respected African ethic of social connectedness, mutual obligation and redistribution. This background of social values, espousing a life within the extended family, was also a major landmark of personal orientation in Rwanda. In functional terms this value set appears as a mutually supportive strategy to stabilise the social community, but brings with it obligations which can hamper individual opportunities. *"You can't have ten people sitting at your home to care about tradition if you want to make a career in this kind of job. You have to choose"* [young Rwandan executive]. Not only are financial matters at stake here, but also the overall situation of an employee's professional reliability and commitment to company interests. Family-related obligations and social or cultural responsibilities are often the cause of temporary absence from the workplace, and are thus incompatible with a job that demands high individual focus (similarly the 'Tonga-effect', Colson 1967). Scott (1976) and Hyden (1980) introduced the understanding of these phenomena as forms of the African 'moral economy'. Beyond such functional and formal terminologies, the affected Rwandan staff members faced individual challenges and life decisions that became the basis from which larger streams of cultural change may be formed in later stages. The context for these considerations can be paraphrased as a confronting relationship between the capitalist enterprise organisation and the embedding society:

- *Capitalist enterprise organisation:* based on individualised and rationalised relationships among employer and employee.
- *Embedding society:* prevailing communal ethic, and social structures that are based on moral affiliations and individual social standing.

Most individuals working for the brewery were aware of these fissures, as much as of the fact that they were triggered by influences from the corporate world outside Rwanda. Although most employees regarded the rational-formal corporate logic as a foreign influence, many aspects of it were seen in a positive way. Quite a few employees saw the company's orientation towards measurable effectiveness and predictable procedures as a possibility to productively make use of their own professional skills in an enabling environment that could bring people in a position to work effectively and be rewarded for it. "To really work, even work hard, without bothering about so many stupid problems around you..." [younger professional].

Nevertheless the intersection of moral economy and formal-rational corporate principles caused occasional friction. An example was the common demand for credit made by employees. It demonstrated a paradigmatic change in the way the company assisted its employees in social matters. Loans were hard to obtain during the time of fieldwork, as the Rwandan financial sector was hardly accessible for most people. Nevertheless the company retreated from its former implicit practice of giving loans to employees and began to assist them in the procedure of gaining formal bank loans. This step was not welcomed by the workforce as it was taken to be the company's declining willingness to care for the needs of its employees. Here a shift becomes visible where the company abandoned a more unwilling than accepted patron-client relationship where the employer *cares* for the employees and entered an individualised exchange of work for money where the employer *facilitates* the employee's individual development but does not necessarily cater for personal needs (on the difficult situation for expatriate employers facing credit demands from subordinates, cf Spies 2009). It must be added, however, that the company's medical care for its entire workforce, including family members, was seen as outstanding. Nonetheless, the shift from care to facilitation was a fundamental change in the employer-employee relationship.

Standardisation

Within the larger corporation each beer brand had to meet the same quality standards in terms of food chemistry and production. Samples of local beers were sent to a central laboratory for testing. From time to time European technicians appeared in order to implement new procedures within the subsidiaries, usually involving a stay of several days per mission. In other parts of its daily operations, the brewery was also becoming increasingly dependant on the mother corporation to sustain its functionality. The intention was no longer to operate on a self-sustainable basis, but rather as an integrated part of global supply chains, respecting international norms and executing a universal process logic. Knowledge, standards, requirements, machines and equipment, spare parts and supplies, all these things were arranged centrally by the mother corporation. "...almost everything is controlled... We work with the [corporate] spirit, this is a great influence" [plant engineer].

As a result of this increasing standardisation the majority of local operations, especially in technical departments, were now done by Rwandan experts, with only remote supervision through responsible central departments (bookkeeping was observed by a different department than work security, for example). The overall goal of these efforts was to establish an efficient and predictable organisation worldwide, based on a structure that to a certain extent was technically optimised and *"doesn't need people"* [plant engineer]. *"The most important [local] people are from marketing, they are not controlled, others are controlled [by corporate supervision]"* [plant engineer]. The corporate centre's aim was thereby to facilitate the subsidiary's independent operation while simultaneously turning it into an integral part of the larger world of the Multinational Corporation (MNC). A Rwandan engineer commented on the increasing influence that standards had on his work. He stated that the brewery *"is not maintaining independence"*. Headquarters' intention was seen as enabling *"remote control"* [engineer].

Connected to this, the introduction of ISO 9000 standards in the Rwandan brewery had been motivated by the corporation's pressure to become a standards-compliant enterprise. A plant manager mentioned the corporate *"standards bible"*, a heavy manual listing all technical and organisational requirements with which to comply. As a matter of fact, ISO conformity had virtually no significance in Rwanda itself. Knowledge of such regulations, let alone the demand for their implementation, was definitely limited during the time of research. It was thus not part of any meaningful *local* discourse. Though these standardisations were of high relevance in respect to the corporate structure and increasingly became an organisation-wide necessity in order to secure ISO compliance in those countries or contexts where this was indeed part of a meaningful discourse. Boiral (2003) elaborates on the introduction of ISO 9000 into workplaces from an institutionalist-organisational view. The processes of institutional isomorphism as described by Neo-Institutionalism (Chapter 2.2) were clearly observable in this context.

One of the major non-technical driving forces of standardisation was corporate accounting. A Rwandan accounting manager had direct access to the corporate system, and he was also supervised by it. No disconnected local paperwork was used for financial reporting and the processing of the company's core data. Hoffjan/Weide (2006:8) see accounting as one of the main elements in worldwide standardisation, and accordingly the harmonisation of internal and external financial reporting, controlling and process management were at the core of this company's unification efforts.

After the position of technical manager had been awarded to an experienced South Asian, the role of technical director, which had always been in the hands of a European corporate expert, was abandoned. The technical manager received a promotion and was intensively trained in order to meet his new responsibilities. On the question of whether there had been changes after he took over, he mentioned enhancing the responsibilities of his Rwandan personnel, and the facilitation of more open and direct communication. From this step onwards, there was no European expatriate present at the central production facility, which represented the ultimate core of the company. Monthly proof samples were sent to central laboratories, as the final means of control. Technical standards were present for every aspect of work, making major surprises unlikely. Members of the local staff seemed content with the new situation, regarding it as proof of their work. The facility was obviously running well enough to remove all European technicians, where in former times not only the position of technical director but also many of the operative jobs were done by expatriates.

However, this increasing homogenisation was not entirely positively received. From a local viewpoint it also appeared as pressure to follow directives that were not always in keeping with the situation at hand. *"They do many things in [European headquarters] which are imposed to the people here"* [Rwandan plant engineer]. One production engineer complained about the new application of standard productivity norms in African breweries, as these were severely lagging when averaged as an output in hectolitres per person per year. The idea behind such benchmarks was the mechanisation of production in order to increase output efficiency. *"But what we need is jobs."* It was not understood as appropriate by all groups of stakeholders that technical efficiency was to be the sole measure of company policy. In this context, occasional acts of protest, sabotage and blackmail were conducted by workers.

Sociocultural legitimation

The whole multinational corporation moved towards a system where single elements and processes were centrally developed and then replicated throughout the operational companies. Its organisation was about to enter a stage of conformity that had the potential to generate a geographically independent 'corporate normality' in the core functions of the technical and accounting departments, thus leading to an eradication of structural difference. Central planning and reporting then provided access and control for a corporate centre that was organisationally distant (Schreyögg 2000:21).

These dynamics notwithstanding, the brewery as an inner part of Rwandan society simultaneously held another view on its own reality. This view was subject to processes of sociocultural and institutional legitimation vis-à-vis the embedding local society. It took the form of 'integrative elements' that smoothened the intersection between foreign interests and the affected local communities. More importantly, the brewery had been treated as a high standing cornerstone of the national economy over many decades, and was deeply embedded in Rwandan material culture (cf Dettmar 1995 in a study on Nigerian-German joint ventures). This rather intangible but deep acceptance of the company as *belonging* to the country, experienced radical changes during the first decade of the new century. These changes were triggered both by a changing market situation and even more so by the corporation's internal standardisation and centralisation processes.

As a local company, the brewery was in need of legitimisation in the face of moral and material expectations of Rwandan society and the authorities. From the viewpoint of expatriate managers this was often seen as a way to bring up unjustified claims towards the company. *"Every day there is something that someone wants"* [former foreign director]. This statement should not be seen as a devaluation of the local social customs of reciprocity, but rather as a realistic account of the fact that the company was confronted with permanent desires and claims attempting to address its social responsibility. Over the last several decades, the local population at the production site had formed special relationship with the brewery that was difficult to experience for foreign management. In a sense of connectedness and mutual responsibility the local community had protected the brewery's facilities from destruction and plunder during the genocide period. It survived the crisis virtually untouched and was able to restart its operations directly thereafter. The brewery had been regarded as a common good belonging to the local public; it had provided work and income, infrastructure, bottled drinks, caritative donations and social stability. *"The people looked after the brewery as it was their own property"* [brewery engineer].

During the time of research, a period of tough rationalisation programmes had led to severe job losses. These measures have been the cause for fear and antagonisms throughout the workforce. A subsequently abandoned idea to severely downsize or replace the old facilities in order to seriously rationalise the production in a smaller new one elsewhere was especially seen by Rwandan company professionals as a threat to their own national standing for which there was no real need. *"That makes us more isolated"* [plant engineer]. *"[...] a money maker, but society is isolating you."* It was clear that these plans had no backing from the local community, and were widely unpopular. *"They will not revolt, but they will not consider it as their own."* In a moral economy the collective opinion of social communities plays an important role, and the step of considering something as 'one's own' is a central element in the process of collective acceptance. External management was widely accepted and often highly respected, but the company's assets were considered as belonging to the local or national community. Exclusive foreign dominance over local assets and resources in such a constellation is not treated as legitimate in all aspects by the local discourse. Foreign management was valued for its competence and efficiency, but not as having an exclusive say over the local means of production. One former high-ranking expatriate remarked: *"Oh yes, they claim that it belongs to them and that the beer belongs to them and that we are only the ones to manage it."* Ponte's (2004) article on the 'politics of ownership' highlights this aspect for Tanzanian companies and foreign investors. It potentially complicates foreign investment in such social environments. Mutual goodwill, trust and a readiness to communicate are important in these settings. When a good state is reached, however, the situation can be a mutually beneficial one. This is exemplified by the locals' protection of the brewery during the war.

A negative effect of the brewery's socio-economic visibility was its vulnerability as a target of jealousy and related attempts at enrichment by third parties. Over a certain period, several influential and not so influential people reportedly felt that they had been forgotten in the face of the ostensible wealth that the company represented. Moral accusations and suspicions of tax evasion were common attempts to exercise pressure. Concerned employees saw it as mandatory for the brewery to strengthen its public relations, and send positive signals to the public in the form of popular activities and symbolic donations, or, at least, not displaying a bad capitalist attitude. *"The opinion of the people is extremely important"* [Rwandan company technician]. Without better public relations the battle was regarded as lost to *"greedy"* interests. One should not act as an *"island"* conducting its business in *"isolation"* [plant engineer]. Taxes, customs, and moral accusations: public institutions and society at large would think of their own interests when they saw the money from the company and could cause for problems, the argument went. *"Business here is not as clean as in Europe"* [Rwandan engineer]. Such cautions do not imply a constant threat of corruption or nepotism (which was comparatively low and well managed in Rwanda). It simply could mean that business is not as distinguishable from social and political life as many company managers wish (on the low differentiation of African societies, Chabal/Daloz 1999). Many employees were unhappy with what they regarded as an unjustified and bad treatment from which their company suffered. They partially saw it as a negative reward for the management's ongoing strategy to decrease non-operative costs and strengthen technical effectiveness according to the ideas of industrial automatisation. *"The Brewery was integrated into society, but the cost was not great."* Criticism was laid on the expatriate management for not being sensitive enough to the balance in which foreign management operated when dealing with Rwandan, or more generally African, environments. *"Take yourself out of society and pretend to work clean... that's a dangerous way that won't fit. It's like this: I can make a problem for you that you don't have... that is how Africa works, you should know the place you work in."*[18]

Changing sociocultural legitimation

The phase of rationalisation and operative adjustments that occurred before the period of fieldwork resulted in heavy job losses, especially for 'non-productive' jobs (cleaning, security, administration, protocol, office servants). The Rwandan brewery had scored low in the ratio of productive to non-productive workers when compared to other African breweries of the same corporation. The magnitude of layoffs was unprecedented and caused intense friction within the workforce. From the general management's perspective it was mandatory to cut costs in non-vital parts of the company in order to remain competitive (particularly due to high tax burdens and increasing competition). Cutting costs was also necessary to allow for new human resources policies. The scheduled introduction of a retirement insurance system for all regular employees demanded that only the 'necessary' size of workforce remained. *"We can go further into social security matters and all that as soon as we've got only real jobs left here. Otherwise we just can't afford it"* [expatriate manager]. This led to a paradoxical situation: the company wanted to provide sophisticated social security programs according to the corporate human resources policies, but in order to be able to afford this in financial terms, all jobs that were not crucial to the core functions of the company had to be cancelled or outsourced. This caused dissent and partial resistance. Yet, three years later

---

18 Note: these issues are unconnected to a potential threat of general corruption, which is comparatively low in Rwanda. The examples are intended to highlight the tensions between the African moral economy and a standardised, decontextualised corporate logic.

when this director had already left the country, one employee commented on his time in Rwanda: *"what we will always remember Mr. [former general manager] for is that he gave us retirement insurance."*

Cultural brokers between the contexts

As we have seen, organisational elements were continuously transferred from the corporate structure to the local company. As a side effect, the local management was permanently faced with the need to fine-tune these new elements to local conditions. This adaptation was part of the brewery's 'unofficial' organisation procedures, and not always visible to expatriate managers. In a sense, the informal part of the organisation merged the two paradigms of the universalistic corporate logic with its European background and the Rwandan frame of reference with its social embeddedness originating in African moral economy. It was not up to the expatriate top management to handle these complexities, which instead were externalised further down the hierarchy and implicitly taken care of by the Rwandan directors and middle managers. Many high level employees were partially socialised into the Western lifestyle and could implicitly assist in the successful local adoption of corporate procedures. This led to a situation where certain regulations and practices were established within the brewery that were not originally part of the Rwandan social environment. Strict alcohol policies, technical and safety standards, rationalisation of supplier-customer relationships, individualised professionalism and many other issues initially caused irritation among the company workforce as well as triggering tensions in the company's interactions with its surroundings. European managers appreciated this enforcement of Western standards as a 'normalisation' of their work and as a simplification of procedures.

As an example, out in the field the company's agronomist acted less as a practical scientist or purchasing agent when taking care of the sorghum harvest that was produced by great numbers of autonomous peasant cooperatives in remote areas. He found himself in the role of organiser, coach, teacher and even diplomat vis à vis the rural crop producers who were mainly living off subsistence strategies and thus not accustomed to customer-oriented market production. The type of sorghum necessary for the brewery's production had only limited availability through the simple mechanism of supply and demand. The agronomist had to convince and even pressure the peasants' cooperative coordinators and village chiefs to adhere to their production agreements. He was virtually 'fighting' for the greatest part of the required quantity of brewable sorghum. This part of his job was done with the help of many unofficial approaches, and practices not found in formal task descriptions. *"They have no idea in Kigali what I'm doing here."* *"If we did things the way they want, [the company] would already be out of business"* [agronomist]. Acknowledging his immediate social responsibility towards the peasants was taken as a precondition of the job. *"If one told them in Kigali what I'm doing here on the road... They can't imagine that... giving people a lift to the next hospital. But, you see, even if I never meet that lady again she'll tell everyone out there who I am and that it was one from the [brewery] who brought her to the hospital, and they will know that I am a good man."*

The sales and distribution staff were controlling a similar process in respect to the handling of the numerous, weakly organised and often not formally educated beverage wholesalers, commercial distributors, caterers or restaurants which were directly supplied by the brewery's trucks. Giving active training to these client groups was a common way of improving their acceptance of the latest rationalisation measures or new distribution and hygiene standards. In fact, the supplier educated its customers.

In an attempt to explain typical shortcomings in these translation processes a Rwandan professional criticised the headquarters' managers for the occasional behaviour of white foreigner's pretending to know things better, thus establishing foreign ways of doing things and not being able to listen to local input. Sometimes, as he said, it was just not worth risking an argument with these superiors but rather for the sake of effectiveness better to listen patiently and later adapt the task to the actual conditions in a way that would work. The expatriate was then just left with his own sense of superior knowledge. *"Just let him be a muzungu"* [Rwandan employee, using expression for 'white man'].

Regardless of these issues, a transmission or translation of topics *from* the Rwandan context *into* a form commensurable with the Western top management was more difficult. Such processes were facilitated by Rwandan directors and high ranking external counsellors, bureaucrats, consultants and politicians, thus through conversation partners at eye level with the expatriate managers. Internal bottom-up translation processes were otherwise quite limited.

Translation and transfer of organisational culture

Within the multinational corporation the transfer of shared standards and procedures served as a powerful means to establish a common set of norms and values throughout its subsidiaries. The basis for these corporate values and norms was, in fact, the typical and common principles of contemporary (implicitly Western) organisation ideology. These principles are hardly worth mentioning nowadays in Western societies with their strict adherence to formal rationalism and economic effectiveness, but in a poor African country recovering from war they gain an almost 'cultural-political component'. In the course of the brewery's organisation development, a change of behaviour in the direction of Western organisational rationalism, was intended.

Viewed from the outside, it became apparent that in organisation development, human resources and the brewery's dealings with corporate headquarters, the inherent cultural differences and the subtleties of local context were not, or only rarely, taken into account. This was especially evident in the course materials used to train local professionals and new managers; they could have been taught in any European business school. The material basically resembled typical management literature. Similarly, the performance criteria were apparently so neutral that they seemed unconnected to any local, cultural or mental aspects. They appeared to be independent from the person teaching or applying them. What makes this matter interesting is the observation that the corporate culture *did* play an important role in communicating the performance oriented 'company spirit'. As part of a far reaching optimisation concept, the norms and values of the propagated corporate culture were implicitly in favour of performance criteria arising out of a capitalist rationalism and an individualised work ethic. Thus, they are part of the 'European' working style. Thus, while culture was not a major focus in the transnational management process, it was a central but hidden component of the multinational organisation. It gained this implicit significance in spite of its almost invisible impact on the 'universal' management concepts. The rules of behaviour taught to African managers and professionals did not explicitly differentiate between African and Western management styles, retaining a certain functional politeness. Officially, these management training sessions had to deal with replacing un-standardised or inefficient work processes with more efficient ones. What had not become official, however, was the fact that the target of these measures was to either transform or overcome working styles and routines that were apparently 'typically African'.[19] Here the key role of African professionals became visible. Their work ethic was, for the most part, compatible with or overtly inspired by the 'universal' rational-Western values of modern business organisation and individual work effectiveness. In their case, a cultural-contextual translation between corporate logic and Rwandan expectation was not complicated, or unnecessary. They were even in a position to become active agents who facilitated its transfer. But as the Rwandan/African context continued to exist, this small group of professionals now had

---

19 Other constellations are equally possible. Especially in South Africa the power relations between the cultures are no longer as self-evident and since the 1990s they have been the subject of constructive debates (Mbigi 1997, Cristie et.al. 1994, Lessem 1996). In the case of the brewery, the economic pattern of enterprise capitalism was, so to speak, seeking to gain entry to a new and previously unexploited field.

a translation issue to solve themselves. They were forced to 'sell' the new corporate regulations, viewpoints and procedures to Rwandan subordinates, and even more so to the authorities and society as a whole.

A reflection of potential differences between European and African contexts was excluded from these transfers. All activities were instead concentrated on operative finances, trainings, techniques, etc. This circumvention of deeper divergences secured a smooth operation, and prevented the organisation from slumping into a loss of direction. Similar but more destructive dynamics were described in the organisations of bilateral development aid by Rottenburg (2002, 2005), who introduced the terminology of the 'hegemonic meta code' to highlight the hidden (or not so hidden) dominance of operative language inherent in the formal-rational organisation logic that has emerged from Western countries.

In order to ease its own procedures, the company was willing to assist public inspection authorities or tax revenue departments in doing their work more effectively. This offer was made for want of a more predictable institutional environment for the company to contend with. Local actors with great influence who were not operating along the principles of formal rationalism were the most difficult to cope with. As part of a worldwide corporation it depended on predictable laws and regulations much more than most of its local counterparts.

In the following I present a brief review of several aspects concerning multinational corporations, followed by a short summary of the ethnographic material.

Global corporate structure – standardization, differentiation, centralisation

Management and control departments of large multinationals need to coordinate sizeable numbers of operations and foreign subsidiaries worldwide. There is a need to develop globally standardised management and control practices, however local customisation still has to be taken into account (Hoffjan/Weide 2006:1). Commercial activities with a worldwide focus are intended to achieve economies of scale which in turn rely on effective procedures and transfers of knowledge. This aspect of multinational corporations is mentioned by Gilroy (2005). He also gives a comprehensive account of multinational enterprises and their implications for the African context (2005:105): "[T]he main advantage of the multinational enterprise, as differentiated from a national corporation, lies in its flexibility to transfer economic resources, information, knowledge and ideas internationally through a globally (or at least regionally) maximising network that offers an almost infinite variety of transactional options." This implies a general possibility to apply the same set of knowledge and processes everywhere. MNC rely on a world where standards are valid across vastly different settings and locations.

From the perspective of a corporate headquarters it seems imperative to standardise the corporate subunits as much as possible in order to enhance control and make performance more comparable and predictable. But local corporate subsidiaries also need to adjust their operations to local requirements. Therefore, multinational enterprises face a conflict between global standardisation and local customisation (cf Hoffjan/Weide 2006:2). Ronge (2001), in his empirical study on the organisational structure of MNC maintaining Chinese subsidiaries, states that increasing rates of worldwide homogenisation and global learning lead to a gradual eradication of country-specific differences. In the future the 'uniqueness' that Western MNC will allow their Chinese subsidiaries will consequently be declining, while worldwide corporate logic will become the most important factor in the formation of organisation patterns and strategies (ibid:126). Thus, subsidiaries in non-Western countries where Western businesses still have less experience or where the conditions remain distinctive are expected to become more regular parts of the corporate structure as soon as the conditions are 'normalised' from a corporate view (ibid:195-202). This position takes a universalistic view of global enterprise structures and expects local contexts to become inserted into global standards in the long run. However, in Africa, there are fewer experiences and such developments are only in their infancy.

Increasing centralisation

Barlett/Ghoshal (1987, 1988) expected a transnational organisational pattern that is network based and coordinated in a regionalised and decentralised way. This decentralised organisation structure was perceived as an adaptation to changing conditions on the world markets. Hedlund/Rolander (1990) envisioned an even further decentralisation and postulated an organisation type in highly industrialised enterprises which they called 'heterarchy'. In this ideal type, worldwide subsidiaries fulfil strategic roles that fit together in a global corporate context. Coordination would be high and specialised but no longer in the hands of a corporate centre (Hedlund/Rolander 1990:25-26, quoted from Beyer 2001a:23f). Beyer's empirical study found that, on the contrary, the decade of the 1990s saw the local adaptation of MNC partially decline and corporate strategy become increasingly centralised once again. Hypotheses of hierarchy-free cluster organisations were not verified. This trend is also reflected in the present case study, with increasing responsibilities drawn towards the central corporate departments.

The changing view on MNC in Africa – local embedding or skyscraper economy?

Perceptions and judgements of MNC have undergone a change since the 1970s in management literature, and also in public opinion. In developmental discourses several favourable aspects of MNC were mentioned with increasing regularity. Most prominently mentioned in this respect are technology and knowledge transfers (for a discussion see Gilroy 2005:107-122). Critical voices point to the problems that arise when multinational corporations grow single islands of prosperity in an overall environment of underdevelopment, with limited possibilities for beneficial diffusions into the hinterland. Foreign investment projects are expected to remain in enclaves separated from the host country, only stimulating ruinous competition between local suppliers (Lieten 1999:121). A 'skyscraper economy' is feared to be the result (Turok 1993). Additionally, MNC are often perceived as possessing a 'preferred bargaining position' vis-à-vis the governments of poor countries, which leads them to keep most of the benefits for themselves (Gilroy 2005:125). I would argue that an MNC's bargaining position in African countries may not always be directly 'preferred', but rather 'exposed'.

Proponents of MNC activity in developing countries expect positive backward-forward linkages between the corporations and local firms, resulting in transfer and upgrading of local skills and technology (ibid). Multinationals frequently offer specific support to local enterprises that are part of their value chain, such as access to finance and capacity building. The beverage corporation from this case study had rising demands in operative competencies to be disposed of by its local distributors and retailers. Hence it had to assist them in meeting these demands (e.g. through a computerisation of distributors' order and accounting systems). Such upgrading policies may result in a gradual closure of opportunities for the informal sectors of an economy, but they also have the potential to strengthen the formalised and higher aggregated sectors. In short, these activities contribute to concentration processes.

In line with these arguments, Forstater/MacDonald/Raynard (2002) described linkages of business and poverty reduction; the topic was also propagated by the World Bank. The latter calls for business action in favour of the Millennium Development Goals (World Bank and World Bank Institute, 2005), highlighting the connection between business and the MDGs (World Bank Institute, 2006), as well as the fight against poverty as a business opportunity (World Bank Institute, InWEnt, Instituto Ethos and The Global Compact, 2005). InWEnt (2006:35) and the UN Industrial Development Organisation (2002) state that one of the most important impacts a business can have is involving small enterprises in its value chain, either as suppliers or distributors of their products. MNC are expected to bring their advanced technology into developing countries, while the receivers are expected to invest in technological learning and absorptive capacity (Gilroy 2005:117). InWEnt (a former German development agency) summarised this issue in positive terms: "In fact, the most important and sustainable impact business can have is simply by doing what it does best: doing business" (2006:12).

Summary

The brewery's organisational culture was driven by a structural evolution from a locally embedded Rwandan company operated by European experts towards an integrated corporate unit operating according to universal standards. While the brewery gradually became 'remote controlled' and managed in a standardised way, the operative responsibilities were increasingly transferred to Rwandan personnel. During these changes the local adaptation of the company progressively declined. Corporate management is now less willing and able to cater to specific local issues than it has in previous decades. The establishment of worldwide corporate standards was a primary goal on the way to enhancing predictability and effectiveness from the perspective of headquarters. From a local Rwandan point of view, this process included a loss of the company's embeddedness within the national culture. The days of the brewery having been 'genuinely Rwandan', as the only producer of drinks and provider of objects central to the material culture (prestigious beers), were seemingly coming to an end. Amidst these changes the Rwandan professionals fulfilled a key role within the organisation. Implicitly they took responsibility for the cultural-structural translation between the contexts of the Western corporation, the Rwandan base of the company and the surrounding country. It is a daily achievement of the brewery's organisation to simultaneously legitimise itself in the face of the mother corporation and the Rwandan host society. The dynamism of its organisational culture is therefore the result of an oscillation between the poles of corporate logic and the Rwandan-African moral economy.

4.3 GERMAN MEDIA TECHNOLOGY CONTRACTORS

International contracting between business partners who do not know each other or each other's working conditions is a special field of Transboundary Cooperations. Arrangements between such actors are of a temporary nature, and the scope of activities is narrowly defined. Nevertheless, several specific aspects make them interesting in respect of our research topic, and thus a case of this type was included in the selection of case studies.

Two German technology companies were contracted for projects where Rwandan customers demanded planning, delivery and installation of large multimedia systems. The first project, which was probably also the first of its kind in Rwanda, concerned an extensive installation of multimedia equipment in buildings with a multi-purpose use for accommodation and meetings. The opportunity of a second contract for a similar project emerged as a follow-up from this engagement. Not being within the exact field of the first company's core competencies, this second project involved another larger company. Contacts between the Rwandan clients and the second company were established through facilitation by the persons involved in the first deal.

First contract, first company
A Rwandan representative in charge of purchasing equipment and taking care of its proper installation was searching for a suitable supplier in Germany. Finally, a small specialised company was contacted and after initial tentative inquiries the first agreements were made. It turned out that aside from being a professional and experienced company, it was also the only one supplying the desired equipment that was also willing and able to do it in Rwanda. The Rwandan customer representative disposed over detailed technical and market information, and was also a tough negotiator. Once the deal was complete a whole array of technical equipment and a full service installation agreement was purchased. The agreement included the personal presence of the German company at the construction site for installation and set-up. Arrangements for transportation of the material were soon made, and a travel date for the German contractor was at first postponed and then urgently fixed by the customer. Travel and accommodation were at the customer's expense, as was providing the administrative and practical framework of the project.

Time constraints on the side of the supplier and the customer's increasing pressure to meet (already missed) deadlines made it apparent that completing the installation work in a short time was necessary, and that this would put the German contractor on a tight schedule. After reviewing the details and descriptions, the company owner estimated the time needed for this project under German conditions to be a couple of days and added extra safety time. Both sides were interested in keeping this period short, and a stay of two weeks was arranged. They agreed that if everything worked according to plan, the remaining days would be spent on gorilla tracking. All materials and tools had to be shipped in as the customer's representative claimed no local responsibility for technical provisions, advising the contractor to be self-reliant. *"Imagine you have to do the job on a small island, bring in everything you need, every little screw, or cable, or tool."* The contractor arrived with two individuals, including the owner, and the reception was both respectful and hospitable. Accommodation and catering were carefully selected according to the host's expectations of what European guests would desire. The German's every wish was taken into consideration, and concerns about food were addressed by not serving local dishes at first and only reluctantly later. In sum, the Rwandan hosts expressedly reflected as many typical European worries about Africa as they could, and aimed at sparing their guests as many of the negative aspects of local Rwandan conditions as possible. The setting in which the Germans were situated consisted of the hotel and the project's construction site. As intended by the hosts, it was almost isolated from the surrounding environment.

On the construction site

In contradiction to what had been discussed in Germany, the construction site was far from an optimal environment for installing sensitive electronic devices. Deviating from the mutual agreements and the contractor's expectations, the buildings were still under construction. From unpacking boxes to installing and testing the equipment, dust and an unreliable supply of electricity made effective work difficult. Consequently, progress was severely behind schedule from the first day on.

Workers and engineers at the construction site met the incoming foreigners with curiosity and respect. It was not a typical sight to see Europeans engaged in manual labour. Workers assigned to assist them were motivated but their lacking competencies in the field of electronics, and the difficulty in communication (mixing English, French and Kinyarwanda) rendered these efforts less effective than desired. The Rwandan representative, who was the coordinating agent, had made the deal in Germany but was not directly involved in the civil engineering and not permanently available on the site. This left the task of speeding up the process and coordinating the Rwandan workers and project managers to the German contractors themselves, who were forced to communicate across language barriers. Thus, despite serious initial efforts on the part of the customer to reach the opposite, the contractors inadvertently became involved in the routines of a Rwandan construction site and a weakly organised civil engineering project. If the German company owner had stopped working under these conditions, demanding that the preliminary stages of construction be completed as expected before the multimedia equipment could be installed, the contractors could only have left the site without real progress for the time being. But in order to sustain cooperation and good partnership, and with the expectation of quick improvement, these unfavourable circumstances were politely ignored when the contractor confirmed his ability to carry out the job under these conditions.

Most payments and shipments had been completed before departure leaving the rest of the operation to be agreed upon without many formalities or definitions other than oral agreements. The venture thus depended on mutual goodwill and a shared understanding of what ought to be done and how. Any decision other than trying to continue would have brought this collaborative project to a critical point. Realising this, the customer's representative was getting worried about whether the contractor would decline to perform his work as the situation was not in a state that allowed for the normal installation of electronic equipment. It became obvious that the quality of work was limited under these conditions. Technical problems hampering the contractor's progress had to be solved by the Rwandan chief engineer, which occurred in a slow manner. Electricity was scarce, masonry and cement works incomplete and transportation occasionally proved difficult. The contractor became the final person to worry about taking care of these problems, as the Germans had to remain mindful of their tight schedule.

After starting to imagine what a failed or disproportionally delayed multimedia project could mean for him, the customer's representative started to get nervous. After trying to coordinate the venture he applied various forms of pressure to several key individuals, and urged the contractor to secure the progress of the project. He was afraid that this *"very small"* endeavour might turn into a negative situation in which he would be personally implicated. It was known to him and all other local persons that failures were unlikely to be tolerated by their superiors without very good explanations. The failure of an international project would be a personal disaster for him, despite the fact that he had only marginal influence on the causes of the complications. The Rwandan representative had no disciplinary control over the personnel on the construction site, but out of an immediate personal interest had to ensure that the foreign contractors completed their work no matter how unfinished the rest of the building was. Here, the informal and cool organisation of the project, which had been refreshing at the beginning, became a liability. All activities were marked by respect for and fear of the superiors, but possibilities of hierarchical flexibility and dependable horizontal coordination were limited. The authoritative structures and the informal mode of organisation made it difficult to alter the situation.

According to the contractor, a similar project under the conditions he knew from Germany would have taken a period of three to four days. He eventually decided that the installation could not be completed on time, and suggested that the representative discuss this problem with his boss. His plan was to postpone the project to a second trip after the major construction works were finished. Initially the representative declined, fearing the repercussions that such an attempt would pose for him and particularly for the chief engineer who was accountable for the slow progress and the chaos at the construction site. The immobilised project had put this engineer in a risky situation. *"Let's contain the problem for now. Bringing it up like this would mean hanging a friend"* [customer representative].

It became visible that difficult situations can arise in authoritative and informal structures where open communication is blocked by fear, and problems are hidden for as long as possible. Out of friendly respect for the wishes of the Rwandan customer representative, with whom the German company owner had a good personal relationship, the work continued until the last evening. Finally the Rwandan was forced to face the situation of informing his boss about the necessity for the contractor to come again. Eventually a second journey was accepted, bringing great relief to all involved, and acknowledging the luck of the Rwandans responsible. Several weeks later the German contractor made a second journey, but the progress at the site was not much better. Only certain issues had been improved and accommodation had been relocated to a technically more suitable but less 'civilised' place. This was a matter on which the contractor had insisted, but which the Rwandan hosts, out of respect, would not have dared to have undertaken at the beginning. Being in a position to host European professionals and feeling an obligation to represent their country as positively as possible, the Rwandan customers had not considered exposing their guests to anything seen by them as 'too African' in order to spare their guests hardships and trouble. During the second stay, the mutual learning curve allowed them to share their ideas when they came together during meals and discussions. Nevertheless the second stay also ended with many long hours of troubleshooting at the construction site before the equipment was installed and running.

Second contract, second company

These activities generated the opportunity for a second contract in relation to another prospective Rwandan customer that was in need of conducting a similar but bigger project. The owner of the first German company decided that the nature of this project was interesting, but not exactly suited to his own core business. So another company from the same region was contacted. After initial hesitations due to their lack of experience with African settings along with active facilitation by the individuals involved in the first project, this second company finally decided to send a representative to Rwanda for an assessment. He stayed in the country for three days. After submitting a final offer, which was accepted, further arrangements were made and a team of engineers travelled to Rwanda to install the equipment within a similar framework as the first contractor. Lessons learned from the first case proved helpful as the second contractor was provided with much more background information, and the team knew what to expect to a certain extent.

The project required two assignments lasting two weeks each. All in all, this second contract was able to be handled under much less complicated conditions than the first. Support through local personnel was offered in advance, but it became clear that the skills required to operate the specific equipment could not be provided by these external workers and the German engineers did most of the work themselves. Their stay in the country was similarly detached from the Rwandan environment, as had been the case with the first contractor. This project was embedded in a bigger, more official and formalised setting, and it can be concluded that it benefited from this as a stabilising structure. The second German company had been reluctant at first to seriously consider submitting an offer to Rwanda. To its management, this request posed a conceptual challenge as it lay outside their previous horizons, and no experience with African customers had existed before.

Further aspects in transboundary contracting
For the first German company the whole affair ended unfortunately, one year later with open payments and missing equipment. Additionally, the customer did not provide feedback as to whether the equipment was working properly or the superiors satisfied. Initial ideas of regular service contracts could never be implemented, and ultimately the contact broke off. This unfavourable situation was the result of a highly ambiguous constellation caused by unclear responsibilities and fear. Implicitly the customer's representative refused to be the person responsible for the lost material, and he delayed enquiries about the open payments. In particular, travel expenses from the second stay were never brought up in open discussion. It can be concluded that even when the financial approval for a second trip was obtained from a superior, the actual amount of the resulting additional costs was either not anticipated by the Rwandan project managers or even hidden from the superior entirely. Whatever the case may be, the Rwandan contacts blamed each other and tried to phase out the contact, fearing admission of these failures. An open admission of the problems that caused extra costs would have been a precondition for a clean end to the contract, but the prospect of affronting a small foreign company was probably seen as less dangerous than risking disapproval from the Rwandan's own strict superiors. Personalised authority and the fear of disciplinary punishment were the primary driving forces behind the organisational methods of the Rwandans; a fact that created great hindrances to an efficient problem solution and instead stimulated a 'management by muddling through'. In this critical situation good relations with the German contractor might have been considered more expendable than the individual position of the directly involved Rwandans in the face of their own superior. Axelrod's (1984) notion of 'end game tactics' seems to apply here. When one party sees itself under pressure at the end

of a relationship, it considers it less necessary to treat the other side as warmly as it had at the beginning. This unfavourable ending of an initially positive collaboration was not triggered by bad intentions or exploitative strategies, but rather was a result of the inefficiencies that arise from the organisation and control patterns found in settings of this type in combination with a lack of experience in handling such matters by both parties.

Seen through the eyes of an external observer, the contracting arrangements could be characterised as attempts to establish a temporary, hybrid glocal setting in which the foreign contractors could operate. From the customers' side sincere hospitality and respect were shown, and accommodation and catering were on a very high level. All efforts were made to ensure a comfortable stay for the international guests. A review of the situation reveals that in order for these arrangements to function smoothly it may have been helpful to reduce the potential of interferences through local 'imperfections'. The hybridity in these settings came into existence because the working environment was already partially disconnected from 'Rwandan conditions' but also not entirely following 'international (or western) standards'. What for the Germans may have been an experience of 'working in Africa', is likely for the hosts to have been an idea of levelling out 'African influences' in favour of the foreign partners. Here the complex situation of connecting the technical contexts of heterogeneous partners became visible in a situation that lacked the facilitation and institutional background in a form that is available for multinational organisations and large cooperations.

4.4 Rwandan Construction Enterprise

There is a small to medium sized construction enterprise within which I was able to conduct a case study. It began operating shortly after the war and has had a turbulent history in terms of growth and partial decline as well as in a subsequent focus on a special customer base. Its main field of activity at the time of research was the planning and execution of public projects issued by governmental departments and donor agencies such as schools, public buildings, waterworks and rural infrastructure. Due to a network of personal contacts, a good reputation, and the owner's ability to communicate in relevant European languages, this company was a preferred contracting partner for many small to medium construction projects funded by European organisations.

The company and its owner

After living and studying in Europe for more than 10 years, Eduard, a Rwandan civil engineer returned home directly after the war and founded his own construction company. He brought a collection of second-hand equipment with him and the motivation to start a business by contributing to his country's reconstruction. Due to his personal background he was well integrated in the European, mainly German, expatriate community and maintained good relationships with foreign organisations. I followed him throughout his working life for quite a lengthy period of time and was thus able to observe interactions with expatriates from the perspective of a Rwandan businessman.

The construction company was situated in an industrial area, where it disposed over a crowded office building, several artisan workshops, stores, and a truck loading field. At the office it employed a core team consisting of three people in administration and planning, around 15 people at the workshops (carpenters, welders) that were supervised by experienced elder craftsmen and a number of truck drivers and technical personnel. When experienced manpower was needed for new construction sites throughout the country, the company owner could call upon large groups of potential workers already known to him from previous projects. The size of the company could multiply quickly according to the situation of its current business. This larger number of people formed a more or less dependable workforce, but Eduard, when asked, would say that the number of people who were *"really working for me"* was only about five or six. Mostly, the required numbers of wage labourers tasked with forming bricks, earthworks and unloading trucks were said to be instantly available on the spot *"out there"*.

Among the most valuable company assets were the workshops with their machinery and tools, and a vehicle inventory that consisted of an off-road car, a pick-up, two 30 ton trucks and a 7.5 ton truck. Gear, machines and technical support used on the construction sites was mainly limited to the trucks and vehicles and a comparatively well-provisioned selection of smaller equipment such as welding tools, drills and portable diesel generators. Equipment in the workshops was old and semi-mechanized, but of good quality. The carpenters used the collection of ancient European machines Eduard had brought with him when he returned to Rwanda, with the oldest dating from the 1930ies. The carpenters' work was beyond the ranged of local artisans, and consequently furniture was often a vital part of Eduard's full service projects. The personnel responsible for these tasks were highly qualified, and Eduard proudly mentioned the superior quality of their work as much as the reliable operation of his workshops.

Company organisation and business structure

Eduard's business revolved mainly around him and his personality and was a typical 'one man show', similar to many companies of a comparable size. Formal company structures were therefore of low importance, and relations with employees as well as customers were handled in a personalised manner. Thus the most essential tool in the company was the contact list in the owner's mobile phone. Through it he accessed a large network of closely and not so closely related affiliates on whom he could draw depending on current needs. His staff, though fulfilling essential functions, was seen merely in a supporting role. Eduard took care of many standard tasks personally, such as acquisition of raw materials, arranging for vehicle repairs and shopping for small tools. *"...yes, they [employees] can do it normally, but... then it is better if I do it by myself because they mostly don't do it right."* This statement reflects on the difficulties Rwandan companies often had with their staff, and the staff had with companies. Commercial and technical responsibilities were therefore almost exclusively concentrated in the hands of the owner, even if this resulted in a state of permanent stress and fatigue. He claimed that this approach was the only way to secure his operations and prevent excesses of irresponsible and fraudulent behaviour.

While standing in a hardware store: *"With me they can't joke here... When I send someone like [an employee] to buy this [special tool] he returns with it costing four times as much, you know... they just make a deal from behind between him and the guy here at the counter and divide the difference among them."*

Such suspicions notwithstanding, he only rarely interfered in tasks such as vehicle logistics, workshop operations and manual labour as long as he had confidence in the individuals conducting them. Occasional problems with this detached form of coordination occurred when deadlines or quality requirements were at risk or staff members exceeded a tolerable threshold of absence. Problems that were most pressing at a given moment were given full attention by the company owner regardless of the problem's nature. These issues could range from planning the next project with an architect or negotiations for getting the essential 30-ton truck repaired to following a technically competent and, therefore, indispensable employee to a funeral function in order to confirm whether the frequent absences of this person had been justified, or whether he had lied about his whereabouts.

Another issue constantly putting pressure on the company was the habit of employees asking for credit or advance payment of wages; debts that were difficult for the company to recover. A steady loss of minor equipment and truck fuel due to employee theft was another issue plaguing the company. The owner's reactions included delaying wage payment and other forms of 'bullying'. But such options of acting out of a superior position were limited. Punishing an able and therefore scarce workforce was much less of an option than trying to convince them to collaborate.

Many workshop artisans as well as several drivers and technicians did not belong to the core personnel and were employed on a short term 'hire and fire' basis. The company 'breathed' temporary employments in accordance with changing project volumes, making it resemble a hybrid institutional arrangement between a 'real' organisation and volatile labour contracts. A strict hierarchy adhering to formal rules was not established in this situation.

Meeting financial responsibilities towards staff and suppliers as well as general coverage of operating costs greatly depended on the temporary availability of cash. Those paid first were business partners or staff members whose cooperation was temporarily most needed. Other payments were made after these priorities had been met, and a number of debts remained open when relations with the potential receivers was of a lower importance. This attitude towards financial obligations was an implicit outcome of under-financing rather than a planned strategy, and thus mainly provoked by a constant lack of cash. Delayed payments from completed projects or urgent problems such as vehicle breakdowns could cause the company difficulties within days. As a result, the workforce could shrink to a core group of staff members or even to only the administrative secretary when times were hard; the quality of the owner's personal life declined accordingly. Eduard's company and household were not perceived as separated entities and were managed as one. The company, considered a medium enterprise according to Rwandan standards, was not subjected to a consistent form of financial control. Nearly all decisions involved expenditure evaluations, making the entire management process very sensitive to the current ups and downs of the company's cash flow. During times of severe liquidity shortage, despite an acceptable contract volume, Eduard could resort to actions such as borrowing 100 euro from the anthropologist (*"to the poor African"*, as he said) which were immediately changed into Rwandan francs by his secretary, and invested in cement bags to be loaded on to the evening truck headed to a remote construction site. *"I'm struggling"*, *"you get your money back"*. Complications resulting from liquidity shortages vary in their severity but have, in principle, to be seen as inherent to the economic strategy rather than as a sign of a temporary problem. Financial buoyancy leads to higher consumption and an ability to manage larger projects, but the general situation of under-financing does not change.

The fragile organisation of a Rwandan medium enterprise

Some of the features making up the Rwandan construction enterprise resemble a typical Western project company. But the totality in the way private matters were seen to be one with professional objectives complicated this definition. The relationships with suppliers and personnel, which were based on permanent negotiation, networking and mutual goodwill, also add to the complexity of distinguishing between the company and the private sphere. This also makes it difficult to draw precise borders around the business and its objectives. Decisions to invest in the business were not only subject to company-internal considerations but could also serve as a means of preventing the owner's money from being taken by relatives or others in immediate need.

Anthropologist: *"Why are you so sure that these trucks are a necessary buy right now? I mean, it's kind of costly."* Eduard: *"Well, yes, but it's a real bargain and I expect this [upcoming project] ... and, additionally, I'd rather put my current money into the company and do something for myself than let my relatives notice that I have cash right now and want something from it."*

No clear distinction can be drawn here between the company and the social environment of its owner. Several aspects relevant to Eduard's company were also mentioned by Heidenreich (1995) in his ethnographic study on Ugandan small scale carpenters. Although Heidenreich's fieldwork was concerned with businesses of a much smaller size and employees with lower levels of education, some parallels rooted in the economic background structures could be found. Most important in this respect are the issues related to an unreliable workforce and the unstable quality of work. Company owners encountered frequent problems when deadlines or quality standards were not met because workers failed to adhere to arrangements. Furthermore, the absence of administrative capacity, efficient measures of cost control and a lack of liquid assets were noted by Heidenreich. Constant delay of payments puts pressure on worker-employer relationships and threatens the sustainability of businesses. The hybrid character of these enterprises is emphasised through their fragile hierarchies. While technical qualifications and suitable work discipline are present, the relations between employers and workers are constantly negotiated and unstable. Every new order has to be arranged for, which makes it difficult to maintain these small businesses in a reliable manner (ibid: 54-64f). It seems that companies of this kind find it rather challenging to establish themselves as sustainable organisations.

Relationship with expatriate customers

Donor organisations, NGOs, embassies, European companies and expatriate project managers were among the construction company's preferred contracting partners, together with national public institutions. Private projects such as housing and real estate posed greater difficulties as those customers tended to be more unreliable and put pressure on prices regardless of quality. Hence the company frequently executed construction work for European organisations. Typical projects included schools, sports facilities and rural infrastructures, which were built according to the donor organisations' social initiatives, often as parts of larger development projects. Eduard presented himself to potential expatriate customers as a competent and experienced local partner capable of solving problems in a way that made sense to foreign experts. He was aware of Europeans' needs as well as what they are likely to fear when dealing with Rwandan partners regarding reliability, quality standards and transparency. Dealing with expatriates gave Eduard the opportunity to behave in a semi-European fashion, dedicatedly expressing cultural openness and relaxed personal manner. This attitude was welcomed by foreigners as it facilitated access to otherwise inaccessible local issues. Despite his almost patriotic and pro-African attitude, Eduard in these situations appreciated the possibilities of communicating freely and without paying attention to the sometimes stiff manners he sensed among many of his compatriot business colleagues. These habits made him a favoured partner both for personal conversation and professional cooperation among a number of European experts at that time. Eduard's linguistic proficiency and open personality fostered relationships in ways that were familiar to Europeans. Over time he became well integrated into the local expatriate community and knew the post-war history of many foreign organisations better than the constantly changing European experts themselves. He was well integrated into the expatriate community to the extent of being invited to social events where he easily mixed with the foreigners. Subjects discussed at these events, however, quite often reflected critical viewpoints or outright cynicism, attitudes that can be frequently encountered within the expat community. Listening to Europeans speaking negatively about their Rwandan experiences angered him, as he felt they were guilty of misjudgement. *"You know, yesterday I've been to this [expatriate evening celebration]. I got so angry! They always have to talk down everything here."*

Due to the personal nature of these contacts and the long track record with several donor organisations, Eduard also became involved in maintenance works for office buildings and housing belonging to the expatriates themselves. This work ranged from renovating whole compounds to fixing a jammed door or painting window frames. Although each assignment was welcomed, and maintaining good customer relations was seen as important, minor repair work made him feel he was being pressured into doing annoying minor jobs. When repairing their own houses, expatriates often became impatient, overly particular or outright fussy and had to be calmed down. In the meantime important business was often waiting elsewhere. *"Look, I'm like the caretaker for the [Europeans] ...but I have to laugh about it silently... she thinks of herself as someone better... that woman, with her stupid door... that's only a waste of time for me"*.

From time to time the company acted as a sub-contractor for large European construction enterprises who were awarded the big donor funded infrastructure projects by the European Union. Due to its good track record, Eduard's communication skills and a reputation as a reliable local partner this field had the potential of becoming an important and lucrative additional market. The work mainly consisted of supportive tasks such as planning and executing community infrastructures. Eduard thereby became a reliable contractor for European companies and a comfortable local counterpart who was able to communicate with the foreign staff of these large corporations. Subcontracting often consisted of smaller roles in large projects that were technically unproblematic but logistically too complicated on a micro-level for foreigners to manage. A road construction company might request that Eduard prepare parts of a slope on a road construction site or an infrastructure contractor could ask him to contribute to the detailed planning of rural installations. Such activities can be seen as fulfilling the role of a 'buffer' between European contract partners and local conditions. From the expatriate's point of view, other Rwandan contractors with less intercultural experience would potentially have become part of their own management problem rather than being part of the solution.

Over the years Eduard's company had become dependent on foreign contract partners and came to specialise in customers related to the foreign development sector. When difficulties or misunderstandings occurred between Eduard and his expatriate customers, they characterised him as a *"rouge"* or *"chaot"*, while he complained of the small budget they proposed and the maximum output they demanded. Other foreign managers attested to his integrity and professionalism. In one bigger organisation a foreign director entrusted key construction and maintenance work to Eduard rather than to his own Rwandan engineers. It was undoubtedly a relief to this manager that he had found a reliable civil engineer to solve pressing problems. *"This one is serious"* [European manager].

Eduard, as an academically educated professional, naturally reflected the opinions and intentions of his expatriate counterparts. He paid close attention to differences, discourses and occasional stereotypes calling it his *"special ability"* to master translation and communication between Rwandan and European life-worlds. *"I always have to think like a Rwandan and like a European at the same time"*, [when mixing up euro and dollars in a discussion]: *"Oh, I should have thought about it. As a Rwandan I should have kept both currencies in mind, you know... Here we must always be ready to translate according to the one we have to deal with."*

Eduard can be seen as a living example of an active 'cultural broker'; as a person who translates social meaning of different origins and facilitates transboundary interactions. Although efforts to foster economic and cultural interchange are often performed gladly, the cultural broker's desire for income opportunities is often attached. In their work, Bierschenk, Chauveau and Olivier de Sardan (2000) describe cultural brokers in the development sector. These 'development brokers' are local agents who are primarily seeking opportunities for an appropriation of foreign resources by negotiating between local and expatriate interests. Eduard, as a variation on this pattern can be seen as promoting the services of his own company by means of his cross-cultural skills.

Concluding remarks

All in all, the company in this field study was made up of an arrangement that falls short of classic definitions of a firm with fixed boundaries and assets. "Within text-book economics, the boundary between a company and the outside world is often conceived as one between 'firm' and 'market'" (Chapman 2001:22). According to the New Institutional Economics, the intermediate form of a semi-organised enterprise such as Eduard's could be classified as consisting of a core resembling a 'real' organisation with a cluster of hybrid arrangements around it that resemble less controllable quasi-market exchanges within the company's own borders (on oranisation theory see Chapter 2.2). The actual behaviour of enterprises of this kind comes closer to a state of an ad hoc organisation than to a classic company structure. However, such set-ups can provide opportunities to participate in the economy at a low initial cost of investment and consolidation. Though initially helpful, in later stages this can pose hindrances to consolidation, when needed. Maintaining and expanding a business in this manner is increasingly difficult when its size exceeds the owner's control capability.

Entrepreneurs operating Rwandan SME tend to follow a particularistic approach in organising their working environment. Unsteady arrangements and low levels of mutual trust often prevent them from aggregating their efforts. In the classic domestic pattern companies tend not to be larger than what can still be controlled by one person. Irresponsible or fraudulent employee behaviour is regarded as the norm. Employers distrust their staff, frequently treat them with disrespect and pay low wages. Similar management patterns were also present in Europe at the beginning of industrialisation. A German textbook on enterprise management from the year 1868 proposed that the best method to be followed by managers is to give clear oral instructions, be present everywhere at all times, personally keep everything in mind and keep an eye on employees (Emmighaus 1868:9, quoted by Kocka 2000:36f). Economic and business strategies under such conditions are often more person-centred than organisation-centred, and short term planning plays a dominant role due to incalculable situations. It must be noted that Eduard's company was mentioned as being comparatively well managed. The preceding comment applies to the general situation in the wider economy. Risk-handling and profit-maximising are approached with further expansion into other, more glamorous business sectors. This leads small-scale entrepreneurs to cease concentrating on their original business. Furthermore, success in Rwanda, and in African economies more generally, does not necessarily mean that one is willing and able to continue a previously lucrative business. Being successful can also lead entrepreneurs to withdraw from their original venture in order to become something 'bigger', a hotel owner or a car importer, for instance. As a consequence, the concept of success is associated solely with social standing made possible by economic achievement, rather than with professional goals or the acquisition of a higher position in one's own industry (cf Sorensen 2000:193). The underlying economic strategy could be defined as 'getting wealthy by whatever it means' in lieu of advancing one's profession or building up a company and feeling responsible for it.

As with many African SME, Eduard's construction company faced a variety of obstacles, most urgent of which was a lack of cash to expand. The need to grow arises from the concentration processes that are starting to become an issue in the Rwandan economy as well. Kappel et al. (2003) mention issues of consolidation and competitiveness for SME in developing countries as becoming a crucial concern within globalisation. Among the most prominent challenges for Rwandan SME is the lack of sources for external financing and the low availability of qualified and responsible staff. Furthermore, weak means of cost control and company planning foster the tendency of remaining a 'one man show', due to the necessities of managing growth, control and responsibility.

4.5 GERMAN CATERING AND HOTEL ENTERPRISES

The subjects of this case study are two companies from the catering and hotel sector. Both are independent enterprises co-owned and operated by Germans who settled in the country years ago. The first company is a relatively large catering and grocery facility with an exclusive choice of foodstuffs that has elevated it to a leading position within the national catering and food industry. The second is a medium-sized hotel and restaurant in a provincial town with an ambitious vision in quality and service standards.

Catering and grocery

This enterprise developed out of an initial training facility for food processing that was established as a European skill transfer project several decades ago. Subsequent to this original purpose, it first established a reputation as the 'German Bakery'. These roots are still visible, even though the food processing capabilities have undergone a strong diversification. After roughly twenty fairly successful years of operation and gradual expansion, the business had become independent and privatised. Now a wide spectrum of European-style foodstuffs was offered, with fresh pastries, bread and meals prepared according to an approximated German tradition and craftsmanship. Additionally, the establishment became one of Kigali's bigger grocery stores and was located in a central area. With the inclusion of a café-bistro, the place turned itself into a meeting point for Kigali's upper-class and European foreigners.

The grocery sold fresh foodstuffs from its own production (meat and bakery) and imported goods from Europe and the Middle East (preserved foods, alcoholic beverages, pasta, sweets, etc.). A slowly increasing demand for Rwandan-made food products was served as well (e.g. processed fruits such as jam, juice or syrup and honey). These local products were of a very high quality, yet too costly for all but the most affluent sections of the domestic population. The grocery's product range, however, was rather exclusive compared to an average local choice, so the Rwandan foodstuffs fit in well as delicacies. The overall price level was high, even by international standards. Correspondingly, the clientele consisted of an exclusive set of wealthier Rwandans and a large proportion of the Western expatriate community. For the expatriates, the restaurant served as a common place for social exchange while the grocery was a likely place for accidentally meeting someone during shopping. Over time, the name and location of the German bakery had become a genuine institution in Kigali. Even though most Rwandans could not afford to become customers, or even accepted spectators, the establishment was something that was familiar to all. Shopping at the grocery or dining at the restaurant came very close to being considered a veritable status symbol. I knew of student couples taking each other out to the bistro, or a representative from a distant parish on a city trip taking exclusive refreshments. There were only a few places in the country that offered this combination of quality and service combined with exclusiveness. Thus it was one of Kigali's locations where the Rwandan upper class mixed with the expatriate community.

Provisions for Western foreigners living abroad

The place provided otherwise largely unavailable foodstuffs frequently demanded by Westerners living abroad. The customer base comprised virtually every German and most Europeans. Even if many foreigners attempted to at least partially adapt to the Rwandan lifestyle, including culinary habits, the imported items in the supermarket-like store were in high demand. The essential ingredients for a variety of European meals were available. While, for example, spaghetti with tomato sauce could be prepared after a visit to a local market, the ingredients for pizza would almost exclusively be stocked here. Typical German-style bread and sausages as well as French pastries were another exclusive and popular part of the offerings. While some foreigners did their groceries completely at such a high-class store, others tried to be more locally sensitive and price-conscious. Nevertheless, everyone made at least one purchase when it came to special occasions such as birthdays, Christmas holidays and private festivities. The requisites for a typical German breakfast, baking a cake at home and similar items from the European world of food for socialising were to be found here.[20]

Store design and architecture were open and simple, with a functional appearance that came close to a Western supermarket. Clients did their shopping in relative anonymity and paid at modern cash registers. This was not standard in Rwanda during the time of research, as most household goods were bought in small *alimentation* stores, kiosks, or at the markets. At that time there were very few places where European foreigners could find a public environment that provided them with a location to shop at and pay as they were used to, thus in their own, culturally accustomed way (self-service store with a large choice of goods, stable quality and provisions, no need to talk to the staff, no need to double-check prices or to negotiate, possibility of paying with large bank notes, money changing service). Additionally they appreciated the opportunity to socialise (meeting fellow expatriates, staff greets regular customers, a place of belonging in a complex general environment in the country). In combination, these factors formed an 'opportunity' which was in regular demand by many the foreign customers. The wish for a certain service standard close to Western expectations was generally a strong one yet not necessarily a daily requirement for most of these foreigners. It persisted in spite of the fact that the expatriate community mostly recruited itself from highly educated and internationally experienced individuals open to other cultures. When someone new came to the country, to take over a position in one of the international agencies, for instance, the German bakery was one of the likely

---

20 The situation has changed since after the time of the field study. Today the concept of supermarket-like stores is commonplace in city centres, as much as bistro restaurants.

destinations on their first unaccompanied city trips. It served as a cultural landmark for Westerners in an East African city that had few orientation points for newly arriving foreigners at that time.

One of the key offerings of the bakery is something purely immaterial. The availability of a functionally familiar environment (supermarket-like) combined with the relative anonymity inside the establishment attracted European customers even more. Most of them were temporarily assigned to a posting in Rwanda, where they were constantly faced with demanding situations. A daily routine in a frequently strange and demanding work environment fraught with potentially stressful intermediations between Rwandan and Western contexts left many European expatriates looking for a brief escape, which could be found by shopping and eating at the German grocery. These expatriate customers often arranged their life in Kigali within social circles of belonging and familiarity in which the grocery staff and management occasionally became integrated. Yet, despite the fact that such personal ties were principally welcomed, the German director had a sober view of his customers' wishes for exclusive treatment. *"When they [expatriates] do their shopping they ask the staff to call me because they want me to serve them personally. But normally I just haven't the time to attend to everyone personally just because they know me"* [German director].

In keeping with the results of Mankekar's (2002) ethnographic study on Indian grocery shops in the USA, the German grocery played an important role in the reproduction of the symbolic and material in the expatriates' Western culture.

An exclusive location

The German grocery simultaneously attracted Rwandans. Wealthy people from Kigali, or sometimes their drivers, found a place to shop and socialize in a high class environment where they could also obtain comparatively special foodstuffs in a convenient way. Many Rwandan customers were accustomed to urban, Western-style food due to periods of living abroad in Europe or America, from living in other African cities, or simply by becoming attracted to a modern, urban, upper class lifestyle. Thus a demand for 'new' food arose resembling modern consumption patterns more closely than what was available through most of the local *alimentations*. The central arguments for buying at such a glossy, high-priced store were taste, quality, freshness or food safety, and availability. Some customers, more obviously than others, also demonstrated their social standing through appearances at the establishment, parking their car in the front while shopping or dining at the bistro. However, it would be erroneous to reduce the dynamic behind this consumptive pattern to individual luxury and social prestige alone. Rwandan society was in a prolonged phase of rapid change and modernization in many aspects of life. The trend of buying food in a supermarket was slowly beginning to spread. The lifestyle of a growing proportion of Rwanda's urban population was rapidly changing. Urbanized housing, work and mobility combined with influences from surrounding countries and international media led to rapid steps in the adaptation of modern-industrial material culture, which for significantly large population groups strongly affected areas such as food and clothing. The German bakery and grocery business served this newly emerging demand.

Together with two or three similar places in the capital, this food and catering enterprise served as a blueprint for an entirely new business model. Other establishments copied this approach, working with combinations of supermarkets selling self-produced fresh foodstuffs and bistro-style restaurants.

The background of a successful business

The company's success was the result of roughly two decades of work. Originally a privatised training facility for food processing, the business has continuously expanded over the years. Intensively trained employees and the enforcement of strict management principles were the director' declared cornerstones for achieving efficient production oriented towards European standards. Since the outset, freshly made German-style bread has been in constant demand by a growing customer base.

As the business started to flourish, its popularity, economic relevance and general 'visibility' helped to sustain its successful operation in difficult times. In spite of the bakery's success this 'visibility' also had its share of drawbacks. A thriving business must be able to defend its claims in a rough institutional climate. Sources close to the company insinuated that attempts to exploit its wealth by various means were more common than they should have been. Nevertheless, despite a rough business environment during the post-war years, the German bakery prospered relatively well. At the time of research the workforce consisted of several dozen employees in a number of departments (e.g. store, restaurant, food processing and administration).

Hardships of cooperative behaviour: After a lengthy and successful time as an entrepreneur, the German director had concrete plans to hand over the management of the company. Anecdotes concerning the candidate search recalled job interviews ranging from totally unqualified aspirants to a promising and well educated individual with a suitable social background who nearly got the assignment, but, during a last test of trustworthiness, proved incapable of complying with the correct rules on handling company cash. In a prearranged test situation he was said to have stolen money just a moment before he was offered a contract. This behavioural pattern was said to be encountered in individuals from all levels of social status and education and must therefore be considered as a major hindrance in the success of many privately operated organisations. The phenomenon is not the same as corruption, which is comparatively low in Rwanda. It is related to a low level of trust and cooperation within Rwandan society.

Rwanda can be regarded as a low trust society. While an exploration of the origins of this situation are clearly beyond the scope of this research, some of its tangible effects must be included in considerations of the present field study. Fukuyama's (1995) approach on societal trust regards it as a vital ingredient for a country's economic success. He makes a distinction between high trust societies and low trust societies. The differences are rooted in the prevalence of family or kin-based affiliations in low trust cultures cooperative ties among partners for professional reasons or shared interests in high trust cultures. While high trust builds, for example, on cooperative ties among partners for professional reasons or shared interests the low trust culture is rooted in the dilemma that individuals are locked in a reliance on their own kin or family group as no other entry points for social cooperation are available. However, I would argue that the dominance of cultural heritage should not be overstressed here when the life conditions at hand exert a much stronger argument to explain these patterns of behaviour.

In quite many aspects of life Rwanda's society was subjected to the effects of a particularly low cooperative capacity during the time of research. This was additionally combined with a short-term orientation of individual decisions at the expense of more durable strategies. Eager climbers started their individual quest for success in a social environment where, so to speak, today's gain was real but tomorrow's prospects were not imagined. These considerations help explain the most pressing structural problem of most African business managers: finding and keeping trustworthy personnel. The director had explicitly entrusted the financial responsibilities to a woman and spoke of her in the highest regard. *"But our secretary, a normal woman as she is, has no problems with it, even when carrying millions of francs to the bank"* [company manager]. It seems that this was not the only company where, after trial and error, vital functions were handled by a 'normal' female secretary instead of a well-connected upper class individual.

Difficult agreements and a tough place for an enterprise: Foreign owned or managed enterprises even more so than domestic ones may have encountered situations where the management itself would speak of forms of exploitation through local authorities, while local authorities would argue that these enterprises appropriated too much wealth by incorrect means such as evading taxes and bringing money out of the country. Such circular allegations are not uncommon worldwide and one of the most feared business risk in developing countries. It is no surprise that they were also mentioned in discussions concerning this case study. Based on personal observations I would conclude that during the time of research the country's economy gradually started to evolve to an institutional level of higher stability and control, while crude forms of ruthless profiteering were on the decline. However, in the more immediate post-war period an enterprise that looked successful could run into situations of hardship. Accusations sometimes were simply based on mutual misunderstandings while jealousy and competition among elite groups could pose risks for an *"unprotected"* business [quote: professional working in an international company]. Inclusion in elite networks was a means of building 'protection'. In a close knit web of mutual belonging and dependency, foreign-managed firms stand out, for good or bad, depending on the situation.

To sum up, the success of a professional production and service company in a sensitive industry, such as fresh food processing, initially depended on the existence of an exclusive customer base able to afford the products. The international community and the steadily growing number of consumers from the Rwandan upper class provided this resource-rich base needed in order to sustain an organisation with special technical demands (processing, food safety, imported supplies, administration). Eating and shopping at the German bakery became a status symbol for certain groups of Rwandans, and a means of social cohesion for many European expatriates. The practical success of this company in professional and business terms depended on a strict management and a lucky hand.

Hotel and restaurant

The second company in this case study is a resort-like hotel and restaurant operated by foreign entrepreneurs in a provincial town. A German-Rwandan couple was independently operating the facilities which belong to a number of regional buildings in public property. Most of the hotel guests, consisting of Rwandans as well as occasional expatriates, came for holidays and weekends, but business related visitors have started to show up as well. The restaurant was also frequented by the local population as a higher class dining destination.

Over the years, the resort and restaurant has evolved into a stable business with more than 10 employees. Given the small size of the local economy on this way it became an important employer in the town. The staff members were carefully selected from the surrounding communities and trained directly in the hotel and restaurant. The managers regarded as a significant success in the face of the initial difficulties that they now disposed over a reasonably reliable and qualified workforce. Another area of their business development was directed at attracting a stable client base to their place. This task delivered the first signs of success of as well.

In addition to their commercial interests, the managers saw a role for themselves as social facilitators with the aim of providing adequate job training to local young apprentices. Their long experience in the catering and hotel sector made them aware, as they said, of a severe lack of capacity and know-how among Rwandan employees and entrepreneurs throughout the food and service industry. The Rwandan manager, during many years abroad, had adopted numerous elements of European life and openly criticised several aspects of conventional Rwandan traits and working habits. Both directors shared the conviction of establishing what they call high quality standards for the services and foods. They accepted this time-consuming task as a necessary precondition for the operation of a business in a medium Rwandan town far away from the capital. It also gave them an important role in a local community that severely lacked education, job training and opportunities.

In the course of their settling down in the town's social fabric the Rwandan-German managers were made aware that not in everyone's opinion they automatically belonged to the place. The need to establish relationships with key persons of the residential elite, and subsequently as well with the local authorities, posed a substantial challenge at the beginning. Their arrival unintendedly worked as a disturbance to the sensitive web of social relationships in the town. The independent and self-confident functioning of the experienced and comparatively wealthy Western foreigners posed a threat to those who hitherto dominated the local status hierarchy (i.e. the classical persons of respect, such as local administration and government representatives, wealthy individuals). Additionally the restaurant was one of the most prestigious dining locations around and the men of the local elite were regular customers, yet partially with outstanding accounts. Soon thereafter a series of accusations was made by official representatives. The entrepreneurs were suspected of sending large sums of locally earned money to Germany, and thereby depriving the Rwandan economy of wealth. The problems resulting from this situation almost put an end to the venture and would have caused a total loss of the invested resources. The situation was resolved after personal petitions by the Rwandan manager high up in the country's administration. This resulted in an intervention from the capital that went in favour of the entrepreneurs and caused a changes in the local governance style. Here, the foreign entrepreneurs had unwillingly played the role of change agents.

Such encounters can be seen as an indicator of the 'exposed' position of foreign actors in very 'local' environments, thus socio-economic fields where most interactions are among individuals from similar geographical or social backgrounds. In such cases of being foreigner of a certain type can become a liability in the sense that such a person automatically is expected to dispose over much larger amounts of resources and means to sustain expenditures than what would be expected from local entrepreneurs. Such monetary wealth was not in fact possessed by these hotel and restaurant managers, and they admitted that from time to time they suffered from the image of the rich European. In the eyes of local citizens, foreign actors adhere to unknown strategies, and when they come from Western countries they are also likely to be less obedient to local authorities. The occasional confrontations take place in a political environment that still is characterised by the exertion of total authority and its acceptance. In such a situation the effects of a small foreign business could at best be described as an example of the transformative challenge arising from entrepreneurship. It must be noted that many of the described issues arise from the fact that the resort was situated in a provincial town and not in the capital, where a higher international presence and faster pace of change lead to a more open environment.

Permanently settled Western foreigners

Despite his ongoing ties to the ever-changing expatriate community, which also formed one of his major customer bases, the German director regarded the presence of international organisations from a critical position. With this point of view he was in agreement with other permanently settled foreigners. The jet-setting lifestyle of many expatriates and the activities of their international organisations were naturally a driving force for a number of local businesses, restaurants, clubs and so forth. Aside from those commercially related aspects that connected them with the international community, the permanently settled foreigners I spoke with rather had their own way of life. In contrast to the clutter of projects, proposals, career options and arranged field trips, the image of the lone wolf character came into my mind when seeking for a way to describe this group of individuals. Their foremost mark of distinction could be seen in their willingness and ability to get along without a return ticket. In many ways they appeared to be disconnected from the daily topics that kept Western expatriates busy. Instead they obtained deep insights into local society and often times developed a strong affection for the Rwandan individuals with whom they were closely connected. Their display of character traits such sturdiness, pragmatism and activeness typically was combined with open cynicism towards the local situation and the international community and a latent frustration about the state of affairs.

From this mixture of powerful and demanding experiences, the permanently settled Western foreigners were not unlikely to develop a set of rather explicit opinions about expatriates working in the organisations of the so called 'international community'. The below quoted informant, being from one of the described enterprises, had built up experiences and emotions over years of life in African countries, and had worked in Rwanda during the immediate pre-war and post-war periods, during which his opinion had apparently been formed: *"Those [expatriates from a development agency] arrive here and have no idea. And then, after around two years, they start to get married, and soon they run into problems. [...] Then they sit in my office, crying"...* *"And then, when you see how the car park in front of the [popular disco club] is crowded with all those off-road cars and pick-ups from [names of various organisations]... This is incredible; you see two, three, or sometimes even more cars from [a German organisation] alone. They all want to be in Kigali, want some comfort and feel important. I say, when you want to do development you ought to be out in the hills where they really are in need of help..."* Here the argument is based on oral reports from local inhabitants and foreign witnesses. Again, in this instance, it is not my aim to inquire into the rights and wrongs of those involved. However, such expressions highlight the mutual perception of different groups of international actors in a complicated social field. It has to be stressed that the experiences on which these anecdotes are built are partially rooted in the period following the crisis of the 1990s. During that time the presence of personnel from aid agencies was much more excessive and often related to high levels of expenditure that correlated with a low sustainability in their projects. Opinions built up during that period are carried forward even though improvements were made to development aid since the beginning of the new millennium (e.g. building on the Paris Declaration for aid effectiveness in 2005). In such statements we also find evidence that a mere distinction between Western and African positions in transnational cooperation is oversimplified. Approaches to the transnational domain are different, for example, in a young project manager with new yet untested visions pursuing a career opportunity, than in an older, seasoned, permanent settler with a foot on the ground in local life and idealism replaced by a combination of pessimistic realism and cynicism.

Summary and interpretations

Throughout this case study I focused on two catering and food enterprises that were managed by German entrepreneurs. Both relied on the intensive training of their employees, and on a high degree of personal involvement of the owners in all daily activities in order to meet their own performance expectations. Both companies were led by managers from a German background and are therefore perceived as foreign entities. Nevertheless, these entrepreneurs were permanent residents with a high proficiency in local manners, and applied strategies suitable to the socioeconomic environment in which they operated. They also were well integrated into local social networking. In sum, these Germans were accustomed to Rwandan peculiarities, and shared the pressure to adapt to the overall conditions with purely local enterprises. In contrast to most activities conducted by expatriates they are not primarily concerned with the affairs of the international community as such. Their economic and personal sustainability depends on their personal skills and the ability to productively integrate into the indigenous Rwandan socioeconomic sphere in settings that are sensitive to external interference. In both cases there were long lasting personal and emotional connections to the country, and therefore the companies were taken as a means of permanent income. This personal situation can be characterised as an 'emigrant' status rather than an 'expatriate' one; thus a 'local with foreign background'. What makes actors such as these vulnerable is their exposure as foreigners standing alone in a dense sociopolitical fabric. Rwanda, during the time of research, was not a cheap and carefree place for independent foreign entrepreneurs to operate a business. The company managers were obliged to involve themselves in every aspect of their companies and, unlike foreign organisations and corporations with international resources, had to cope with the same conditions as every other local enterprise. Independent enterprises of this kind cannot count on the availability of specialised arrangements that place them in protected arenas, as is the case with bilateral projects or large multinational corporations. Those more 'official' organisations are part of settings which, by diplomacy or sheer economic weight, remain shielded from the harsh reality of the local environment. To be absorbed by these dynamics is a substantial risk encountered by independent, foreign, small and medium enterprises. Nevertheless, it is important to note that the population in general and the public institutions in particular are interested in foreigners as entrepreneurs and are willing to receive them openly. This unquestioning openness towards newness combined with the potential returns on investment make Rwanda an interesting place for international SME and entrepreneurs despite possible hardships.

4.6 A Mixed Arena: Energy Crisis and Millennium Development Goals

This case study describes the proceedings around two intersecting transboundary formations. These emerged from the complicated situation of the Rwandan electricity supply, and the implications of certain European donor policies for the micro strategies of local protagonists. During the time of fieldwork, methane gas extraction from Lake Kivu and subsequent generation of huge amounts of electrical power held the promise of a bright future. Proposals had been made and withdrawn, and the country's infrastructure was much more open. To begin with, a national energy crisis that was caused by acute shortages of electric power seriously affected both the economy and social life in urban areas. During this time a donor programme was instigated with the aim of bolstering rural electrification as per the Millennium Development Goals.

A severe energy crisis in Rwanda throughout the years from 2004 to 2006 confronted both the population and the recovering economy. Hydroelectricity is the major power source in the country, and long periods of drought led to a situation where the turbines used more water from the reservoir lakes than could be refilled through rainfall. Overuse of lake water for power generation in previous years meant that electricity had to be rationed. Additional complications arose from the poor technical condition of the small national electricity grid and the old machinery. Irrespectively, the greatest portion of rural settlements did not have access to electricity, but those urban areas that were connected to the power grid were subjected to regular breakdowns and rationings. The population as well as most enterprises severely suffered from exorbitant energy prices and unreliable supply. Several programmes emerging from donor institutions aimed at improving this critical situation. Two of them are important for the ongoing activities that contributed to this stage of the case study:

First, the national power and water energy utility came under the temporary management of a European technical consulting company. The consultant had won a tender to manage and rehabilitate this deficient public company within a couple of years. This arrangement was made under pressure from the World Bank and later on seemingly failed, which brought the utility back under government appointed management.

Second, a European donor country had instigated a rural electrification programme in line with its self-obligations to reach the Millennium Development Goals. It was decided that some of Rwanda's Micro-Hydro power plants were to be reactivated under the management of the local private sector. This programme was initiated with private sector promotion in mind and took the form of a Public Private Partnership (PPP).

The main protagonist within this complex of technical infrastructures and policy making is a small German-Rwandan investment project that was initiated to participate in the PPP scheme but was later abandoned in the preparatory stages because of unfavourable conditions.

A transboundary arena and the involved actors

Throughout this case study I am going to outline the proceedings of a transboundary arena that brought together several different stakeholders: European donors, Rwandan authorities, European consultants and small-scale entrepreneurs. The centre of this arena was formed by the national power utility, to which all electrical and water infrastructures in the country belonged; the focus of the fieldwork was directed at the proceedings of a small Rwandan–German investment project. The following actors were the most important:

- Rwandan–German project group for Public-private partnership project consisting of German engineer, a Rwandan entrepreneur, and a German coordinator.
- PPP-programme for rural electrification conducted by a Rwandan Ministry and the embassy of a European country. Overall planning was done by a related consulting company of the same country.
- Bilateral development agency of another European country, later taking over the PPP-programme as an executive agency, technical experts.
- National power and water utility, initially under the management of a European consulting enterprise working as a World Bank contractor and subsequently under governmental control again.

The energy crisis

"Power shortages slows down hair salon business – A recent survey by the Business Times has revealed that power cuts have greatly affected hair salons."

"Rwacom is losing 30% of its products – [...] According to the production manager, the factory is losing 30% of their products, which are destroyed during the production process due to power problems." (both quotations: Business Times, April 18-19, 2005)

During the time of this case study, the estimated access to electricity in Rwanda ranged between 4-6 percent of the population, with a strong majority of connections in urban areas. This figure represents an exceptionally low level of coverage

(World Bank/Public-Private Infrastructure Advisory Facility, 2005). Per capita consumption of energy (i.e. electricity and oil products) in Rwanda is among the lowest in the world, even compared to neighbouring countries. The capital city of Kigali alone accounts for roughly two-thirds of the total number of electricity customers and demand for power. At the time of fieldwork, electricity was an unreliable commodity due to frequent breakdowns, expense and restriction to urban areas. In the face of these challenges, the provision of public infrastructure was a contested field of national development policy, and for the population it came close to a symbol of improvement in daily life. During the years 2004 to 2006 and onwards, electricity prices rose sharply and are beyond the financial capability of many urban households, while rural areas remain largely unconnected. Power came to be considered a 'necessary luxury' similar to the use of mobile phones. Thus power cuts and increasing prices were a common conversation topic. The national electricity grid was in poor condition; technical losses, electricity theft and lost payments due to organisational weaknesses were common.

According to public figures, the national peak demand in 2005 ranged around 45 Megawatt, with forecasts projecting a strong increase due to expanding economic activity and a huge backlog of unserved need. In technical terms, Rwandan power generation in this era was dominated by one major hydroelectric plant and several big secondary hydro plants which were running below capacity due to water shortages. The peak demand at early evening hours had to be covered by huge Diesel generators which were privately operated under a special contract.

Rural electrification / Millennium Development Goals

In this situation, only a few of the roughly 25 Micro-Hydro plants that had existed prior to the 1994 genocide were still operational. Most of these small-scale facilities were located in geographically remote places and found to be in bad technical condition. Out of considerations unrelated to the national power crisis they were re-discovered as environmentally sound sources of rural electrification and thus became the target of a Public Private Partnership initiative issued by a foreign donor institution. Among other individuals from the private sector, a group of two Germans and one Rwandan became interested at this point. They attempted to start a small electricity company in order to turn this situation into a personal opportunity.

At the beginning, the embassy of that European country issued a public announcement concerning a lucrative PPP-programme. The Rwandan private sector and local cooperatives were invited to submit proposals to rehabilitate several of the Micro-Hydro facilities with the help of a fair subsidy. The initiative for this programme originally came from the European country's ministry for development cooperation. It stands at the end of a series of interconnections, deriving its impetus from a self-obligation of that country in respect of the Millennium Development Goals (MDG). In accordance with its European partners it had promised to do something in support of the Millennium Development Goal of poverty reduction. The MDGs as a whole represented a political plan for improving central aspects of human living conditions worldwide by the year 2015. They were officially established at the Millennium Summit in 2000 and adopted by all UN Member States in 2002. An Africa Partnership Forum in 2005 also confirmed them for this continent (ECA 2005) and demonstrated the African governments' commitment to the initiative (African Union 2005, 2005b).

However, MDGs as such are rather abstract goals. In order to become meaningful in practice they had to be reduced to more tangible programmes and activities. Thus, in due course, the ministry for development cooperation of that European donor country decided to approach rural development in several poor countries as a viable means of reducing poverty. Finally, a programme was formulated to connect a large number of poor rural households in a selected number of poor countries to electricity. Contributing to the Millennium Development Goal of reducing poverty by enhancing rural income opportunities through electrification – a logical chain from a general idea to a specialised activity in the eyes of a donor institution. Infrastructure was quickly identified as a necessary precondition for most development efforts, and rural electrification was considered of central importance in this regard. One way to promote it in Rwanda was found in the rehabilitation of several of the non-operational Micro Hydro power plants. Since the 1960s a number of these small hydroelectric facilities provided electricity to hospitals, communities, small factories and other establishments, but became inoperative due to a lack of maintenance or war-related destruction. To round up the programme, the idea of promoting the Rwandan private sector was suggested. In order to give local businesses and cooperatives an opportunity to participate in the rehabilitation of the Micro Hydro facilities, a public private partnership (PPP) programme was launched to attract local investors. The possibility for local generation of sorely needed power and the economic opportunities arising from the PPP scheme fell on fertile ground among entrepreneurs, cooperatives and profit-seekers. Against this background the Rwandan Micro Hydro programme became the last step in a long 'translation chain' (Rottenburg 2009, 2002) that, without the original intention of doing so, linked the global debate surrounding the MDGs with the ongoing local energy crisis.

The position of the donor institution

The ministry of the European donor country acted as the 'principal' but never appeared directly on the scene. It testified to its presence by setting up strict conditions for ensuring that the quickly growing number of people interested in profiting from this programme still contributed to what the ministry defined as its development goals. This was intended to be achieved through key figures for each private project in the form of a required number of rural households to be connected to electricity by 2015, and technical details such as cost per connected household, cost per installed kilowatt hour, total lifespan and total cost. The European ministry initially contracted a European consulting company to start the programme in several countries at once and then handed responsibility over to the development agency of a neighbouring European country contracted to execute this programme in Rwanda. The side of the donor institutions in this PPP programme consisted of the following actors:

(1) *Donor ministry:* The official intention to promote the Millennium Development Goals aside, another internal aim was likely to have been involved at the foundation of the whole Micro Hydro issue. Internal policy debates increasingly questioned the effectiveness and relevance of development aid, and the ministry was in need of some good projects with a direct 'grip' and determinable outputs. It was stated that the donor party was interested in the rural electrification programme because it allowed for tangible results in a number of key indicators (electrified households, empowered women, etc.).

(2) *Programme consultants:* The initial design of the PPP initiative was carried out by a European consulting company with a track record in worldwide rural development projects. All initial contacts and facilitations in Rwanda were conducted by this company.

(3) *Development agency as executing contractor:* Further preparation, execution and monitoring of the programme were later subcontracted to a special branch of another European country's development agency that specialises in such not-really-market contracting arrangements, which maintained a strong presence in Rwanda. This form of cross-contracting between Western donor agencies is officially conducted in a similar way to 'real' corporate business, but as with all donor agencies it ultimately relies on public funding, business-like behaviour notwithstanding.

Attempted German-Rwandan investment project/ Public-Private Partnership

The aforementioned Public Private Partnership (PPP) programme attracted one Rwandan and two Germans who formed a project group in order to seize the opportunity of investing in Micro Hydro power. They intended to establish an independent small-scale business by means of acquiring the donor subsidy, locating a suitable Micro Hydro site and exploiting it commercially by selling the generated electricity to the power grid. Cases of smaller European investors becoming interested in regenerative energy in tropical countries are not entirely uncommon, and occasionally donors are in place to provide a financial and administrative background (e.g. European investor and a World Bank in Ugandan Micro Hydro Power, East African Business Week, June 19, 2006).

Within the context of the PPP programme this Rwandan-German project group was an atypical formation. Spanning a transnational background, it was able to communicate effectively with all sorts of stakeholders in the field, ranging from embassies to local farmers. It was also strictly committed to commercial interests, whereas some other PPP applicants, such as rural cooperatives, prioritised supplying their current facilities or communities with power. While bigger transnational enterprises and small humanitarian organisations are common, there existed almost no institutional environment within which experiences or even expectations were available on how a transnational micro-business could be established. The German protagonists saw a mixture of personal opportunity, commercial interest, a motivation to do an exciting and useful job, combined with a potential for adventure. The Rwandan entrepreneur saw a commercial opportunity coupled with the possibility to contribute to the development of his country.

Public private partnership frameworks are designed to acquire cooperating private partners intended to act as local executioners of the donor's global developmental goals. In this case the goals were related to the MDG programme, and the private partners were expected to fulfil a predefined role in the project design of the donor agency. Eligible project proposals fit the donor's technical and formal expectations as a precondition for approval. In order to enhance the formal appearance of the project design, the group of three considered a professionally correct approach that would conform the donor's interests and meet expectations. The Rwandan project partner, as the oldest and most experienced in the group, suggested that one of the Germans should take the formal position of director. *"I don't want to be racist, but I think when dealing with [the donor institutions], it's better that the director is a white person."* In interactions with Rwandan counterparts this Rwandan project member would then have taken the lead as the 'general representative'.

The intended micro hydro location and its owners

All Micro-Hydro facilities are constructed similarly, but geographical conditions and the differences between the installed aggregates result in each site possessing unique characteristics. A suitable location for the German-Rwandan rehabilitation project was identified through a review of various feasibility studies. It was a rather small facility located in an isolated village, where contact was conducted through a representative of the Catholic Church who practically fulfilled the role of the local administration. This person was in charge of legal matters concerning the micro hydro facility, and therefore the primary negotiation partner during the visit. At the second stage of negotiations, higher-ranking church officials had to be involved as well. It turned out that the clerical authorities were indeed interested in the rehabilitation of this hydro power facility, seeing potential for a mutually beneficial situation. The Rwandan businessman's excellent reputation ensured that a contract was signed quickly. For a poor, rural village in a remote area this potentially new connection to Kigali and Germany was a good bargain. A church official mentioned that the arrangement was satisfying because it would allow them a certain minimum control of their asset. Apparently, other actors, including governmental authorities, had previously attempted to seize control of the facility in a less favourable manner. The church was therefore quite pleased that someone now wanted to operate the facility while paying for it, instead of attempting to expropriate the church. As a matter of fact, signing contracts was a rather delicate process in Rwanda, which had a socio-economic environment with a low prevalence of trust and reliability, and a legal system still in its formation phase. Long-term investments, which essentially rely on stable contracts, were thus not without risk. But *"...the Catholic Church? That's different"* [local businessman]. Aside from its wide ranging and omnipresent engagements in education and health, the Catholic Church is one of the major economic powers in Rwanda, holding considerable assets mainly in real-estate and retail business. Even though the Germans at first were wary about this trust into the church their inquiries revealed that its overall juridical and business reputation was excellent. Different informants valued its formal correctness and commercial professionalism.

What is the right kind of private investor?

The general aim of a public-private infrastructure partnership is the provision of infrastructure access to the population at fair prices through a private provider under an official license. It can be difficult to find the right kind of private operator for such schemes (cf Chowhury 2002 for rural telecom). Investors are additionally required to provide professional and financial guarantees to ensure the seriousness of their offer, and to prevent the 'winner's curse' of being awarded a subsidy contract only to be unable to execute it due to a lack of capacity (for similar concession matters in Peru, ibid. 2002:13). The Micro Hydro project was designed for a grid-parallel operation, feeding the national power network directly and exclusively. All low voltage lines, connecting buildings with the grid through a high voltage transformer, were owned by the local community and were in poor condition. The potential investors' aim did not involve maintenance of these installations or the community's accounting of electricity payments. Such a plan enhanced the technical and financial feasibility for the investors because it aimed at minimising cost and local responsibilities, although it reduced the overall gain for the local community.

Complications

Interferences came from a parallel programme issued by the United Nations' agency for the promotion of worldwide private business development (UNIDO), apparently following a similar Micro-Hydro agenda of its own. This caused occasional confusion, because UNIDO conducted its own feasibility studies, and later also opened its own call for tender for local project proposals. The German-Rwandan application was almost filtered out in the pre-selection process because the jury for irresolvable reasons believed that this project was already being subsidised by UNIDO, which almost brought it to an end. In later stages of the Micro Hydro programme this parallel donor activity caused serious interference once again. Both the European donor country and the United Nations had similar activities running, and disbursing their funds in some cases resulted in a competition. The available number of utilities was partially and accidentally included in the plans of two large subsidy systems. In certain cases more than one local investor attempted to take control of one of the few truly lucrative physical Micro Hydro sites, backed by their respective donor agencies. Another, yet smaller, incident was the attempt of a Rwandan medium-level bureaucrat to advocate the rehabilitation of a certain Micro Hydro site to several stakeholders, including the German-Rwandan project group. It turned out that according to a field specialist's judgement this particular site was not at all suitable for modern hydroelectric exploitation but that it belonged to the jurisdiction of this official's home town. According to the terminology used by Bierschenk, Chauveau and Olivier de Sardan (2000), this official acted as a 'development broker', who tries to channel development resources to his own community by manipulating the intersection of local and foreign interests.

Equity, credit and subsidy

Start-up companies that rely on subsidies and external financing may encounter a need to deal with circular requirements in order to secure access to private equity, donor subsidy and bank credit simultaneously. It may turn out that a bank loan becomes a realistic option only when private collateral or financial buoyancy from subsidies is readily available. The subsidy in turn depends on proof that the private part of the project is on safe financial grounds and already supported by a bank and/or private equity. The private investors, however, wish to make final commitments only when the other sources of capital are available, and the risk is partially divided among them. A balance must thus be struck between individual prospects and the bank's and donor's requirements. In the case of the German-Rwandan project group, options for increasing capital on their own were limited, so they wanted a bank loan. Obtaining such capital through a bank credit was almost impossible in Rwanda at that time, a situation that made many entrepreneurial initiatives difficult. In a general sense, African businesses were usually financed through informal channels while the financial sector had typically been unable to make external capital available to the standard entrepreneur. So the project group prepared for a situation in which they had to simultaneously present a sufficient financial plan to the donor agency, including a bank loan, and to present sufficient securities (i.e. collateral) to the bank. Here, their German background proved helpful in relieving them of many formal tests of trustworthiness usually applied to local applicants by the donor agency.

National energy provider / management contractor

For roughly one and a half years before, the Rwandan national power and water utility had been managed by a European engineer-consulting company under a five year contract. This arrangement was the result of a World Bank initiative aimed at rehabilitating the utility's deteriorated technical installations and upgrading its commercial operations. The policy's intention was to subsequently prepare the utility for a privatisation process. As one of the major obstacles to post-war recovery, its performance in customer management and billing procedures was very low. The donor's initiative targeted these shortcomings, including solutions for electricity theft and the huge technical losses (cf World Bank/Public-Private Infrastructure Advisory Facility, 2005:34ff). Around the beginning of the millennium the World Bank increasingly demanded the introduction of privatisation initiatives in the national utilities of several African countries. This was intended as a cure against unsustainable operations caused by exceedingly low prices and weak management. In fact, many African electricity and water providers were primarily guided by political motives while their technical and commercial conditions were widely neglected or unsuitably scaled down as a result of inadequate capabilities. Placing the national power and water utility under external management must be understood in this wider context. Indeed, refurbishing this institution so as to transform it into a self-sustaining public company ready for privatisation originated in World Bank directives and not in a genuine interest of the national policy makers. Various voices from national stakeholders and the general public were sceptical of these plans and feared that the government might lose control of a central asset of national interest.

Nevertheless, the need to drastically intervene in the current technical state of these utilities had become obvious through the fact that the overall condition of all power and water infrastructures had deteriorated in recent years to a level where their operation became unpredictable. Many of the technical and organisational shortcomings could be attributed to the long-lasting impacts of the war. Like most Rwandan organisations the national utility had lost a lot of its experienced personnel. To counter this critical situation, the five year management contract was considered a "most immediately significant form of PSP [private sector participation]" to transfer management responsibility to a private operator under a competitive contract with performance criteria (World Bank/Public-Private Infrastructure Advisory Facility, 2005:38). The schedule of this management contract was tightly packed, aiming for numerous technical and organisational improvements ranging from a baseline assessment through diverse forecasts, the formulation of a business plan, implementation of financial planning and reporting, information management, quality monitoring, customer survey, loss reductions, tariff review (read: increasing prices to commercially sustainable levels), environmental protection and training. In brief, the objective was to turn an under-equipped and technically deteriorated public utility into a sustainable, professionally managed, up-to-date and ready to privatise company within five years. Management took over in the form of several European long-term experts, backed up by additional visits from special consultants. These expatriates had to take care of many large and small issues personally and at once, and faced an immense workload.

The consulting company had entered a contract that demanded the fulfilment of predefined benchmark criteria in order to get the whole payment out of the contract.

"The importance of ensuring that the management contractor is subject to strong and clear performance incentives cannot be overemphasized. However, this aspect of the contractual framework highlights the fact that the arrangements proposed over the next five years should also be seen as a collaborative partnership between the private sectors, government, and donors." (World Bank/Public-Private Infrastructure Advisory Facility, 2005:39)

This arrangement required the European management to commit themselves to a self-imposed obligation for measurable outputs in a situation that was unreliable and politically highly contested.

Foreign management and domestic circumstances

Much of the framework was controlled by the Rwandan government, or simply remained beyond the influence of any actor. Refurbishing a deteriorated public utility in a developing country is difficult from a technical and organisational point of view. Additional complexities originated from issues beyond the control of management but had an impact on its performance. In brief, a foreign management team in a Rwandan public company subject to political guidance had to balance the transfer of technical and organisational expertise to this organisation. Meanwhile they were left to deal with the need of arranging for a symbiosis of their work with the local conditions and political demands. What at first was intended to be a clean implementation of universally valid technical standards later on led to technical adjustments in employment and tariff policies, the implementation of new strategies and other disturbing effects that brought the management under pressure from the public and the authorities. The expatriates became subjected to local power struggles and a complex administrative environment while simultaneously trying to secure the establishment of the predefined technical criteria. This may be considered as one of the worst positions in which a contractor can become involved. The anthropologist Rottenburg (2002, 2005) describes a similar setting that took place in an organisation development project in an East African public utility. In his example the contractor/consultant ultimately loses while the financier (donor) and the owner (national or local authority) both retreat to their initial positions, leaving it to the consultant to resolve the practical problems that are undoubtedly in existence. Technical needs notwithstanding, from a nationally conscious viewpoint such privatisation processes can also be perceived as unwelcomed inroads for Western capital interests into domestic affairs. Ponte (2004) recounts a similar situation in Tanzania, describing efforts to protect local interests against external dominance in a case where an industry sector is driven to open itself up to foreign involvement. He points out that accusations of nepotism are not sufficient and that these "politics of ownership" must also be seen as attempts to secure national sovereignty and legitimate domestic property.

In our case the differences in perception of what was right and wrong led to frictions that caused the expatriate management to be replaced by Rwandan executives. These changes also affected the Micro Hydro programme, as arrangements made with the expatriate management were not part of the new energy policy to be followed by the new Rwandan management. This marked the beginning of serious trouble for the small German-Rwandan project.

The activities of the national utility's external management were no longer seen as an ideal embodiment of the clean and abstract technical standards which were also meant to be implemented in Rwanda. This caused the external consulting company to lose the symbolic bonus it initially possessed as a representative of a technically advanced European country. The more the foreign managers became absorbed by the domestic situation, the less their reputation as the embodiment of technical prodigiousness. Even to the point that they came to be seen as exhibiting habits and strategies that were contrary to national interests.

In many developing countries the political demands put on public infrastructure are inherently contradictory. From a political standpoint, tariffs as well as foreign influence have to be kept low. In terms of technical concerns, compliance to functional standards and systemic effectiveness must be ensured and documented, which also serves as a means to re-establish commercial sustainability. However, the initial plan to approach a state of financial sustainability, which was agreed upon by all stakeholders, apparently meant an increase in electricity tariffs, a move no longer accepted by the government.

It is my assumption that arrangements between the domestic authorities and foreign business leaders were not without their specific set of complications. Another case of a *"boss sacked"* in a Rwandan company with the government as a major stakeholder seemed to possess certain parallels. In that case an international conglomerate acquired a management contract for one of the bigger hotel and conference centres in the country. A difference in opinions between the foreign company and the Rwandan stakeholders lead to the publicly announced statement that the foreign director apparently "did not meet some issues related to performance as per the contract" (Rwanda Development Gateway, September 4, 2005). The relevant wording is *"as per the contract"*: in such joint-ventures the first round of negotiations seems to be purely rational and the plans are apparently devoid of non-technical contexts. The intended partnership is expected to be mutually beneficial. It usually is seen as an opportunity for implementing standards of international quality in a developing country. Yet they simultaneously pose a risk to the foreign partner who may inadvertently become responsible for the functional establishment of these standards under local circumstances that are beyond his scope. The foreign partners enter the contract because they are technically capable, but still can't control local circumstances that are not favourable for the introduction of that technology. These circumstances are nobody's fault in particular, but they are the bottom-line of that which makes a developing country what it is. In order to complete the story, however, it must be noted that this situation developed alongside another important issue in the Rwandan energy sector. Namely, the scheduled construction of new power plants running on methane gas from Lake Kivu. One such project had been initiated under the management of a foreign joint venture and later abandoned; several months later a Rwandan venture started its methane gas project. New and shifting priorities arose from the promising source of cheap and accessible energy that Lake Kivu seemed destined to become. In relation to this prospect the government's interest in decentralised, rural, small-scale projects with comparatively small power outputs declined.[21]

A mixed arena

Taken together, the intentions and activities of the donor ministry, as reflected through the PPP programme, and the interests around the national power and water utility with its changing management already formed a multi-polar setting. When small-scale protagonists like the German-Rwandan project group became part of that setting, the situation gained the character of a temporary transboundary arena (temporary because the timeframe for this special constellation was limited). The energy crisis was at its most turbulent peak when the city's lights went out at evening hours and new alternatives were only to be seen on the horizon. At that point the Millennium Development Goals and their offspring, the Micro Hydro programme, were promising in light of the recurring energy shortages. Their transboundary character became apparent when the nature of the activities triggered by them was closely observed and tracked down to the respective stakeholders. Very distant and rural places in the Rwandan hills were touched by middlemen acting on behalf of their own pockets and, after all, in the name of those academic constructs.

The national utility as a two-edged principal

From the utility management's perspective the whole affair concerning the rural electrification PPP went in the wrong direction right from the beginning. It intended to spend donor money on small, grass-roots projects in remote areas when

---

21 The methane gas deposits in Lake Kivu are agreed to be of great value for the adjoining countries. Situated between Rwanda and the neighbouring DR Congo, the lake is believed to be a unique energy resource with huge deposits of natural gas dissolved in its deep waters (Doevenspeck 2007).

at the same time the maintenance of the national main grid was pressing and of utmost importance for urban and economic development. The domestic engineers would have wished the subsidy to be invested in these national assets instead of dislocated, small facilities. On the organisational and technical front the whole Micro Hydro PPP nevertheless relied on the support of the public utility, as it was needed to fulfil the role of technical and administrative facilitator. And this even more so for those small projects that wanted to connect to the national grid, as was the case with the German-Rwandan group. The grid-connected private Micro Hydro projects aimed to obtain favourable provider contracts from the national utility, consisting of an attractive offtake price per generated kilowatt hour. For them in particular the situation became unfavourable when the political strategy changed following a replacement of the utility's directorate.

It turned out that the donors had established an incoherent institutional framework in which the national utility had to play a double role as (1) a potential client of the newly planned independently run small-scale power producers. It was seen as obliged to buy their generated power and refund them at attractive prices despite the fact that it had no money, and (2) as a facilitator with the task of assisting the private small-scale project groups in their preparation of the technical and formal aspects of their investment projects, and later on to authoritatively evaluate their proposals. The utility received a considerable sum from the donors to compensate for these efforts.

It became obvious that the donors had designed two different roles for the national utility and that these roles contradicted each other. In this situation the overall strategy of the new utility management was the ultimate reason for the German-Rwandan group to abandon the project because attractive prices for the generated electricity could no longer be realised. The utility management based its argumentation on the profit calculations it obtained from the PPP-project's business plans because it was called in to assist them, and it saw the calculated profit margins as being too high compared to international standards.

Key figures, commercial facts and disbursement pressure

Changes in the strategy of the energy provider were finally followed by initial steps towards a new national energy policy. This policy was not oriented towards small-scale power generation (instead having the large-scale Lake Kivu projects in mind), and this posed a sudden problem to the PPP-investors as the return rates per kilowatt hour diminished as soon as the utility management became re-nationalised. The contracting donor agency, which was responsible for the local execution of the PPP programme, feared that not enough private small-scale projects would survive under these conditions because it had to guarantee that a sufficient number of individual PPP projects would connect a sufficient number of rural households. In order to secure this goal all other factors were seen as secondary, including the problem that not all the project proposals that were seeking donor funding complied with the highest standards in planning quality and transparency. The agency's programme coordinator admitted that none of the seven proposed projects would in fact adhere to European standards and that he had personal doubts about several of them. *"None of the projects would be admitted in Europe like this"*. But to fulfil the assignment he depended on a sufficient number of local private partners to execute the rehabilitation projects. The donor organisation's central task of connecting a fixed number of rural households to electricity depended on it. This agency was thus forced into a position of facilitating questionable project proposals in order to fulfil its goal.

Dialogue between the private German-Rwandan project coordinator and the donor agency's official programme manager: Coordinator: *"When we don't get the [amount of] Francs per kilowatt hour, we're out."* Programme manager: *"Then I've got a problem!"* Coordinator: *"Why?"* Programme manager: *"Because I have to find someone else as quick as possible then."*

The executing donor agency had to fulfil the assignment according to pre-defined figures: number of PPP partners, connected households, cost per generated kW/h and cost per connected household etc., and now faced its own version of the common disbursement pressure.[22] Had the constellation been situated within a strictly commercial setting under market conditions, this short dialogue probably would have had an alternative ending: [Programme manager, fictively: *"If you won't do it under these conditions, someone else will do it. Bad for you"*]. Such an argument was initially brought up by a consultant related to the donor agency, but it later became clear to the German-Rwandan project group that in reality the donor agency needed them as much as they themselves had wanted the subsidy.

Withdrawal and cancelling of the project

When it became clear after intense negotiation that the final price per kilowatt hour was far from their initial expectations, and other possible solutions such a compensating governmental subsidy on top of the basic tariff, were not particularly helpful, the German-Rwandan group decided to cancel the project. Most of the sister projects were not abandoned in the face of severely declined profit opportunities. Some of them were much bigger and belonged to cooperatives that did not directly depend on profits from selling electricity. Another explanation

---

22 Disbursement pressures, as much as donor competition, may lead to seriously weaker development projects, Wolff 2005:247, footnote 14.

was given by the Rwandan group member as he claimed to know several proponents, and commented on their insincere strategies. He later also noted that the German-Rwandan group should have boosted their proposal to justify the application for an artificially high subsidy, as this was considered usual practice. The Rwandan group member mentioned: *"I should have been more aware when [one of the Germans] prepared the financial plans. We should have made it bigger because now we're the smallest project of the whole programme and the additional amount of subsidy could have helped us much now. We've been too honest"* [Rwandan group member].

In order to gain an overview of the situation, major incidents are summed up from the viewpoint of the German-Rwandan PPP-project in a rough chronological order:

- Successful submission of preliminary proposal for pre-selection procedure.
- Cooperation with national power utility and communication with project consultant.
- Long period of waiting and incidents of miscommunication in several instances.
- Contact and cooperation with local community and regional church authority.
- Communication with management of national power utility and project consultant who both facilitated the PPP-proposal.
- Diplomatic and technical affairs, donor subcontracting of PPP programme to another development agency.
- European management is expelled from national power utility, strategy and management changes affect the Micro Hydro programme.
- Communication with new management and policy makers, attempts to secure a commercially interesting tariff, private investors and donor organisation depend on new utility management.
- German-Rwandan group abandons the project as commercially unviable.
- Donor agency officially closes the proposal of German-Rwandan group, the sister projects from the same PPP programme were under way for a lengthy period of time and delayed. Lack of governmental facilitation and poor coordination of interests, complex situation with multiple stakeholders.

The three individuals involved in the project group were motivated by entrepreneurship combined with the prospect of a personal adventure for the Germans and retirement provisioning for the Rwandan. An additional incentive was the possibility of contributing to the development of a rural community. This set of motivations led to a quick withdrawal once it became clear that their expectations could not be met. In terms of the donor agencies' strategies it can be said that their disbursement pressure roughly equalled local interests concerning profiting from the project. As a result, they quickly found themselves in a locally dependent position. The disruptions around the national utility demonstrated that the energy sector was among the Rwandan policy fields still in the making, and a dependable institutional environment for external actors did not yet exist.

The observation of this small but complex transboundary arena revealed an intersection of different interests that were concerned with the same issue from different angles. Similarly but in a very different context Obi (2001) described the complex intersections in the transboundary arena of the Niger delta, where oil companies and political elites competed with international NGOs and local protest groups. In this case, too, more than one original Transboundary Cooperation took part in a wider issue. "The juxtaposition of multiple transboundary formations operating in the very same locale is one for which our analytic tools are not well developed" (Kassimir/Latham 2001:273).

4.7 INDIAN TRADERS

In many East African countries, Indian immigrants have formed communities of considerable size and relevance to the host country's society. Since the first migration waves during the time of British colonization, a distinct population group emerged under the name of the 'Indian diaspora'. From the early influences of the colonisers until today, settlers, workers and entrepreneurs from the Indian subcontinent have become visible important protagonists in several regions of the globalised world, including Rwanda and East Africa. The activities of these Indian overseas communities are an almost ideal entry point for the observation of a distinct variety of Transboundary Cooperations. Based on a case study of an Indian trader in Kigali, I will present some perspectives on Indian businesspeople as a transboundary form on their own, based on ethnic origin and enterprise. In a second step I broaden the view and take a look at certain aspects of the Indian diaspora in Rwanda that are related to the study of Transboundary Cooperations.

The African Indian population in East Africa

Considerable numbers of Indian emigrants have settled in different parts of the world as an effect of labour migration among the British colonies (both forced and independently). Until today they have formed a dedicated diaspora population of considerable size that is based on kinship, mobility, social networking and cultural belonging. The Indian businesses operating in African economies and the numbers of hired Indian professionals throughout the continent are all part of this wider context.

Indian professionals are frequently contracted in Africa because of their academic and practical skills and their readiness to go abroad. They often combine their professional standing, the ability to function well in the context of a developing country and a requested wage level that often fits local budgets. They can be found in responsible positions in education, health and management in many African countries, including Rwanda.

But at least as characteristic as these academically skilled labour migrants are Indian entrepreneurs, operating businesses of all sizes and types. Often they take an active role in the local economies of their host countries and are highly visible in their local markets. The classic occupations included those of import-export traders, retailers, moneychangers and general businesspeople who largely make up the popular image of the 'Indian' throughout African societies. Traders, shops and retailers selling imported goods are the most visible representatives of this group's activities in Rwanda, as much as foreign exchange offices and several factories in urban areas.

Due to a lack of local production facilities in Rwanda during the time of the research, most manufactured or processed goods had, and still have, to be imported. The opportunity is taken by a competitive mix of native and East African, Chinese and Indian trading businesses. The local Indian entrepreneurs frequently channel their affairs through trading networks on the basis of personal contacts and relationships. In this way they are linked to Asian suppliers and overseas distributors. The retailers, who conduct the local part of the business, sell the goods in their stores and outlets, thus building on the infrastructure of these informal networks. In fact, they work as bridgeheads for trade networks that often are spanned across several countries. In Rwanda, most of these businesses were originally almost exclusively situated in Kigali's commercial centre, where they formed a local manifestation of the 'Indian Diaspora'. Nowadays the commercial activities in Rwanda have largely expanded and enterprises are to be found in all parts of the country.

Overseas Communities

The term 'diaspora' signifies a distinguished category of social belonging, forming a scattered population group that consists of migrant communities in distant regions of even unrelated parts of the world. It is not limited to the Indian context and in fact has its main origin in the Jewish context from which is was adapted as a general academic term. Robin Cohen (2008) devoted a book to the phenomenon of 'global diasporas', describing the relationship between the worldwide migration of cultural communities and their identity. In the case of the 'overseas Indians', a shared conviction of cultural affiliation and ties to their homeland is common. Therefore, next to the major Indian languages are the regional tongues and (sub-)cultures, which are practised overseas as well. In the terminology of the Indian government, individuals belonging to the Indian diaspora are either called "Non-Residential Indians" (NRI) when living and working outside India, or "People of Indian Origin" (PIO) when also born abroad. Although its members were visibly present in Kigali's social and commercial life, the Indian community in Rwanda is comparatively small in absolute numbers. In fact, it is not even mentioned in the Africa section of the Indian government's "Report of the High Level committee on the Indian Diaspora" (NRI & PIO Division, 2001). This report outlines the history and worldwide situation of the Indian diaspora from the viewpoint of the Indian government. It describes the situation of Indian communities in the East African countries of Kenya (100,000 persons or 0.36% of population), Tanzania (90,000 persons or 0.28% of population) and Uganda (12,000 persons, being an insignificant proportion of the population). Despite these rather small percentages of the overall population, members of the Indian communities occupy influential socio-economic positions within these East African countries. Rwanda, as well as Burundi, is not mentioned in this report due to the much smaller size of the communities in these two countries.

An often-noted characteristic of these communities is their efficient local integration in formal and economic terms. At the same time they are maintaining their own social and cultural infrastructure. The aim to settle permanently or semi-permanently in their host countries goes hand in hand with the adoption of a role as permanent strangers (Sorensen 2000:80). In several important aspects, the situation of many Indian (more generally South Asian) migrants in African countries is very different from that of Western expatriates. For individuals from Western countries their comparatively short periods of residence often times are directly related to assignments in the local branches of Western organisations.

For the remainder of this chapter, in the face of a considerable variety of activities conducted by Indians in Rwanda I will concentrate on the transboundary relationships in the rather classic example of an import-trading and real-estate business.

An Indian entrepreneur

In the following section I introduce an Indian trading enterprise in Kigali. Mr. Mandar, the owner, came to Rwanda as a young man along with his brother. While the brother moved on to other countries in search of further opportunities, Mandar was left to stay with the new trading business they had started. With some interruptions he had spent most of his life in Rwanda. In the course of 30 years he became a successful businessman and a person of respected social standing. The character of his commercial activities as well as the form of their practical organisation, and his lifestyle too, can be seen as a prototype of his generation's manifestation of African-Indian overseas business.

Mandar's commercial activities were based on import and retail, real-estate and some foreign exchange. Aside from his Rwandan business, he also owned a parallel company of roughly the same kind in other East African cities. His stores offered a variety of relatively high priced, upper-class items for private homes and business needs, consisting of different kinds of household equipment, furniture, domestic appliances and office supplies. These goods were mainly imported from India or Dubai, where Mandar disposed over the relevant connections to suppliers and cargo handlers. Occasional products of East African manufacture were also on sale in his stores.

One of his core businesses was the official distribution of a special Indian product range that was marketed internationally. In this market segment his toughest competition came from another Indian brand that was similar. Selling a genuine technical product of Indian origin had a symbolic value to him beyond the purely commercial aspects and he made significant efforts to bring it to the Rwandan market.

Furniture was another important product category for Mandar and had previously been a priority for his business. Originally he was interested in selling high-class furniture from local manufacturers. This was planned as a convenient means to substitute imports and thereby cut costs and complications. It turned out differently and during the time of this research he was very critical about the reliability and quality of local supplies. He once tried to set up a domestic production facility himself but explained that its operation had been disappointing due to an unsatisfactory quality of work and unsolvable difficulties on the organisational side.[23]

"General business"

To Mandar, the way in which he had started, built up and maintained his enterprise was the most obvious one and he called it doing *"general business."* Both of his main branches, retail stores dealing in imported goods and real-estate, had been developing well over a long period and were the source of his wealth. He adapted his habits and style of business to the conditions in Rwanda and skilfully secured

---

23 This judgement expresses the trader's individual experience but also highlights the situation of many Rwandan artisans and manufacturers. More on this topic in case study 4 (Chapter 4.4).

his belongings during the difficult years of political instability and civil war. This enabled him to participate in the economic rush of the post-war years. His basic approach to business was to maintain exclusive relationships to overseas suppliers that gave him an advantage in the local market. Over an extended period of time until the first decade of the new century the simple ability to sell valuable goods and equipment has been a means for success, even in a highly restricted economy.

Better supply and changing customers

During the time this research was conducted, the situation of traders changed significantly. Business strategies such as 'marketing' and 'customer care', widely common in other parts of the world with mature and oversaturated markets, had only started to gain importance in Rwanda. Originally, the domestic situation was that of a largely supply driven market at the expense of the customer. As long as the trader possessed access to the right supplies and managed to have items in stock that were hard to find elsewhere, price and service were of little consequence and customers were almost obliged to visit the store ('caveat emptor'). Such is the situation in an under-provisioned, landlocked and poor country with an economy in crisis mode. Compared to other countries of the region, Rwandans over an extended number of years faced harder obstacles to buying technical or commercial goods due to a simple lack of reliable and affordable suppliers. Under-provisioning with imported goods went hand in hand with a very low demand or even ability to apply these products. The few traders that were able to service this closed-off market were in a situation of convenient profits. Indian trading businesses proved capable of operating reasonably profitably in such situations due to their effective networking, personally tied chains of supply, personnel from the own family, and a comparatively flexible shift of liquid capital across countries. Mandar was one of these traders from the pre-war time and the surging economy in the post-war period. Similarly, in real-estate, he found optimal conditions for his business of renting out commercial spaces to local entrepreneurs after the war. This was a time of high demand for readily usable building structures while space was limited and rents were high. Those first new buildings erected after the war met a medium standard at best, but that did not matter.

Yet, as a matter of fact and despite all ongoing economic and political difficulties, the Rwandan economy had steadily become more vibrant. In the last couple of years before this study conducted, the first serious competition to Mandar arose. Entrepreneurs of Mandar's generation had to adapt to a new situation with additional competition from local entrepreneurs and foreign traders, and also especially with the government tightening its fiscal regulations and enforcing new commercial rules. The first post-war years had been tax-free and unregulated for the traders. At the same time customers often had to buy whatever was on display without any real bargaining power. However, this raw stage of a cut-throat economy was slowly nearing its end. Additionally, new waves of younger competitors from Rwanda, neighbouring African countries and Asia entered the market. The sweeping changes brought on by civil war and the resulting population movements saw a dramatic evolution in Rwandan society, paralleled by a first wave of modernisation in the major domestic industries. Even if the Rwandan economy at that time was not comparable to technically and commercially more evolved 'emerging markets', the new generation of local entrepreneurs started their own trading enterprises and used their own connections to Dubai and Asia. *"The young businesspeople are very shrewd."* Mandar saw his old convenient market position coming under pressure and tried to expand his product line in new directions while searching for a new competitive advantage.

A lifestyle between integration and diaspora

Mandar was considerably well integrated in Rwandan social life in terms of knowing places, local affairs, culture and language. He spoke Swahili to his workers and understood Kinyarwanda; in public he conducted himself like a wealthy Rwandan. On the other hand, his private life was focussed on the Indian community and a selected group of expatriates. Private relationships and work related contacts were carefully kept separate. In his relationships with most native Rwandans he usually remained defensive if not restrictive and would not let himself be subjected to risks arising out of being too trustful.

A younger woman from Mandar's extended family, Urja, worked with him and lived in his household. She came from India in order to seek her own opportunities, driven by the hope that one day she might be able to go to the USA. Mandar accommodated her because he had the resources and was in need of a trustworthy business aide. She took on the job of supervisor in charge of overseeing the staff and monitoring the money. Thus Urja assisted in the administration of Mandar's company, providing her commitment and labour in exchange for personal opportunities. In this role she was representing Mandar's interests towards both his customers and employees; as a relative she became Mandar's most trusted business associate.

Despite being wealthy, Mandar's public behaviour showed no traces of abundant luxury or consumptive excesses. He kept a low profile, in contrast to successful Rwandan businesspeople, who often represented their material successes more openly. Mandar, like other Indians, did not see an imminent reason to make such impressions on the local public. His relevant social context was his extended family that was scattered across several continents. Within these family circles, reputation and hospitality were exchanged, children were sent on visits to relatives living in India, Africa and America, keeping family bonds alive. These connections were occasionally reinforced through meetings, festivities and weddings. Occasional travel, talks on the phone, sharing home videos or pictures; this was the social world in which the Indian businessman saw himself situated. Even though the realisation of a good personal standing in Rwanda itself was desirable for Mandar, the last frame of reference was presented by his de-localised kinship community.

Friendly relations in Rwanda outside this personal sphere were more limited. Meeting people in Kigali without the purpose of business was a rare but welcomed opportunity, and people suitable for such interactions were carefully selected. Mandar openly explained his decisions on why he liked to meet a person and also did not hide the distinctions he made in levels of trust and affection between family and kinship, nice and harmless strangers (such as the anthropologist himself), and those he tried to avoid. Mandar was constantly shifting between the social world of the diaspora and the local context of the Rwandan upper-class. As a result, after three decades in the country, his personal habits were no longer typically Indian, but this only became apparent when he visited India. In his home country Mandar would easily stand out as a person living abroad, as someone not deeply rooted in the traditional culture of the region he once came from. Over the years, he began to call Rwanda his home even though he maintained a sort of separation between himself and the Rwandan social world.

Management, trust and organisation

The company's business consisted of several main activities. Two shops and a number of secondary facilities sold imported goods. Several stores and commercial spaces available for rent made up the real-estate side of Mandar's enterprise in Kigali. In another East African city his representatives managed a similar business on his behalf.

Management was centred in Mandar's hands and predominantly focussed on control. All decisions and responsibilities, every initiative, idea and strategy came exclusively from the owner himself while the staff, consisting of more than 15 people, narrowly followed his instructions. While the main store was overseen by his relative Urja, Mandar occupied his office where he was supported by Rwandan administrative staff. He kept meticulous notes on all sales, items, stores and financial movements as well as on the arrivals, departures and whereabouts of his employees. Every event involving decisions or money was directly overseen by Urja or Mandar while the staff received orders and executed supportive functions. The

Rwandan employees rarely found the courage to air their opinion and refrained from taking risks, which, together with the strict controls, resulted in an authoritative and hierarchical organisation.

Both Mandar and Urja complained about their employees' unreliable behaviour and poor quality of work. According to their explanations, the whole business suffered from unmotivated and uninspired staff. Workers not only did their job in a slow or incorrect manner but were also not to be fully trusted. *"No, normally they don't work well"* [Mandar]. Accordingly, the wages were low and workers had to be supervised almost constantly. This situation put a strain on the social relationship between the staff and the employer, leading to prevailing accusations of exploitation and mutual distrust. In fact, both Mandar and Urja distrusted the Rwandans in their business as a matter of principle and saw this opinion constantly verified through their own experiences. Incidents of theft and mismanagement were among their daily troubles, followed by workers being lazy or unmotivated. Mandar had begun to install electronic surveillance equipment in the hope of containing the problem of theft in branches he could not observe personally.

On untrustworthy clerks in responsible positions stealing money: *"I'm losing money on this, you know, so I can't sleep at night"* Anthropologist: *"Hmm, but why don't you just fire them?"* Mandar: *"That doesn't really help... they are able to manage the shop well otherwise, and any other person would do the same... cause the same problems."*

Obviously, Mandar was unhappy with the situation. He suffered from an unproductive and distrustful atmosphere. Under these circumstances he saw no opportunity for treating his staff in a more relaxed manner, as he feared immediate exploitation. On the whole, owners and employees seemed to be caught in a vicious circle that was not too uncommon in the Rwandan economy at that time. They were mutually dependant on one another and had to cope with a distrustful environment in which strict hierarchical control had become the lowest common denominator. In this setting the employees lacked the incentive to perform better. Instead they saw themselves being subjected to a suspicious and autocratic boss who seldom gave positive feedback and also paid low wages. This situation made it hard to find and retain qualified staff that could have resulted in a positive change. Thus cheaper, under-qualified staff and young part-time workers were hired instead. In order to strengthen his position, Mandar employed a trained clerk from India. His duties included maintaining the main shop while overlooking and managing the sales. It was hoped that a native Indian without any other local involvement would be better in meeting the business owner's expectations. Mandar recruited this man and arranged travel and paperwork for him and his family. In the end, however, he was also dissatisfied for similar reasons. Taken together, in spite of a thriving business, the company's situation was far from optimal, and the owner began to worry about the future.

On top of these worries, the actively maintained distinctiveness of the local Indian community further contributed to a certain uneasiness in commercial life. As it is often the case, the social separation at hand can, and will be, explained in ethnic terms. In this way, the conflict of interests in the domestic trade economy also became a confrontation between different sorts of people. A Rwandan who had formerly worked as a clerk in an Indian shop paraphrased his experiences: *"All they get...it is sent to India and they are very hard to understand...it is a funny race of people"* [former Rwandan clerk]. Similar patterns replicated themselves in other commercial relationships, mostly between traders and customers or among competitors.

Many of Mandar's family members had spread across the world and had their own businesses to look after, some making fortunes on other continents. Once a brother living in America was seeking investment opportunities and considered Rwanda for a new venture. Mandar recalled how he had been reluctant to advise his brother in favour of putting money at risk in this country, fearing that the harsh conditions and high uncertainties were unfavourable. His brother had once moved to Canada, and so Mandar was aware that his relatives had become accustomed to the more predictable and stable environment of this Western country. He clearly did not wish to be responsible for any risks in Rwanda. Explaining his reaction he states: *"I am content with whatever I have here... and, so after all I told and explained my brother to keep his money in [North America]"*.

Summing up, one could say that Mandar's commercial activities represented a business model that had been successful over a longer period but slowly ran the risk of becoming outdated. New competitors increasingly challenged his market position, and workers either refrained from accepting the tough conditions or were under-qualified. Entrepreneurs of his kind had started their ventures within market conditions that allowed an efficient supplier to dictate the market to customers. For a certain time, traders with the right supplier contacts had been in a position to reap huge profits from selling exclusively imported goods.

Cultural diaspora, business and lifestyle

Motives for the almost characteristic mobility of migrating Indian individuals and their families are mainly related to the need for generating an income. The hired Indian professionals in management, health and education are usually employed by local institutions such as universities or hospitals or the larger companies on the basis of their personal skills and academic knowledge. Traders and entrepreneurs, in contrast, often come from backgrounds where economically motivated migration was already common in the family but not directly related to a higher formal education. These individuals either start their trades abroad as an accessible means to make a living, or they inherit an already existing business. Many of today's successful entrepreneurs from the Indian diaspora were born abroad or migrated at a young age. A new enterprise often begins with the sale of Asian consumer goods obtained from international suppliers, or directly from Indian manufacturers. The necessary contacts in many cases are formed through personal networks or the extended family. The network behind a new venture can also provide initial support in the form of logistical assistance or awarding of credit. Examples of diaspora-owned businesses in the Rwandan capital Kigali are to be found in several retail stores selling IT equipment, clothes or household goods. Links to suppliers in Dubai or Eastern Asia provide a source of cheap goods, while local distribution is handled by smaller retail shops. These traders often have notably well organised stocks and readily available products, when compared to some of their competitors. They help each other out in cases where a particular shop might lack an item demanded by a customer in order to finalise a sale, at least among their colleagues. Such cooperative behaviour is not typical among Rwandan traders. Managing one's enterprise easily consumes the greatest part of these entrepreneurs' daily lives, while leisure activities mostly centre on the family.

When it comes to destinations for migration or investment in new ventures, the judgements are made on a purely technical-pragmatic basis. Decisions concerning new locations are mostly oriented on the experiences of familiar individuals and personal background abroad. Official data such as reports on political stability and macroeconomic trends or formal industry surveys, which are so important for Western investors, are devoid of the specificity and deep personal experience vital for the classical Indian overseas entrepreneur. From the viewpoint of the researcher, this weak connection of individual estimations to formal data has a definite cause: the commercial strategies of these small to medium scale South Asian entrepreneurs enfold their viability often in precisely those places or industries that are not optimally served by native local businesses. The emergence of such Transboundary Cooperations can often be attributed to possibilities of handling or exploiting asymmetries in the balance of global and local contexts. In the old Rwanda, having better access than locals to valuable Asian supplies was a structural condition that applied to several South Asian communities. They could sell imported goods on their own terms where no other means existed to get hold of these products. In situations such as these the diaspora can prosper without much integration. In a classical sense, many Indian SMEs in African countries are ready to deal with unstable environments where native entrepreneurs are not yet in a sufficiently competitive position.

Historically, the phenomenon of the Indian diaspora was related to British colonial policies of forcing or semi-forcing Indian labour to move to other continents. These movements, while initially forced, established themselves as a migration trend in search of income opportunities while economic hardships prevailed in India. Thus migration was, and still is, usually not motivated by political, religious or ethnic pressure (NRI & PIO division 2001:xii). Instead the pursuit of personal interests is guides most of the diaspora's decisions. One's own social and cultural life abroad is reproduced in community events and activities, and is mainly concerned with maintaining the cultural identity and individual or collective livelihood. Migrants involved in business or those who are professionally employed by local companies or administrations are typically interested in, and critical observers of, both the local and global news and seek to know what is going on in their host country. But they often do not involve themselves personally in local affairs and retain the distanced view of an outsider.

Indian individual living in Rwanda: *"I have seen five governments in this country."* Anthropologist: *"Has there been a best one for you?"* Indian individual: *"All of them were good as long as they stayed in power, but all of them are bad as soon as they lose power."* (Note: the author made no inquiry into historical facts at this point)

In comparison, Western individuals in African countries, expatriates and tourists alike, often seem to be more interested in expressions of local cultures and emotionally more attached by humanitarian issues than Indian migrants. However, in fact the distraction from local affairs expressed by Indian individuals is only half of the truth. Their immediate grasp of the local context often is much stronger than what is possible for most Westerners. This seems to be an effect of the underlying closeness in living conditions which is also expressed by the term 'south-south'-cooperation.

Cultural closeness as an economic strategy

Northup (1995:60) maintains that migration is an important part of the Indian social world connected to income and work related motives. With respect to the diaspora's characteristic maintenance of its cultural identity, Falzon (2003:679) identifies the "ability to recreate a culture in diverse locations" within Indian migrant communities. Social life is largely centred on an active in-group community, regular social events and a practice of continuous information sharing. This also includes well organised efforts in the form of semi-official printed information such as the Rwandan 'Indian Yellow Pages', covering the whole local community.

As a workable definition of what a diaspora is, Tölölyan calls it a "semantic domain that includes words like immigrant, expatriate, refugees, guest workers, exile community, overseas community, ethnic community" (1991:4). Having established a vital diaspora culture, Indians (and South Asians more generally) share a history as a distinct and exposed immigrant group in East Africa. Several older studies have treated these groups in country specific and historical aspects: Bharati (1972), Ghai/Yash (1970), Kuper (1969) while Morris (1968) worked on ethnic discrimination in their case. Sorensen (2000) gives a broad historical account of the economic and social activities of Indian traders in a Ugandan provincial town, which bears partial resemblance to the situation in Rwanda. Indian traders remain separated from the local population around them and in their individual orientations rely almost exclusively on their own communities. Sociocultural segregation and self-proposed maintenance of their ethnic distinctiveness contribute to a locally common image of the South Asian diaspora's 'unassimilability'. This goes along with adapting to the capitalist ideals of hard work and entrepreneurship, but not with blending into local lifestyles. Such observations can not only be made in East Africa, as similar patterns were also observed for Indian migrants in industrialised countries: for the North American context, Mankekar (2002:80), or Indian IT professionals in Germany, Oberkircher (2006).

Collective economic success goes hand in hand with high internal differentiation and social stratification. Mankekar (2002:92), Dhaliwal (1995) and Wadhwani (1998) see class distinctions playing a role also within diaspora businesses and identify social and economic exploitation. This may not only happen between owners and employees but also between owners and dependent family members, especially concerning the labour of poorer relatives.

A different view on the subject is taken by Broadman (2007) who presented a comparative study of Indian and Chinese commerce on the African continent. According to this author, Indian investments are much more integrated into the surrounding local societies than Chinese ones and benefit from the active presence of Indian communities in Africa. With long established diaspora communities being present in several countries across the continent Indian investors, as much as the Indian government, possess a distinct advantage over their Chinese competitors. Active political support of these migrant communities from the Indian government is nevertheless limited due to the resistance of African governments in accepting such external interference (Biallas/Knauer 2006:8).

"Indians are cheating" vs. "You can't trust Rwandans"[24]

The local market conditions for imported goods in many African countries often provide Indian traders with favourable opportunities according to their own methods of translocal exclusivity, stable supplies and high prices. Trading and import

---

24 The quotes were taken from Rwandan and Indian interview partners, respectively.

businesses in these situations virtually dictate the local markets and may not always be concerned much about customer care. Rwandan clients thus often perceived themselves more as potential victims than as valuable customers (however, the idea of customer care was both rare and new in many Rwandan businesses as well during the time of research). Without going into the dynamism of ethnic differentiation, it can be noted that in the context of buying and selling, Indians are often seen in light of ethnic stereotypes as much as they themselves argue in culturalist terms about Rwandan habits. Antagonisms on the basis of ethnic ascriptions are common, and they roughly go like this: Indians lament the complications of conducting their affairs in Rwanda. They see a need to protect themselves against exploitative and dishonest local business tactics, administrative arbitrariness, and unruly employees with poor working habits. Rwandans in turn regard cheating and conspiracy as typical threats posed by Indian businesspeople, who are seen as ruthlessly inflating prices in order to make profits and other even more shadowy deals.

Bank director: *"We really want European investors."* Anthropologist: *"But there are also many Indians in business now, and they warn against some problems here, for example in the [taxation procedures]."* Bank director: *"What I don't like about the Indians, they can never do clean business."*

Cooperation and trust

An Indian living in Germany with family ties to East Africa sums up the economic advantages of ethnic networking:

Anthropologist: *"What are the main differences between Europeans and Indians when it comes to doing business in Africa?"* Indian from Germany: *"The family joint system. Indians have more success at the moment and they are doing much more. Basically, we have a big advantage all over the world which basically lies in the family joint system. Look, I can go to Kenya tomorrow, or to South Africa, or Dubai. I just have to make a phone call, and somebody will be there for me to give me a place to sleep and to tell me where to go. You can't do that, just like that. If you go, let's say, to South Africa, you pay much more, hotels and so on. And over there you don't get any insider information about the place you were coming to. What I'm saying, Indians are not more intelligent or better in business, no, it's about this family network."*

Social networking here takes place in a mixture of strategic cooperation, personal reputation and a sense of belonging that is mainly ascribed to individuals of the same ethnic and social background. Connectedness is a valuable resource to Indian migrants, as they depend, for better or worse, primarily on their own community, due to their avoidance of deeper social bonds or resource sharing with the local society (see also Sorensen 2000:194). While the Rwandan society is subject to low levels of trust and cooperation among its members ('low-trust society') the Indian community is not affected by such liabilities. On the contrary it seemed to turn its natural differentiation from the host society into a benefit as this situation brings about the ability to set its own standards. While Rwandan businesses usually found it hard to work together trustfully the Indians assisted each other and devoted their awareness to the members of their ethnic group more productively. On this way their distinctive pattern of belonging became a beneficial resource for the members of the ethnic community. An Indian informant admitted that this distinctiveness can go very far: *"The own language is the basis... Sometimes Indians are kind of excluding and don't allow outsiders to be part of their inner community. I can somehow understand why the African guys tell you this. Our people stay with their own language and keep their things secret... they say don't teach anything to your staff, 'namaste' is enough."*

This empirical observation confirms to Axelrod's (1984) well-known statements about group-internal cooperation of a minority within a majority of non-cooperating outsiders. Axelrod developed his formal approach in the context of game theory, where the "tit for tat-rule" prescribes that among participants cooperative behaviour shall be rewarded with cooperation and non-cooperating behaviour shall be answered by a termination of any cooperation until the defective actor cooperates again. The theoretical result is a self-policing group that promotes a collectively stable environment of exchange, while non-cooperative individuals are excluded. Under suitable conditions such a group can develop a momentum to grow and provide its members with options to reduce their transactions with defective outsiders, concentrating on group members instead. The economically optimal behaviour of minority groups in competitive environments closely resembles this model. Individuals apply a cooperative ("nice") strategy to handle their community internal behaviour. At the same time interactions with (assumedly non-cooperative) outsiders are rather harsh, or reduced where possible. And as soon as the group is big enough for the individuals to conduct a significant amount of their relevant transactions among each other, it can survive even when the surrounding social environment is uncooperative.

Shared language, spiritual beliefs and cultural events together with a preferred treatment of group members reify the special status within which the migrant group's individuals see their social life embedded. Yet, their commitment to the in-group goes hand in hand with a partial reduction in individual independence. Individuals become subjected to peer curiosity, group pressure and narrow cultural or moral standards.

This ambivalent issue of local integration combined with the perceived commercial successes that have partially led to considerable wealth make the overall acceptance and political standing of Indian communities in East African countries a delicate issue. One fear is that the local native populations might question their loyalty towards their African host country (NRI & PIO Division 2001:100). However, the activities of the Indian diaspora in their host countries usually are centred on business, livelihood and cultural life. In order to prevent possible antagonisms, the representatives of Indian communities in African countries make use of various opportunities to symbolically demonstrate their commitment towards their countries of residence (example: Indian community delivers public disaster relief in Uganda, The Monitor, November 12, 2007).

Cooperation patterns

A comparison between Rwandan and Indian cooperation patterns provides a first impression of a very special collective relationship. Rwandan society in general has to cope with a relatively high level of distrust as well as an equally strong tendency towards defection among its members. Typical patterns of activity within the Indian diaspora, in contrast to its African host society, are instrumentally supportive and mutually facilitating even though personal rivalries might be fought out in the commercial sphere. This in-group stabilisation corresponds with a separation from the outer social environment and an active reproduction of the collective sociocultural boundaries. Gambetta (2000) mentions the importance of trust for social cohesion, but also delves into the topic of reducing the dependence on trust by an establishment of stabilising social structures. In other words, suitable social structures can effectively decrease the need to rely on trust. Axelrod's (1984) famous findings from his work on cooperation (as mentioned above) can provide explanations of the empirical situation: An effective group strategy is the reciprocation of both cooperation and defection. When, in relation to the present, the future is important enough, cooperative behaviour can become collectively stable. When the actors are likely to meet again, or when they must depend on each other to sustain themselves in an environment of outsiders, the implicit drive to accept these rules is high. This means that if everyone in a closed community is cooperating, there is no better advice for a particular player than to cooperate as long as others cooperate, and to reciprocate a defection. In this sense Indian traders in Kigali worked together astonishingly well. When, for example, a customer entered a store and asked for a particular item that was unavailable the owner could instantly borrow the product from one of the neighbouring stores and sell it at his own profit in order to make the deal. Even though such collegial help is not at all limited to Indian traders, the extent to which Rwandan traders were able to benefit from mutual cooperation was much lower. In many instances their lack of cooperation prevented Rwandan businesses to stabilize or even get started and left them vulnerable to the commercial impact of their Indian competitors.

Diaspora in comparison across context and time

I found that the ethnic and economic strategies attributed to the Indian overseas communities in East Africa possess a striking similarity to the way in which Davis (1999) described the historical state of Jewish merchant culture in 18th century Europe. Despite all the differences in context and time that can reasonably be asserted I nevertheless introduce some elements of comparison. European Jews at that time lived together in merchant families that spread across the continent and, as is well known, engaged in a variety of mercantile and financial activities. These communities maintained their cultural distinctiveness and a certain sense of cosmopolitanism in spite of their integration into the host societies and a normal residential status. In many aspects their social structure is that of today's diaspora cultures. This is not as surprising as the word "diaspora" itself originates in the Jewish context. The underlying social structures of migration, community and commercial cooperation seem to be stable over the centuries and can also be found in other ethnic groups over the world.

According to Davis, the merchant families made no distinction between their business strategies and family affairs. A full integration of private life, the extended family and the realisation of business opportunities formed the inevitable basis of sharing risks and establishing rationally advanced enterprises. "Crossed-over strands of action and communication networks buzzing with diamond prices, bills of divorces, bans, bankruptcies, and [spiritual affairs] seem to heighten the energy of enterprise, religion, and family life all at once" (Davis 1999:73).

Similarly, entrepreneurs from the Indian diaspora keep themselves separated from the host societies despite a strong integration and a good formal assimilation into local settings. Living in closed communities corresponds with economic integration and adaptation to local conditions. The historical Jewish communities exploited the advantage of ethnically organised distinctiveness in a similar way, allowing the community members to

"stage their own social dramas quite apart from the criteria of the world around them and to invest in trading relations with meanings that went well beyond [monetary value]. [... these were the elements] that make business an *interesting* activity, arousing energy and intensity. Here was a payoff more durable and less dangerous than usury. Such elements facilitate extensive networks, even while allowing people to air their doubts about each other, or perhaps we should say *just because* they allow closely linked participants to air their doubts about each other. They also make possible the information flow and rapid movement of goods [...]." (ibid:75, emphasis given)

Cultural closedness and secrecy were thus historically found to enhance personal opportunities: Their

"keeping of secret account books gave merchants a sense of protection for their family interests and was also part of the process by which a conceptual distinction [was maintained...]. Thus, the sense of inside space created by account books and other records in Hebrew characters was more than a family space; it was a larger Jewish space. Within it, Jewish traders established shifting partnerships with each other and had heated fights before rabbinical courts." (ibid:73f)

The use of Indian languages in host countries provides a very similar opportunity, starting with common forms of Hindustani or Hindi and culminating in regional or local Indian languages only intelligible to a very select in-group. Communities based on such patterns are able to maintain their own inner dynamism that functions independently of general societal trends.

"The economic drama that emerges is a ceaseless quest for information on the part of all participants – about products, people, and their trustworthiness [...]. The accompanying exchange is, if anything, 'hypercommercial', but it flows through a world in which the homogenization and impersonality considered essential to modernity are not present. Instead there is a fine division of labour, a specific identification of people by their origins [...] and a strong preference for personal contract and witnessing." (ibid:79)

Regarded as an economic pattern, such a socially embedded strategy possesses certain comparative advantages, which are based on a strong background of cultural bonds and shared social responsibility. Conducting transnational business in this manner, fostered and protected in a sphere of culturally closed ethnic communities, is most probably very different from doing business in the spirit of 'colour blind' modern capitalism. Ethnic networking can be regarded as a mercantile strategy at the frontiers of capitalist expansion, making commerce viable under difficult conditions. But it is not supposed to be a way to diminish social distinctions.

5. Analytical Framework: Three Aspects of Transboundary Cooperations

In order to derive further insights from the ethnographic material it will now be assessed with the help of an interpretative framework. We are looking at the organisational substructures inherent in the different kinds of Transboundary Cooperations that were part of the fieldwork. The following comparison is therefore less interested in the ostensible activities and formal missions of the observed organisations (e.g. the tasks involved in running a development project, conducting trade, manufacturing, consultancy or diplomatic representation). Instead, here we concentrate on the underlying assumptions and activity patterns that are rooted in the organisational 'sub-consciousness'.

Analytical framework with three aspects

The framework applied in this chapter represents the outcome of a conceptual process based on literature research and numerous iterations of grounded theory. The following three main aspects were identified:

(1) *Local Embeddedness.* Assessment of the depth and type of intersections between a transboundary organisation and the local social environment. The extremes are a wholly assimilated or a locally disconnected organisation.
(2) *Institutional vs. Technical Orientation.* The nature of organisational objectives and their operative orientations can be derived either from their technical environment (task fulfilment, technical effectiveness, market success) or from their institutional environment (seeking legitimation, compliance to institutional demands, symbolical approval).
(3) *Management of Heterogeneity.* Implicit structures and epistemic preconceptions of global heterogeneity upon which a Transboundary Cooperation is built. The approach consists of the two comparative concepts 'diversity vs.

difference' and 'operative universalism vs. operative relativism' (also see Chapter 2.3).

In the following sub-chapters each of these three aspects is put into a theoretical background and set in relation to the fieldwork.

Comparative assessment

The technical aim is to achieve a stage of comparability between the case studies. In order to enable this, the field studies are decomposed into thematic elements, which are then grouped according to the three analytical aspects. The comparison is semi-standardised. I have chosen a form that abstracts some phenomenological uniqueness of the field data in favour of structural aspects. This helps to identify commonalities and interrelations between the case studies. It is a trade-off between the valuation of uniqueness in field data and a general analytic interest.

5.1 LOCAL EMBEDDEDNESS

Regardless of their *glocality* (see Chapter 2.2), as soon as transboundary actors carry out their operations they act in *local* places. In this chapter I am going to inquire into the relationship between the operational core of Transboundary Co-operations and the Rwandan socio-economic environment. This first analytical aspect covers the question of local embeddedness. It asks whether and to what extent Transboundary Cooperations are locally assimilated or autonomous. In this respect, questions arise about the tendency and/or ability of related actors to blend into the local social environment, as well as the intensity of the influence the local setting exercises on the procedures of a Transboundary Cooperation.

High and low levels of local embeddedness

Transboundary actors may be subject to influences on their tasks and operations, which originate in dynamics rooted in the place they work. An actor's local embeddedness can thus be conceived as a combination of domestic entanglement, involvement, participation, responsibility and the social pressure of local communities. Experiencing local embeddedness implies that transboundary actors become an integral part of the situation in the host country and start to depend on what is taking place in that location. They become subjected to local possibilities and constraints, and ultimately have to prosper and survive under local conditions. Strongly embedded transboundary actors consider their circumstances under the same conditions as Rwandan actors. For them, a 'local standing' is important and cannot easily be abandoned or reduced without cost. The German grocery, an example from case five, is a highly embedded company and totally subject to the Rwandan environment. An example of very low embeddedness is the *Deutsche Welle* radio relay station near Kigali (which is not part of this study). This facility is virtually autonomous and disconnected from its surroundings, technically self-sufficient, and visitors are only accepted on personal invitation. Most of the case studies range in between.

Transterritorial deployments

Not all Transboundary Cooperations are locally embedded. Cooperations and activities across the boundaries of social spaces can take various forms, where transterritorial deployments are one extreme of a wider ranging isolation from the local environment. This term is associated with activities that may be considered as 'external interventions' of a limited sociocultural depth. In the following steps, I make use of Latham's (2001) concept in the adapted form of "transterritorial enclaves". According to Latham, the word 'transterritorial' initially means "the movement of a social entity across the boundaries of a territory from some external place, where the entity retains in that territory its identity as external" (Latham 2001:75). By preserving their external character, transterritorial deployments are separated from other transboundary forms such as international arenas and translocal networks. "A transterritorial deployment [...] is an installation in a local context of agents from outside that context. The place from which they are deployed is typically some kind of organizational platform (e.g. the headquarters of an international agency [...], a transnational corporation [...], or even the capital of a Western state)" (ibid.).

A typical diplomatic embassy can be considered as very 'transterritorial', as such installations often operate as isolated outposts on virtually alien ground. The small German-operated hotel from case five, on the other hand, has only very few operational determinations derived from Europe. In fact, it became part of the local economy. Therefore, both organisations are subjected to different transboundary processes in the Rwandan environment. It is obvious that hotel managers have different backgrounds and experiences divergent from diplomats, yet, what is to be presented here are some structural implications: how deep does the operational core of a Transboundary Cooperation penetrate into the local field? To which extent does it (unwillingly?) become interconnected with the local social and institutional landscape? An embassy can and will stay almost disconnected from its host country since its objectives, its provisions and its staff are intentionally kept self-sufficient. An embassy's main job of diplomatic representation does not necessarily require the diplomats to delve deep into their host country's society. For instance, a former economic advisor at the German embassy in Kigali bluntly admitted to his Rwandan and German visitors that his knowledge on intricate business affairs in the country was naturally limited and instead praised the insider information he received during the meeting (the anthropologist was one of these visitors).

Typical for transterritorial deployments is their narrow and specialised contact with their surroundings.

"Transterritorial deployments are by definition specialized in relation to any local social order they enter since they rest on the forward placement of a defined and delimited organization from outside. In other words, they move along relatively narrow bands of intervention or engagement with local order. An organization, individual, or institution could never carry with it the range of culture, politics, and social relations that are encountered in a given locale. The most extreme from of this external movement is extra-territorial, where the deployed organizational form (e.g. military or consular) carries its own culture, laws, and juridical authority (or in the case of a 'factory', its own system of economic extraction and trade)." (Latham 2001:76)

Diplomats and similar representatives usually understand those aspects of their host country that are relevant to them in a rather instrumental way, and do not necessarily aim at profound interpretations.

Transterritorial enclaves

External organisations with shallow local interconnections show a tendency to refer almost exclusively to their internal structures and background, especially for the legitimation and orientation of their daily operations. In such situations the guidance of an international head office or the existence of extensive formal regulations would play a lively and important role in everyday activities of the local agency. Deployments with a rather limited local entanglement are tied to an active management of their organisational boundaries in order to keep local demands at bay.

"If deployments are (in principle) limited, then how are the boundaries of their specialization enacted 'on the ground' and defined or identified by planners, practitioners, and local recipients of the deployment? This is really a question about the scope of the involvement of the organization deployed – how much of political and social life 'on the ground' is drawn up into its purview and range of self-defined responsibility." (Latham 2001:77)

I call social-organisational entities that are subjected to these dynamics 'transterritorial enclaves' (in the sense of a functional state of being for a 'deployment'). Other ways to characterise the state of transterritorial self-isolation is to describe it in terms of a 'black box', which highlights its perception as a closed unit from a local or native perspective. It could, furthermore, be seen as an 'island' that exists self-sufficiently in a diffuse and unapproachable environment. It is not only in Rwanda that expatriates tend to arrange themselves in enclave-like lifestyles. An ethnographic account of diplomatic life by Niedner-Kalthoff (2005) is indicative, among other publications, as well as Evers/Gerke's paper (2005) on the situation of development experts.

The possibility of self-containment is also an important aspect when evaluating the impact of multinational enterprises in Africa. Foreign corporations sometimes aim at profiting from distinctive local opportunities to be exploited by operations of limited scope, such as mining in closed areas, special management contracts and so forth. Sometimes, however, they become drawn into the totality of the local context, not always to their own benefit. In this regard, I point to the risk involved in making close arrangements with parties who wield local power in weakly legitimated patrimonial governments and criminal states. The threat of loss for an external actor can be substantial. Where the initial intention has been to set up an efficient foreign enclave, for example, a politically protected mining enterprise or an especially profitable investment safeguarded by the 'good connections' to local potentates, further affairs might draw the foreign actors into a totality of local politico-economic practices. When a seemingly limited transterritorial enclave forcefully goes native, it is likely an incident of foreign resources being exploited by domestic profiteers, who have greater influence in the long run. "Foreign businesses, which dependency theorists would consider to be part of a network of imperialist interests, were in fact most often the dupes of the prince with whom they negotiated" (Bayart 2000:231, on the situation in the Congo).

Local assimilation

The opposite of transterritorial enclaves are transboundary actors who become assimilated into the local context. In terms of adaptability, openness and partnership, a state of local assimilation may initially appear as generally desirable. It can serve as a countermeasure against the typical handicap of foreigners' communities, namely a disconnection from the deeper streams of the local environment (which is also a form of organisational blindness). In some fields of activity, such as the execution of development projects, it may even be considered a practical and ethical task to actively blend into the host society: foreign development experts have to fulfil their assignments *in* the country, *with* local counterparts.

Yet, there are constellations where transboundary actors become deeply drawn into local currents, far beyond their desires or expectations. Foreign small to medium businesses and NGOs, in particular, may face complexities arising from aspects of the local settings which, by nature of the social fabric, must be dealt with in totality. Work habits and administrative procedures are only the most common examples of this. And despite official proclamations of the opposite, working with local customers, target groups or suppliers under the conditions of the undifferentiated domestic institutional environment can cause problems for foreign actors, which cannot be solved with foreign approaches. This might lead to situations where it becomes increasingly difficult and ineffective for foreign actors to remain outside the sociocultural and economic contexts of the host country, even when they originally wish not to interfere locally or lack the capacity to do so.[25] At this point it becomes constructive for transboundary actors to know who is who in the local arena, what is going on and where one's own position lies. Yet, for foreign-owned SMEs a very high degree of local assimilation can also pose a liability, and in extreme cases an outright threat. Social pressure or the dependence on habits and customs of employees, target groups and local institutions is difficult to handle for foreigners with limited resources. SMEs and small NGOs, by definition, have limited resources, but are most likely to be drawn as a whole into the host country's setting. In this context, Rwandan informants often admitted to the importance of foreigners becoming amenable to local adaptation. On top of this, warnings were not unusual concerning risks to be encountered by external actors. Among these were social pressure, accumulating issues of inefficiency, and local exploitation strategies that aimed at the diversion of resources from the foreigners to local channels by legal but creative methods. *"You must know the place you work in"* [Rwandan official's friendly advice on this matter]. I do not speak about corruption or forced misappropriation here but instead of mostly informally and implicitly emerging forms of symbolic or strong resistance to the unadaptive foreign conduct.

Local and transterritorial influences on transboundary activities

The following three questions aid in grasping the matter of local embeddedness:

- Is there a deeper need for or interest in the transboundary activity connecting or adapting to local contexts in order to fulfil its objective?

---

25 Arguments to attract potential investors are largely based on the notion that foreigners who comply with the formal requirements will expect no further complications and conduct their 'business as usual'.

- Is there a possibility of the Transboundary Cooperation remaining separated in order to resist deeper involvement in local contexts where desired?
- Is the nature and extent of its own local embeddedness reflected by the organisation's members or employees?

Transterritorial enclaves and local assimilation

In a hypothetical continuum between a strong 'local assimilation' and a locally disconnected 'transterritorial enclave' it is helpful to have a rough understanding of where a specific Transboundary Cooperation lies. Thus I have built upon the previous considerations concerning local embeddedness to create a working concept for a typification of the case studies. Here, we try to determine where a given case stands: is it locally involved and assimilated, or is it a self-centred transterritorial enclave? The following lists provide some important characteristics to look for:

Table 1: Local assimilation vs. transterritorial enclaves

Local assimilation
What does it mean for a Transboundary Cooperation to be locally assimilated?
• Operational decisions reflect local (micro-) dynamics and attempt to adapt. • Operational decisions are increasingly bounded, or even determined, by local micro-politics and local institutions. • Objectives become streamlined towards local settings and actor constellations. • Decisions are increasingly made in relation to the personal connections and standing transboundary actors have in the local scene. • Objectives may arise or significantly change because of location specific circumstances. • Remaining informed requires knowledge of local news. • Personnel is hired due to that person's strong local connections. • Institutional legitimation is directed towards the local frame of reference.

> **Transterritorial enclaves**
>
> *What does it mean for a Transboundary Cooperation to be a transterritorial enclave?*
>
> - Operational decisions must increasingly consider, or are determined by, intra-organisational dynamics.
> - Objectives become streamlined towards inter-organisational values, policies and constellations emanating from the overseas head office, regardless of local conditions.
> - Personnel is assigned predominantly because of internal loyalty or competence.
> - Remaining informed requires knowledge of news from the organisation's head office.
> - Local connectedness is not a primary requirement, neither for staff nor objectives.
> - Institutional legitimation is directed towards the foreign/external frame of reference.

Assessment of case studies

In the remainder of this chapter I apply the concept of local embeddedness onto the seven case studies. This is done by assessing each case and filtering out the empirical elements that are relevant to the aspects of local embeddedness and the related working concept. The result of this exercise is a collection of findings. In a synthesis (Chapter 6), these findings will be a source for broader analysis.

[Case 1] Bilateral development agency

The policy of this agency is to directly place German development assistants into the local structures of their Rwandan counterparts. Far-reaching involvement into operative duties cause a deep assimilation of the development assistants by the local circumstances. This happens despite the fact that the policies and goals set by the local branch office of the development assistants are more directly related to and influenced by its German head office than the context of the targeted project partners in the host country. The guidelining values and goals of the development organisation are therefore not primarily influenced by domestic issues in the target country (Rwanda). Instead, they are derived from the German head office, which bases them on developmental-political priorities. Individually, however, the foreign development assistants are inserted into the Rwandan environment in spite of their organisation's centralised orientation. It should nevertheless be mentioned that the activities from this rather small development agency from the case study still show a comparatively high adaptation to its local target environment, and a comparatively deep involvement in local contexts.

[Case 2] Multinational beverage corporation

Relevant parts of the brewery's technical and commercial operations are adapted to local conditions, but the organisational core is increasingly orientated towards the corporate structure. Here, a shift from a post-colonial brewery's primarily local focus to an integrated subsidiary applying corporate-wide standardisation becomes visible. This leads to a parallel occurrence of local assimilation/adaptation and the emergent characteristics of a transterritorial enclave at the same time. Decreasing local assimilation does not lead to abandonment of adaptation. Instead, the process becomes increasingly selective. The rising importance of internal corporate standards is the driving force behind this shift and aims at a worldwide homogeneity of corporate procedure. This goal is of such high importance to the corporation as a whole that the environmental fit of the local subsidiary becomes less relevant. The organisational practices in the brewery are highly respected by its employees even though they deviate from the social norms of the host country.

[Case 3] German contractors for media systems

The contractors were, per definition, present for the limited time frame of a short project. Arrangements were set in place that did not involve becoming part of the local scene. Instead the project setting was intended to work as a 'temporary enclave' without much interconnection to the local environment, out of hospitality and with the aim of allowing quick progress. The intentions notwithstanding, the contractors gradually became assimilated to the local work environment due to the nature of their tasks and the need to get their job done in the local environment. Their customer proved incapable of maintaining the planned distraction of the German contractors from the rest of the work environment. Throughout the working process, therefore, a hybrid micro-environment established itself where the external contractors had to virtually fend for themselves to ensure the project's success, facing local complexities in lack of provisions, organisation and internal management. The contractor, being an SME with little previous experience in such situations, was overstrained with the unanticipated local complexity while the customer's representatives were overstrained by the emergence of organisational difficulties.

[Case 4] Rwandan construction enterprise

This local company is a preferred contracting partner for foreign actors from the diplomatic and development fields, which are often structured as transterritorial enclaves. Drawing on his international experience, the Rwandan owner understands the requirements of both local Rwandan and foreign/Western ways of thinking and working. Due to the personality and intercultural competencies of its owner, the company therefore possesses the ability to deal with foreigners in a way that facilitates the acquisition of reliable local engineering services. The company is contracted for the execution of donor projects and the maintenance of properties. Its owner's reliability and cultural adaptability reduce the complexity of interaction for the foreign staff, which otherwise would be subjected to the complexities of the local environment in a much more unfiltered way. The Rwandan owner acts as a cultural broker, customers benefit from his communicative abilities and international experience. The construction company itself is a strictly local organisation with all related characteristics. It is a challenge for its owner to keep up the exclusive relationships with foreigners when at the same time his company faces typical local constraints that threaten to scare them away (e.g. shortages and breakdowns, manpower complications, lack of liquid money).

[Case 5] German food and catering enterprises

The first example, a German grocery and food processing company benefits from its symbolic connectedness with German and European culinary culture and food quality. It attracts financially buoyant native and international customers. From a technical and commercial point of view, it is totally assimilated into the Rwandan environment. The second example, a German hotel and restaurant mainly serves Rwandan clients and possesses a less international ambience, except that its quality standards are at a generally competitive level. It is a local facility operated by foreigners, which is also reflected in the sometimes special treatment received by the local authorities and public (which can have positive and negative effects). Both companies and their owners are part of the local economy and are inclined to deal with it in the same way as native Rwandan enterprises. Additionally, being regarded as foreigners, they have to cope with exposure to domestic influences such as public opinion, authorities, etc., and due to the greater visibility higher scrutiny is attached to their activities.

[Case 6] A mixed arena

a) Donor agencies managing the PPP-programme
Similarly but stronger than the development agency in case 1, the PPP donor agency follows internal requirements of meeting programme goals and delivering

correct figures. It displays many aspects of a transterritorial enclave, even though the overall project goal is rural development, thus targeting conditions in poorest areas in locally feasible ways. The agency is experienced in the country but the final focus of decision making is set by the need to meet the internal project goals (e.g. delivering a number of local partners, funds disbursement). Political interests of Rwandan stakeholders and selfish strategies of its private partners remain mostly obscure to the agency, or are partially tolerated in order to meet project goals.

b) Attempted Micro Hydro investment project
Full assimilation into the local environment, but strategically taking dual roles of Rwandan and expatriate actors, depending on the situation. Code switching is applied by the small bi-national team: Rwandan or German identities are played out, depending on the situation. Cultural brokerage is used as a means to get access to both the rural community management and the administration of the international development agency. At the end the dependencies on the complex Rwandan context resulted in overreaching difficulties and finally the abandonment of the project.

[Case 7] Indian traders

The members of the Indian community were more often than not actively preserving their social and economic identity and autonomy as a group. This took place through self-separation of their 'own' ethnic community from the outward 'others' of the host country. Nevertheless, a strong technical and commercial adaptation takes place and Indian trading enterprises have sometimes mastered the complexities of the local social economy effectively. The observed Indian trading business was a genuine part of the local economy, while its owner himself was only very selectively integrated into the host society. He was known and well-connected but his personal affiliations and trust did not reach beyond the bonds of his extended family. Within the terminology of this research, Indian communities might be called 'assimilated enclaves'; they play an active role in the local environment and work with local means and employees as any native enterprise would. But from an insider's view they appear as local hubs of international networks. The logic of their decision making is essentially driven by local effectiveness and they therefore pay close attention to domestic developments. However, their ethics and the allocation of their resources are driven by dedicatedly in-group-oriented decisions that are largely unrelated to circumstances in their country of residence.

5.2 INSTITUTIONALISATION VS. TECHNICAL ORIENTATION

Throughout this second analytical section the focus rests on the impact of institutions and institutionalisation processes. I propose that the intensity of institutional influences in an organisation is one key factor that shapes the patterns of Transboundary Cooperations. The point of departure in this context is the question of whether a Transboundary Cooperation's primary institutional legitimation is derived from *technical* or *institutionalised* environments. The idea to apply this concept for the understanding of collaborations between European and African actors was first introduced by Rottenburg (2002, 2009). I will first explain the idea of institutionalisation and then present a working definition for empirical use. The term 'institution' was introduced in Chapter 2.3, as well as some of the core concepts of the Neo-Institutionalist organisation theory. For readers unfamiliar with these, a brief overview is included in the appendix (Chapter 8.2, Sociological Neo-Institutionalism, see also Chapter 8.1, Institutionalisation Test).

Institutionalised organisations

According to Neo-Institutionalist theory, the major aim of organisations is to achieve a state of legitimation in respect of their institutional environment (see Chapter 2.2). Institutional environments are shaped by laws, public expectations, social norms and values. "Organizations that incorporate societally legitimated rationalised elements in their formal structures maximize their legitimacy and increase their resources and survival capabilities" (Meyer/Rowan 1991:53). As a result of this tendency, compliance with general institutional and societal expectations as well as a high conformity to standards are advantageous. Although these 'intangible' conditions are key elements for organisational prosperity and survival, they do not affect technical outputs or practical efficiency. "Formal structures that celebrate institutionalized myths differ from structures that act efficiently. Ceremonial activity is significant in relation to categorical rules, not in its concrete effects [... It] has ritual significance; it maintains appearances and validates an organization" (ibid:55). Two examples for institutional legitimation typically found in industrial societies serve as an illustration: First, the time table of a public bus has to be implemented regardless of the number of passengers actually boarding the bus at a given time because, at least in the classic sense, the primary effectiveness of *public* services is measured in terms of correct service delivery and not in terms of efficiency (seen as merely carrying the most passengers per busload). Second, and similarly, doctors have to treat patients according to acknowledged medical *standards* regardless of the *actual* curing effect that the patient is going to experience. Adherence to medical standards is a prime measurement of clinical effectiveness because the occurrence of cure is beyond ultimate control of the medics.

"[O]rganizations fail when they deviate from the prescriptions of institutionalizing myths: quite apart from technical efficiency, organizations which innovate in important structural ways bear considerable costs in legitimacy" (ibid:53). Still, organisations and actors in general, may follow highly institutionalised orientations in one aspect and more technical 'hard-fact' orientations in another. In this context, a very important instance of institutional legitimation, or even 'institutional myth', in transboundary management (and not only there) is the application of 'generally agreed accounting standards' (GAAS). Whether or not an organisation complies with these international standards of finance and bookkeeping can enhance its standing and reputation vis-à-vis its foreign project partners. Such displays of legitimation are invaluable, especially for today's African actors.

Institutional and technical environments

From the viewpoint of Neo-Institutionalism an organisation lives in two kinds of environments. On the one hand there are the *technical environments* with their challenges of efficiency and material-physical competitiveness, and on the other hand there are *institutional environments* with their demands of conformity to accepted standards and good relations with providers as well as symbols of legal and normative legitimation. Technical and institutional environments are not independent from one another. Structural elements, which were once introduced to enhance technical efficiency, can later be adapted by other organisations due to their symbolic value (the reason being: showing off one's effectiveness can be a symbolic asset in itself).

As a consequence, organisations and corporate actors can be typified according to the extent of their institutionalisation. "At one end are production organizations under strong output controls [...] whose success depends on the management of relational networks. At the other end are institutionalised organizations whose success depends on the confidence and stability achieved by isomorphism with institutional rules" (Meyer/Rowan 1991:55). In a somewhat simplified way, the organisation types under investigation here, private business and development aid, reflect somewhat opposite directions in an organisation's environmental orientation. While ever increasing institutional demands can also be found within commercial enterprises, their objectives are reflected in the annual balance sheet, and successes or failures are often causally allocated. In extreme situations business managers can always justify themselves by retreating to the position of securing the company's financial sustainability and shareholder interests. Such an argument wins the discussion mainly because it refers to indisputable material goals. With non-profits and donor agencies this is different. Goals such as 'poverty alleviation' or 'facilitation of democracy' are abstract formulations where successes or failures cannot be accredited causally to single actors (Kühl 2004:259). Success is demonstrated on symbolic and representative levels rather than through a blunt equation of earnings and expenses, low downtimes or rising market shares. The chief reason for these organisations' existence is not primarily to generate material profits or tangible outputs, but to contribute to collective or political goals such as development. Their goals, their success factors as well as some of their resources are of a symbolic nature (which does *not* mean they are not real).

Goals and values in organisations

The context of institutionalised organisations can further be exemplified through a distinction between organisational goals and values. According to Kühl (2004: 236), *goals* direct the focus on procedures and means that are needed in order to achieve certain ends or requirements to a predefined extent. They are measurable guidelines in the process of operational action and resource allocation. *Values*, by contrast, are rather general rules about the appropriateness of activities and provide a general frame of orientation. By their very nature they have no steering qualities. Connected to considerations about policy implementation in development agencies, the same author further demonstrates that highly institutionalised organisations are oriented on abstract values rather than on concrete goals.

Organisations with clear-cut goals, measurable output requirements and precise technologies are most likely technically oriented. In contrast, organisations are much more likely to be subjected to institutionalisation processes when they are subjected to a set of more abstract goals and complex ethical or political values and where these values are to be reached only through sparsely precise technologies. In highly institutionalised organisations, their own values are so unspecific and generally 'good' that hardly anyone could advise against their use. This makes it attractive to endow otherwise vague agendas and agencies with abstract values in order to give them a solid base from which to argue and justify their activities. It is, for example, quite logical that poverty should be alleviated or that aid projects should be sustainable. While these basic values are both powerful and compelling, they appear to be tautological. Tautological explanations are present when a negation of the proposed value would lead to an alternative which is self-evidently out of question. Nobody, in this example, would seriously advise against fighting poverty or making projects more sustainable (cf Gälweiler 1986, Kühl 2004).

It should be stated explicitly that the technical and institutional environments of a given organisation are not situated in a conflictive opposition or negative relation towards each other; rather, they are two separate dimensions of the organisational environment (cf Walgenbach 1999:327ff). Despite the temptation to see the relevance of the Neo-Institutionalist approach predominantly for non-profit organisations, its value lies in the analysis of the institutional side of any type of organisation. To "identify technical features with for-profit firms and institutional forces with non-profit or government agencies is no longer viable" (DiMaggio/Powell 1991:32). Yet, when comparing different organisation types with each other (e.g. local enterprises, development agencies, multinational corporations, diplomatic representations, etc.), some tendencies of the institutionalisation effects can be observed that are related to the type of organisation.

At the end of this book I have included an institutionalisation test that provides a preliminary picture of an organisation's degree of institutionalisation (see appendix). It is an adapted form of a test compiled by Kühl (2004) to highlight the institutionalisation of development agencies. Readers with a practical interest in organisational analysis or the assessment of their own Transboundary Cooperation may find it helpful.

Highly institutionalised organisations

Rottenburg (2002:93ff) applied the terminology of institutionalised organisations to the analysis of bilateral development aid in Africa. The development sector, and with it various kinds of donor agencies and related organisations, is a very likely candidate for institutionalisation processes. Besides its high-standing societal value, the very notion of 'development' itself is diffuse and open to interpretation: "By now development has become an amoeba-like concept, shapeless but ineradicable. Its contours are so blurred that it denotes nothing – while it spreads everywhere because it connotes the best of intentions. The term is hailed by the IMF and the Vatican alike, by revolutionaries carrying their guns as well as field experts carrying their Samsonites" (Sachs 1992a:4). Development organisations thus have to work in settings that abound with unclear definitions and policies instead of clear-cut directions.

As mentioned above, technical efficiency in itself is not necessarily the final criterion for organisational prosperity. In many circumstances the needs for institutional legitimation are also high. Highly institutionalised organisations are characterised by their affinity with blurred separations between efficiency and legitimation. Such organisations are efficient according to their own logic exactly when their institutional legitimation is maximised. They usually derive legitimation from adherence to agendas, policies and the higher purposes they were set up to follow (well-known examples: development, aid, science, medicine, care, culture, peace, etc.). On the technical front they have to deal with programmes, projects, cooperation partners, official contracting and evaluations.

Organisational actors of the highly institutionalised kind may possess a tendency to overvalue their own importance and reputation due to their affirmative self-centredness and the lack of other external acknowledgement than formal and symbolic appraisal. A donor agency does its job well when it disburses the scheduled funds, conducts the scheduled projects and, in so doing, gains the approval of the evaluating entity, for example a consultant or supervising ministry. It is not a meaningful question in this context whether and to what extent these activities made the targeted people less poor, healthier or more democratic. It is simply not feasible to change the totality of other people's lives through a development project and everyone knows this. Therefore that ultimate aim of a development initiative, e.g. making people less poor, cannot really be appraised even by the most sophisticated evaluation procedure. What can be measured are internal dummy figures that may (or may not) be suitable to serve as indicators, documenting the fulfilment of the project's objectives. Such a figure was the number of households connected to electricity in the case study about rural electrification ('a mixed arena', case 6). It could say something about the internal state of the project but would not directly reveal anything about how well the targeted population was doing, even though these people's life situation was the initial reason for directing a rural development programme at the Rwandan countryside. What follows from this consideration is that the real effects of activities with an institutionalised, non-technical, major goal cannot be effectively measured, and even if they could, their fulfilment could not be ascribed to single projects or actors. Accordingly, even non-technical and non-market organisations, such as most of the development agencies, have to manage their scarce resources and legitimate their activities in terms of efficiency (cf Preisendörfer 2005:151). But certain fields of their activities exist where technical efficiency is not the most relevant indicator. Development aid is, to a large extent, one of these sectors.[26] Besides, development aid, healthcare, education and many civil society groups are vivid examples of fields

---

26 There will possibly be opposition to this statement in the way that development organisations nowadays would also be subject to competition and market pressure in order to acquire projects. But, nevertheless, virtually all transactions in the field take place in a politically guided 'pseudo-market' and have not much in common with a free allocation of supply and demand. The application of market-rhetoric itself sometimes serves as a means of institutional legitimation for the non- or pseudo-market players in the official development sector.

in which values other than technical input-output relations are of great significance. Their formal legitimation is built almost entirely on important human values and not on expectations of gains or returns. [27]

Institutionalisation vs. technical orientation

For the interpretation of the case studies I made use of the following indicators to identify a Transboundary Cooperation's institutionalisation or technical orientation.

Table 2: Institutionalisation vs. technical orientation

Institutionalisation
Criteria for strong organisational institutionalisation
• Principal objectives consist of abstract values. • 'Making no mistakes' implies 'complying with procedures'. • Survival and resources of organisation depend on positive evaluations. • Key figures are symbolic, representative or derivative while core activity remains ambiguous. • Tools: budgets, agendas, evaluations, policies, standards. • Dependence on external funding and legitimation of own activities. • Future of organisation/actor depends on institutional/symbolic fit.

---

[27] At least in the classical sense. But even profit maximizing actors in healthcare are never allowed to neglect the primary concern for 'health' if they want to retain their legitimation. The usual primary concern for 'the market' cannot reasonably be applied by healthcare enterprises. It is common for such companies to promote their concern for human wellbeing in their image campaigns.

> **Technical Orientation**
>
> *Criteria for strong technical orientation*
>
> - Principal objectives consist of steering goals.
> - 'Making no mistakes' implies 'securing output'.
> - Survival and resources of organisation depend on technical effectiveness and/or market success.
> - Key figures are concrete and direct measurements of core activity.
> - Tools: control and supervision, verification strategies (i.e., assessment of primary effectiveness, marketing research).
> - Dependence on acquisition of customers, partners or clients to generate returns.
> - Future of organisation/actor depends on technical fit.

Assessment of case studies

Again, in the remainder of the chapter I assess the case studies in the light of the theoretical concept that was previously developed.

[Case 1] Bilateral development agency

This development agency is a highly institutionalised actor type. Organisational prospects primarily depend on institutional legitimation. Being legitimated here implies that the activities are in line with the developmental policy of the German head office and its ministerial control. Regardless of their individual projects, the German development assistants are obliged to follow these overreaching regulations in all their activities in the field.

The measurements for success in the work of the development agency reflect the goals and values of the organisation. The absolute success rate of completed projects (or other transactions) comprises not only the quantity or turnover rate, but predominantly the successfully executed goals that transport the organisational values. The number of projects is less important than the fact that these projects are conducted according to the underpinning goals and values (which are directed at human capacity development). In fact, hypothetically, a technically successful transaction that wouldn't meet the normative goals and values would not be considered a correct transaction within this type of organisation. The direct opposite would be a 'body leaser', thus a competitive market driven personal secondment company that seeks to increase its turnover by any suitable means and with little concern for values other than individual profit maximisation.

[Case 2] Multinational beverage corporation

The brewery is part of a multinational corporation and therefore subject to its corporate- wide steering and requirements. Its success is, for the most part, measured in terms of annual net profit but also in terms of market share, product quality and general standards compliance. Basic operations are guided by a strong technical and commercial orientation. This is also highly valued by the Rwandan technical staff because of the side effect that also a certain degree of stability, dependability and transparency is promoted in this way. This stems from the fact that foreign companies in developing countries often try to strengthen such values, as their own rationality to a large extent depends on them. However, increasingly also new institutionalisation processes are triggered by requirements set by the corporate head office. Additional non-technical demands arise from increasing standardisation, control and reporting. These trends cause a local subsidiary to invest efforts not only to cater the local markets but also to meet the formal demands of the centralised corporate control. Internal legitimation of a local brewery increasingly depends on institutional correctness and legitimation. This occurs in the form of generalised accountancy, technical and quality standards, formal and bureaucratic requirements and human resources benchmarks. In brief, the brewery applies a technical orientation towards its local field of operation and towards corporate controlling. Additionally, it applies forms of institutionalised legitimation towards the corporate organisation in order to internally legitimise its local activities. These institutionalisation processes seemed to gain higher importance during the drift towards centralisation.

[Case 3] German contractors for media systems

Overall an almost purely technical orientation is applied. The judgement of work consists of measurable and comparable technical characteristics. Projects shall be technically functional and manageable, and the companies measure themselves through their cash flow. They are contracted because of their technical capabilities, and the customers do not issue any institutional requirements for the specialists to be contracted.

[Case 4] Rwandan construction enterprise

Formally established procedures are largely absent in this company; the symbols and habits of a formal-rational organisation are hardly in use. Strong technical orientation together with a high level of trust and professional legitimation vis-à-vis foreign contracting partners through the personality of the company owner.

[Case 5] German food and catering enterprises

Strong technical orientation. Market success and commercial sustainability are the primary goals. However, in several circumstances institutional legitimation becomes necessary towards local/national stakeholders to counteract the effects of being regarded as a foreign business. Institutional legitimation for these enterprises means effectively complying with the Rwandan ethical, political and cultural sphere of influence.

[Case 6] A mixed arena

a) Donor agencies from the PPP-project

The donor agencies that issued the PPP programme did this from a purely value-based approach. As is usual in the development sector, they apply an institutionalised rationality where the requested adherence to the norms and goals overrules any technical consideration. In the case study rural electrification as a highly valued developmental goal stands central in spite of a nationwide energy shortage both in industry and the capital. The local project sites are tested for their compliance to the programme goals before they are finally accepted. Generally, there is a strong institutional orientation towards central project benchmarks. The agencies involved depend on the fulfilment of agreements and contracts to successfully execute the development programme. As the activities are non-commercial and regulated through guidelines, success is measured by evaluation. When a local partner seems to be helpful in meeting goals, the agencies tend to be quite uncritical towards that partner's behaviour. This stems from a high dependency on technically capable local assistance.

b) Attempted Micro Hydro investment project

Technical orientation on physical feasibility and individual gain. Secondary institutional legitimation towards donor agency and local community administration in order to secure access to funding and local acceptance. In reality, this was an individualist's activity.

[Case 7] Indian trader

Pure technical orientation. Formally institutionalised procedures are almost absent; and even the symbols and habits of formal-rational organisations are only used to represent authority within the company. No need for representative behaviour in front of customers, no relevant relationship to domestic reputation gatekeepers (like the media) or any other discourses. High institutionalised legitimation to the ethnic diaspora group, which, however, had no bearing on individual commercial activities.

5.3 MANAGEMENT OF HETEROGENEITY

How do international transboundary actors perceive the nature of the social boundaries they cross? And how does this shape their behaviour in the local arena? Hidden beneath the apparent struggle of local against foreign knowledge and underneath many alleged clashes of cultures or civilisations, specific sets of pre-conscious assumptions about global heterogeneity are in place. These assumptions heavily influence the perceptions of the actors involved and implicitly govern transnational organisations.

How does this happen? The foundational principle of how social and cultural heterogeneity is integrated inside an organisation's own boundaries also says something about its institutional intent. It sheds light on paradigms and attitudes at work between African, Asian and Western spaces. These foundational assumptions can change but are often stable over extended periods, as they are embedded in an organisation's substructures.

In this light, the question of how the actors from the case studies integrate the effects of differences and diversities is an empirical one.

In this section, these issues are raised on the operative level. In order to assess the *management of social and cultural heterogeneity* in the field, I am going to apply the concepts of heterogeneity from Chapter 3, as outlined in the following two terminologies:

- *Difference* vs. *diversity*. The two basic ways of conceiving social and cultural heterogeneity.
- *Operative universalism* vs. *operative relativism*. Multiplying the applications of one logic, which in practice is universalism, or customising the operative logic for specific contexts, which in practice is relativism.

The case studies are measured with these concepts in order to determine how they manage heterogeneity on the operative level.

Difference vs. diversity

Earlier in this book, the notion of alien and familiar strangeness has provided the base for the more accessible terminology of 'difference' versus 'diversity'. These terms explain the foundational relation of a social entity with a distinctive counterpart (which can be actors, institutions, or organisations):

(1) *Diversity:* These are shallow social and cultural distinctions between individuals and groups, with a potentially disturbing or stimulating and creative effect. They are easy to regard as socially constructed and do not contradict elementary humanistic and moral notions (e.g. the idea of human rights). They also mostly do not contradict 'rationality' to a large extent. The concept of 'diversity management' implies that these variations are still manageable and are all part of a common ground of understanding. Accountability is implicitly expected, and performance is measured against policies and standards. Human variation is acceptable within the 'business logic' of a common frame of reference. Any variation that lies outside this 'business logic' is by definition no longer accountable.

(2) *Difference:* Incomprehensible 'otherness' in social and cultural relations. Human backgrounds, deeds and beliefs can be regarded as incomprehensible or incompatible. Definitions of belonging and grounds for reasoning may be incommensurable among counterparts. Such broad differences are not necessarily negative, but they are endowed with a higher potential for confrontation. 'Difference' in this context is an epistemic and practical experience where the gap between the 'own' and the 'other' can no longer be bridged by one's own established principles, thus leaving open spaces of indetermination. In operational terms, difference means that one side has assumptions and ambitions about the relationship that no longer correspond with those of the other side. This is a cause of disorientation, friction, or radical newness. The following table enumerates the empirical criteria of 'diversity' and 'difference' that were developed in Chapter 3.2.

Table 3: Key characteristics of 'diversity' and 'difference'

Key characteristics of 'diversity'	Key characteristics of 'difference'
• Lies within own scope • can be explained in one's own terms • 'shallow' divergences • other's position is commensurable with own principles • accountable • transfer of basic items possible • potentially creative enrichment or only a minor problem • diverging contexts can be covered by one 'business logic'	• beyond own scope • cannot be explained in one's own terms • 'deep' divergences • other's position is incommensurable with own principles • unaccountable • translation even of basic items necessary • potentially pejorative perceptions or perceived as threatening • diverging contexts cannot be covered by one 'business logic' • hermeneutic approximation

Operative universalism vs. operative relativism

The distinction between operative relativism and operative universalism looks at how global heterogeneity is reflected in the working structure of a Transboundary Organisation (as introduced in Chapter 3.2). The term 'operative' indicates that only the level of observable organisational activity is considered here, rather than the propagated values, policies or mission statements. The two concepts are now briefly laid out.

Operative relativism

Here, an actor's paradigm is one of epistemic and functional distinctions between socio-geographical spaces. These distinctions form the base of the actor's transboundary organisation. They can take the form of a respectful relativism, but in fact are built on unequal relationships. It is not the aim of these transboundary arrangements specialised in operative relativism to overcome the inequality between the connected contexts. Such schemes cannot work when there are no differences. Many, but not all, are exploitative; others may have the best intentions in mind but are nevertheless built on an understanding of inequality and uniqueness. All these actor types are based on asymmetry, and they exist because they make use of specific local circumstances or structural inequalities on the global scale. Some types of Transboundary Cooperations are specialised to exist under such heterogeneous global constellations but are not tied to specific locations. These kinds of Transboundary Cooperations exist *because* of the necessity or possibility of applying two sets of standards at the two ends of a transboundary relationship.

Operative universalism

This mode of operations sees the process of human civilisation as adhering to one set of logic, and common fundamental principles. It also provides the underlying assumption of mainstream modern Western culture and capitalist expansion. This means that everything complies with the same fundamental structures, and all inherent diversities (cultures, meanings, colours, habits, materials) are, in fact, part of one universal approach, which can be managed through a common rational-political process. When dealing with people and places around the world, this concept makes itself relevant as well.

Operations based upon universalism have to fine-tune their activities to fit local environments. Adaptations are necessary in developing countries or other places considered 'exotic'. The universalistic approaches of today are sufficiently accommodating and astute to appreciate the local situation of places where they are expanding, but only as a means of getting a foothold in the scene. Soon, the newly taken place will become a subject of the universal principle. Transboundary operations based on operative universalism gain additional effectiveness when their underlying logic can be replicated across places, locations and continents. This replication leads to global scaling effects, which are safeguarded by diversity management in order to catch heterogeneous elements.

One of the most prominent applications of this paradigm is the transfer of knowledge and resources from European (or Western) to African societies. This pattern implicates that any rational transfer only makes sense when one can expect that the same socio-technical principles are at work at the place of implementation as at their place of origin. Also, multinational enterprise management builds on the notion of a general validity of rational organisation. Diverging viewpoints and local variations are allowed as long as they remain on the common ground of functional diversity and accountability. Conclusively, universalistic Transboundary Cooperations assume a fair amount of operative *sameness* and exist *despite* the occurrence of local circumstances that complicate their activities. If possible, they would apply the same basic structures all over the world.

Dual occurrence of operative universalism and relativism
Elements of both positions, operative relativism and, at the same time, universalism, can be found in the underlying structures of specific types of Transboundary Cooperations. The same holds true for the notion of heterogeneity in terms of diversities and differences. In such instances, I speak of 'dual occurrences' in the organisational mapping of heterogeneity. Certain cases in my fieldwork have displayed this characteristic.

Assessment of case studies
Now the case studies are, once again, placed in relation to the working definitions.

[Case 1] Bilateral development agency
- *Diversity vs. difference:* Foreign development assistants are directly embedded in the social environment of their counterparts, which is a goal of the organisational set-up. These experts are supposed to apply their professional expertise in a setting that is characterised by the contradictive rule sets. These are the 'universal principles' of societal development (as typically transferred from industrialised to developing countries) and the local knowledge and practices based on the given values, conditions and heritage, which have their own inner logic. Under such complex conditions, the maintenance of an official development partnership is regarded as a value with its own merit, regardless of the output (think of the institutionalised legitimation of this actor type, cf Chapter 5.2). In this situation of good partnership under heterogeneous and partially incompatible assumptions about the goals, the emergence of 'working misunderstandings' is not uncommon.
- *Diversity* management in these project settings (as opposed to *difference*) is the official mode of action. There would be no safe ground and no reason to conduct development aid if it were not for the assumption that there is something to transfer from the West to Africa, and that such a transfer can only work in the absence of *difference*.
- *Operative universalism vs. operative relativism:* With the foundation of bilateral development aid, a universalistic approach to principles of development and societal well-being (e.g. democracy, market economy, education, human rights, female empowerment) is applied. This universalism is the very reason and core basis for conducting foreign aid. Simultaneously, however, a powerful form of operative relativism is applied in all kinds of tangible activities. The development sector conclusively works with a double measurement. The dual occurrence of universalistic and relativistic elements becomes visible as an oscillation between the universalistic transfer of Western ideas and the acknowledgement

of the independence of the Rwandan partners. Being something like the cornerstone of each bilateral cooperation, their independence is constantly reflected and propagated. The autonomy of the receiver is a high-standing value in itself. This value is also a help up in circumstances where it hampers the effectiveness of the developmental transfers. Otherwise development *cooperation* would make no sense. This, in turn, triggers stricter requirements and higher evaluation efforts on behalf of the donor. The German engineers' project stands out as an example of this: the experts attempted to maintain a necessary transfer of their own Western ideas, while at the same time the indigenous structures had to be respected, which resulted in the poor project outcome that fell short of the German agency's plan.

[Case 2] Multinational beverage corporation

- *Diversity vs. difference:* Since the beginning of the brewery in colonial times, a fundamental shift has taken place in the perception of heterogeneity. At the beginning it started with an assumption and open acceptance of difference between Europeans and Rwandans and their respective frames of reference. The differences were seen as almost natural. Today the multinational corporation exercises a worldwide diversity management. Several decades before expatriate technicians were assigned to an 'exotic' workplace in order to run the company under exceptional (tropical) conditions. Nowadays the African subsidiary is part of the corporation's diversity spectrum and subjected to its real-time accounting and human resources development. This process resembles an evolution towards 'total diversity' without parts that are unaccountable from the corporate centre's point of view.
- *Operative universalism vs. operative relativism:* In general, the multinational corporation replicates its central business strategies on each continent and aims at economies of scale. The core logic of a MNC is that of operative universalism. As the case study illustrated, the transfer of corporate processes and standards implicitly depends on internal translation of Western ideas to the African context. This act demands that local cultural brokers handle the adaptation and proliferation of the external/corporate issues among Rwandan staff and stakeholders.

[Case 3] German media technology contractors

- *Diversity vs. difference:* The Germans are contracted by a top-modern representative of the customer. Both parties reached an understanding of the project with a diversity structure in mind. Later on, the German contractors experienced

a breakdown of the accountable project setting, rendering the prospect of 'business as usual' impossible.
- *Operative universalism vs. operative relativism:* A commercial transfer project that was ultimately based on the assumption of generally applicable technical and commercial rules. The implicit assumption of universalism, however, was limited from the beginning of the project as agreements were made for the contractor to provide all materials and skills necessary to establish working conditions at the site. By this it was silently acknowledged that the customer party would not hold itself accountable for any complications. The work environment became a temporary hybrid space between universalistic and relativistic understandings of the situation, which did not lead to a lasting cooperation.

[Case 4] Rwandan construction enterprise
- *Diversity vs. difference:* Personal relationships with expatriate customers as well as proficiency in Western communication habits help to overcome epistemic and operative differences. The company owner's core ability lies in preventing his expatriate customers and partners from experiencing 'difference'. He aids foreigners in maintaining a sense of control and understanding in a strange environment, acting as a cultural broker who manages the impact of heterogeneity between external and Rwandan counterparts.
- *Operative universalism vs. operative relativism:* Generalised and rational technical universalism mixed with a pro-Western orientation, but also claims of Rwandan uniqueness in personal, technical and political discussions. Both standpoints share a parallel existence.

[Case 5] German food and catering enterprises
- *Diversity vs. difference:* Not applicable in this case, as the companies are local social entities. They manage their transboundary relationships by themselves and are able to balance the requirements of the Rwandan context with their own backgrounds.
- *Operative universalism vs. operative relativism:* International quality standards and German culinary ideas were adapted to the local situation. The question of the operative mode is not applicable in this case.

[Case 6] A mixed arena – the energy crisis and Millennium Development Goals

a) Donor agencies from the PPP-project

- *Diversity vs. difference:* Accountability is one of the key factors in the programme design. The local project partners and the development agency itself are required to meet target figures, and all proposals have to comply with predefined benchmarks. An approach with diversity management was therefore intended, and unaccountable elements not allowed in the programme design.
- *Operative universalism vs. operative relativism:* The agencies applied different frames of reference for their judgement of the contexts of the donor country and the Rwandan setting. None of the local partner projects, which were to be subsidised, would have been admitted if European standards had been applied. Upholding these standards was not feasible in the African partner country, and continued cooperation was more important than formal-technical purity and political clarity. The intention of the rural electrification programme originated in the Millennium Development Goals, which itself largely is a universalistic approach to development and societal well-being. This universalism is also the fundamental reason and theoretical base for conducting foreign aid. During the project's execution, however, forms of relativism were applied on the operative ground. This development programme worked with a double measurement of technical and political standard that was separating the context of the donor's and the receiver's societies. On this way the receivers could be 'saved' from the inflexibilities and technical challenges of complying with Western standards. At the same time when such a double measurement is in place, the local decision makers are able to retain a higher level of control and propagate their own interests within the framework of an externally funded programme. This dual occurrence of universalistic and relativistic elements causes a circular tension between the universalistic transfer of Western ideas and the acknowledgement of the independence of the Rwandan partners.

b) Attempted Micro Hydro investment project

- *Diversity vs. difference:* One of the entrepreneur group's biggest assets were their personal relationships with the most important actors from the field. With their combined backgrounds they had access to most Rwandan and European decision makers. The ability to communicate in Rwandan and European manners alike helped to overcome the difficulties of the differences in the field and to win the trust of all stakeholders. The role that is played well by this a group is that of an intermediator between the contexts of the European donor programme, the interests of the domestic institutions (e.g. the energy provider) and

the rural self-administration that represented the interests of the village. Without such an intermediator a workable connection is difficult, especially as the relationships are partially based on a model of difference. It is not surprising that this private entrepreneur group was also the first to abandon the project as it suffered most directly from the incompatibilities in the programme set-up.
- *Operative universalism vs. operative relativism:* The set-up of this project was streamlined to the context of an African developing country and could not have worked in the European donor countries. The same is true for the would-be entrepreneur group. Their primary goal was to benefit from donor funding without too high formal requirements and start their own business in this way.

[Case 7] Indian traders
- *Diversity vs. difference:* The Indian business community was organised around the notion of social distinctiveness. Rwandans, as with all other persons, were treated as an 'out-group' and therefore not accountable in private matters. Neither the possibility nor the demand for a deeper interaction with the exterior local environment arose, so the relationships primarily remained on the level of suspicious difference. Facilitating relationships with employees targeted surface issues.
- *Operative universalism vs. operative relativism:* Combined with a sociocultural separation towards others, the Indian traders in Rwanda applied a tested and trusted commercial strategy that had also worked elsewhere. Business models and supplier connections were re-applied and modelled after those of Indian activities in other East African countries. Their commercial and organisational structures could therefore be considered as 'group-exclusive universalism'. But seen from a different angle they also qualify as social exclusiveness (see 'ethnic capitalism' in Chapter 6.4).

6. Synthesis: Most Important Patterns and Types in the Field

We will now take up the building blocks from the case studies for a synthsis in order to gain an understanding of the patterns and types of Transboundary Cooperations. During the previous chapter, an assessment of the field data was laid out. The empirical material was broken down into relevant components of information and subsequently grouped according to the three analytical positions. In this way we arrived at a high level of comparability among the case studies. Now, in the present section it is time to make use of this analysis in the form of some generalizations and typifications.

What we do in this chapter

We will systematise our observations and draw conclusions in order to make the findings comparable to similar settings as well as practically applicable for those working in related fields.

To begin with, I will return to the question of local embeddedness and the institutionalisation phenomenon. I will then move on to discuss the issue of heterogeneity management in development aid organisations. After these considerations, a synthesis of four practically relevant archetypes of transboundary organisations is developed. Subsequently, a final comparisons concerns modes of production in transboundary capitalism as well as their possible influence on local communities.

6.1 INSTITUTIONALISATION AND LOCAL EMBEDDEDNESS

We have seen that the intensity of *local embeddedness* and the processes of *institutionalisation* (Chapters 5.1 and 5.2) play important roles in the operative behaviour of Transboundary Cooperations. What I aim to do now is to demonstrate some structural links between the degree of a Transboundary Cooperation's local embeddedness and the strength of its organisational institutionalisation. In a simplified schema there are four combinations possible among the two dimensions of embeddedness and institutionalisation:

1. Strong 'technical orientation' and 'locally assimilated'
2. Strong 'technical orientation' and 'transterritorial enclave'
3. Highly 'institutionalised' and 'locally assimilated'
4. Highly 'institutionalised' and 'transterritorial enclave'

In the following step, the practical effects of these four combinations are highlighted in the form of four exemplary descriptions ('spotlights'). Each spotlight is characterised by one of the four combinations of institutionalisation and local embeddedness, and stands for a typical kind of transboundary organisation found in Rwanda and on the African continent.

Spotlight 1: Strong technical orientation and local assimilation

The German hotel and catering enterprises were typical examples of Western foreigners doing business in an African country. These enterprises usually serve domestic markets and employ local personnel. In general, they have become part of the local economy, and thus with its opportunities and drawbacks. The observed companies are able to draw upon their own German expertise and resources to establish their businesses, but the relevant theatre of activity lies within the local scene. Such transboundary organisations essentially become part of the local, national, cultural and political setting in which they operate. One could say that they run the risk of becoming absorbed by the local context. Their strong technical orientation demands measurable output, mostly in the form of task effectiveness and commercial success. There are no directions, guidelines or restraints coming from external sources outside the country. Such an organisation relies on the local market to obtain everything it needs or otherwise uses the same means for international sourcing as indigenous enterprises. Its client base is essentially locally based. SMEs owned by foreigners frequently have to cope with the suspicion that they are extraordinarily wealthy and have unlimited access to Western resources.

They are, however, effectively independent and not supported by big Western organisations, in contrast to the numerous international non-profit agencies operating in the country. What makes them genuinely 'transboundary' is their adoption of a dedicatedly 'foreign' background, individually and businesswise, to a new environment.

Spotlight 2: Strong technical orientation and transterritorial enclave

These types of actors were harder to find in Rwanda and are more common in resource-rich areas. A foreign owned organisation, which was not part of the case studies, resembled the combination of a 'technical enclave': *Deutsche Welle*, a radio relay station in the outskirts of Kigali. The word 'enclave' describes perfectly this closed security area. It consists of extensive technical installations used to transmit German shortwave radio and TV to a large portion of the southern hemisphere. The compound includes vast antennas, housing for expatriates and personnel, and structures that contain everything needed for technical and organisational self-reliance. German engineers live in the closed-off area with their families. Together with their Rwandan staff they have to maintain the functionality of the transmission station. Their primary goal is the management of operations and minimisation of breakdowns. Engineers rarely need to leave the compound for reasons other than occasional shopping (which is often done at the German grocery), administrative or leisure activities. All tasks are dominated by technical aspects and comply with German standards (e.g. electrical safety, engineers' work contracts). Excessive institutionalisation processes are kept low even in the absence of any local or commercial interests because all activities are technically measurable and effectiveness is immediately visible. Values and goals other than technical ones are not important. Here, the transboundary character remains limited to the interactions of the Germans with the local workforce and the technical hosting of an FM antenna for Radio Rwanda. The overall contextual and operative interactions with the Rwandan environment are weak.

Spotlight 3: Highly institutionalised and local assimilation

A definite organisation with such a combination of characteristics was not part of the case studies. Actors of this kind can be found in Rwanda in greater numbers when one looks at small privately operated foreign NGOs and aid initiatives. They typically depend on charity funds, grants, donations or subsidies in order to sustain their activities. Their basic functions primarily consist of delivering aid to recipients belonging to their 'target groups' and secondly, but essentially, granting symbolic reward to their donors and activists. This combination of success factors places them in the realm of institutionalised organisations.

Among the protagonists of the presented fieldwork, the individual development assistants from case study 1 can be attributed to this highly institutionalised and locally assimilated type of transboundary actors. Although the formal core of their own organisation, the German secondment agency, qualifies for the next type (i.e. transterritorial enclave), the development assistants themselves are deployed into local partner organisations and take part in the Rwandan 'business as usual'. When it comes to their daily work experience, they are, so to speak, assimilated by the local environment.

Strain in this situation can arise from a potential loyalty conflict between the practices and directives of the institutionalised core of the foreign organisation on the one hand, and the needs or 'real' issues of the target environment on the other. Often it is not hard to come across deeper incompatibilities between the issues relevant to local environments and the programmes of foreign organisations. Individual expatriates in these situations are frequently burdened with the task of balancing both. Usually, they are inclined to pursue their mission competently and demonstrate a high commitment to their organisation's values. They must also, however, cope with the stark reality of the host country, a process that often brings with it intense personal experiences.

Spotlight 4: Highly institutionalised and transterritorial enclave
Development actors such as the secondment agency from case 1 are easily identified as institutionalised organisations, and increasingly they also behave as transterritorial enclaves. This may appear counterintuitive at first, but I regard it as an outcome of a major shift in the general approach to development. Contemporary development assistance sees itself in a position of being able to deliver policy advice or 'government advisory services' to target countries. According to these newer priorities, the manners in which bilateral and multilateral development aid are conducted almost resemble those of Western business consultants (critically, Hüsken 2006). Budget aid is directly delivered to the state coffers of recipient countries, supplemented by advisory and bilateral consulting approaches.

There still exists a proportion of 'classical' development aid where foreign experts are appointed on the basis of their professional background and sent to a project in the partner country. It is a trend that these more physically operative agencies of foreign assistance now also tied to centralised policies and programmes. Their activities are now strongly determined by objectives that are broken down from high-level key concepts. The fulfilment of these objectives is constantly evaluated, leaving less room for local adaptations. Institutionalised organisations lack immediate feedback regarding their efficiency from the external environment, while a sense of 'work well done' mostly implies that the organisation is in line with the expectations of the controlling department on the next level of hierarchy. Together these practices are put in place in order to secure the responsible and appropriate use of public funds and donations, to secure the values of aid and humanitarian development, and to maintain good relationships between countries. In the increasingly ambiguous and multi-faceted environments within which development is carried out, this safeguarding become ever more necessary. At the same time, and with increasing prevalence, this leads to a situation where expatriate agencies, on the operative level, act like remote islands in their host countries. Such agencies are able to conduct projects with an officially evaluated success rate of 80% or higher.[28] However, under these circumstances their activities barely touch upon the basic 'reality of the local' in their respective local environments. They reside in glocal settings, which are specialised in catering to institutionalised transboundary agencies. A more extreme form of 'institutionalised enclaves' can be found in national embassies. Diplomatic representations usually have no tangible or operative responsibilities in their host countries except political and cultural representation. They are to a great extent independent from everything around them and function regardless of the situation in the host country.

In order to showcase the embeddedness-institutionalisation relationship at a glance, the illustration below suggests the placement of the case studies within a two-dimensional matrix that resembles the above combinations. Three additional types of organisations, which were not included in the empirical material, are added to complete the picture. The structural links between the degrees of local embeddedness and institutionalisation become visible by combining them in a four-quadrant matrix. Cases were placed in positions within the quadrants according to their specific combination of the two structural characteristics.

---

28 Just as an example from Germany: GTZ (2005), report on impact monitoring.

Diagram 1: Relationships between institutionalisation and local assimilation

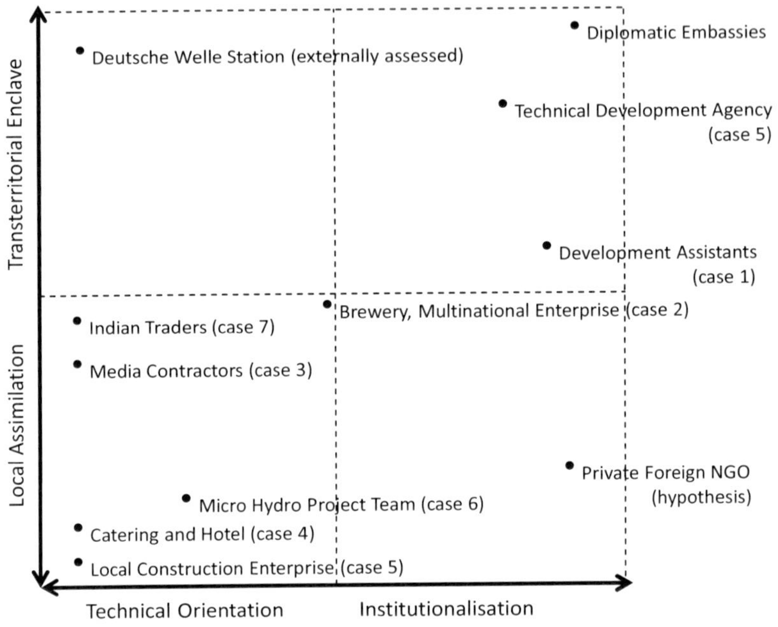

```
                    Transterritorial Enclave
                              ▲
                              |                    • Diplomatic Embassies
         • Deutsche Welle Station (externally assessed)
                              |
                              |                    • Technical Development Agency
                              |                      (case 5)
                              |
                              |
                              |                    • Development Assistants
                              |                      (case 1)
                              |  • Brewery, Multinational Enterprise (case 2)
         • Indian Traders (case 7)
                              |
         • Media Contractors (case 3)
                              |
                              |                    • Private Foreign NGO
                              |  • Micro Hydro Project Team (case 6)   (hypothesis)
         • Catering and Hotel (case 4)
         • Local Construction Enterprise (case 5)
                              |
    ──────────────────────────┼──────────────────────────▶
     Technical Orientation        Institutionalisation
                    Local Assimilation
```

Please note that no quantitative measurements have been made and the diagram is of a purely illustrative character.

6.2 HETEROGENEITY – STRUCTURAL INCONSISTENCIES IN THE AID SECTOR

Actors approach their social environment according to their own assumptions about how this environment functions on a fundamental level. Such is common sense in the social sciences. In terms of social boundaries, whole fields of transnational relations are structured in accordance with their own specific notions of social and cultural heterogeneity. In this regard a unique issue, predominantly encountered within donor agencies and similar actors from the development sector, became increasingly relevant during my research. I am speaking here about a typical simultaneity of mutually excluding epistemic logics located on different normative and operative levels within these organisations. These logics are not integrated, as it is part of the system that they remain separate.

When the foundation of an organisation's basic operative pattern is built upon the simultaneity of two mutually exclusive assumptions, and when both assumptions are also inevitable for the continuation of the organisation, I call this a *structural oscillation*. The author Reckwitz defines the term 'structure' by stating that in a broad sense structures are the level of the 'general' or 'generic' in the social world. They mark phenomena that are time-resistant and collectively relevant (1997:32). Thus, what I am now going to describe is resistant over time and collectively relevant for an entire field of activity. This chapter now discusses two elements of structural oscillation, which mainly appear in the foundational principles of development organisations. The result is manifested in a specific set of behaviour that would be startling to observe in common private business.

Oscillation between difference and diversity

Assuming that a reader is, like me, from the Western world, an essential question inevitably arises: namely, what are we going to realise, or to grasp, from the intellectual space of the African continent? How deeply do we understand? Despite the new trend of identifying business opportunities across Africa, the sense of humanitarian emergency still prevails and largely outshines other perceptions. From this fact a veritable movement of aid, resources and people is set in motion to provide help, which is essentially a favourable trait among humans. Now, donor agencies and aid organisations must demonstrate that they require money for their projects to taxpayers and charitable donors. In pursuit of this interest the image drawn of the continent has to be dark, bleak and somehow essentially African. Developmental and humanitarian help is assigned but it can only be prolonged as long as someone out there is acknowledged as desperate and poor. It is almost inevitable that Africa must remain poor when considered from the position of these organisations. Locations often become project sites rather than ordinary places in ordinary countries; their main similarity lies in the presence of certain grievances against which the projects were set up.

A donating society granting aid to other parts of the world leads donors and receivers into a delicate relationship. The cause of much of this delicacy is the idea of *improvement*, which is inherent and directly connected to the practice of help. According to Gronemeyer we all too soon assume that "only through help is the recipient raised to the level of true humanity. This implies a view of the cultural and spiritual superiority of the giver" (1992:57). What is remarkable here in the context of organisational legitimation is a shift from difference to diversity during an act of developmental aid. One of the initial causes for commencing a new cycle of foreign aid is the donor's perception that the recipients are somehow *different* in that their way of life is unfavourably distinct and probably also worse. Aside from efforts in disaster relief, the most common denominator in applying such an approach is national economic strength. Africa as a whole is associated with a grave need for externally induced development programmes because its appearance is one of foreignness and poverty. I do not question whether this perception is right or wrong; it is a central point of departure for all forms of official foreign aid, which could otherwise not be sustained. It must be a notion of difference that enables the development sector to commit resources, political initiatives and manpower to projects that would otherwise never be accepted at home (or in 'developed' areas). Effectiveness, diligence and local responsibility are often rather low and frequently no longer accountable and explainable within the standards applied to activities in Europe and the West.[29]

Subsequently, the notion of *diversity* is applied when the tools of intercultural project management come into play, standardised country reports are issued and the mutual commonality between donor and receiver is taken for granted, thus allowing for the transfer of new ideas and solutions. In fact, the goal lies in the transfer of the donor's ideas to the receivers by way of making them appear desirable.

In the realm of values and normative legitimation, development aid depends on the notion of difference among the world's regions. At the same time, on the level of action and operative legitimation, diversity management must be taken for granted since the strict evaluation procedures would never work otherwise. Donors and receivers officially agree on technical standards and shared project goals that adhere to the tenets of formal-rational modernism (cf Rottenburg 2009, 2005). Whatever happens can always be justified, either normatively, by using the discourse of difference, *or* operatively, by applying the discourse of diversity.

---

29 Contradictory to these statements, official evaluations of projects mostly indicate success rates of 80% or 90%. Wolff (2005) questions these figures and skilfully elaborates on the practices of evaluation and de facto self-evaluation throughout the development sector. It should be noted that these organisations depend on positive evaluations in order to sustain their institutional legitimation. For them, positive evaluations are one of the most valuable assets and therefore carefully maintained.

Oscillation between operative universalism and operative relativism

The policy and practice of development aid is based on a notion of asymmetry between donor and recipient. If both were regarded as equal, there would be no need for intervention. There have been many attempts to overcome this principal asymmetry in the practical operations of the aid industry which have met with little success thus far. A noteworthy distinction becomes visible when multinational corporations and international donor agencies are compared with regard to the question of operative universalism and operative relativism. While a multinational corporation aims at economies of scale by also using this universalistic goal rhetorically as an argument to justify its policies, a donor agency cannot simply do the same, even when it implicitly would like to roll out its ideas and projects across as many countries as possible.

A slightly simplified comparison between both organisation types reveals that the corporation unquestionably has the directive power to manage its internal affairs according to its own strategies and standards regardless of diplomatic or other concerns (as long as it adheres to laws and respects local customs). The main consideration is that local environments only have to be regarded in the way and to an extent the external management considers suitable. No external obligations arise for internal management decisions as long as efficiency is maintained. Asymmetry is a normal element in hierarchies within companies, and the opinion of the boss is usually determinative. This is the way that universalistic practices and ideas are brought down to 'alien grounds': the corporate subsidiary modernises its local subsidiary according to global standards, and whoever disapproves is free to leave the company or cease buying its products. More often than not people choose to remain. Local governments and communities attempt to acquire their own share from the corporate subsidiary's resources, provided that the corporation does not threaten job loss and withdrawal from the country. All in all, the pattern of MNC subsidiaries is quite a simple universalist approach.[30]

Donor agencies, on the contrary, apply a more complex pattern. Legitimation for the execution of development aid is derived from a twofold argument: (1) the recipient is in need of assistance and (2) there is something worthwhile that can be transferred from donor to receiver beyond simply money. Ideas and concepts of development are always connected to the act of giving aid.[31] Here, a subliminal

---

30 This rather positive view on MNCs is justified in the case of locally productive foreign corporations. I return to this issue later in the chapter.
31 Note the distinction from humanitarian aid and disaster relief, which do not aim at structural development but rather at caring for short-term emergencies.

universalism is already in place as the ideas and concepts that originate in the donor country are to be deployed across recipient countries. The possibility of spreading the means for suitable development serves as a foundation for the legitimation of implementing costly projects in 'underdeveloped' countries.

Simultaneously, however, these same donor agencies must promote the independence of receivers, be it countries or target groups. It has been repeatedly demonstrated that overly universalistic development approaches often bear the mark of colonialism and are also not particularly participative. They confront the targeted population with foreign projects and ignore local knowledge, thereby severely decreasing effectiveness. For this reason, today's development policy is collaborative and officially guided by the receiver's demands. In fact, no act of development assistance can take place unsolicited. Recipients of aid must formally apply to the relevant agency or through relevant channels in order for assistance to be granted (or aid to be dispensed). Local knowledge and determination must form the basis for proper cooperation, self-development and human dignity.

Since the act of development cooperation implies the transfer of ideas from donor to receiver, the actors involved are likely to be entering an asymmetric relationship. This relationship becomes possible because the receiver has, in the eyes of the donor, proven to be at a stage of development that justifies certain means of foreign assistance that would be withheld from more advanced counterparts. In this light, development agencies mostly exist to spread a modernistic universal idea to counterparts. They use non-universalistic means in order to do this. At the core of this dynamic lies a necessity for the *special treatment* of recipient countries/target groups *because* they are in need of help.[32]

Inconsistencies in the regime of these transnational discourses and resource flows are deeply rooted beneath the visible bustle of daily activities. Over the last decade the details of the aid world have changed drastically, yet the basics remain the same:

"Even the self-criticism of development aid manoeuvres itself into a paradoxical situation. It regards its opposite numbers in the Third World as comprehensively needy, backward according to valid standards of normality, and subject to an essential catching up process. And at the same time it broods tormentedly over the arrogance of the rich nations, makes

---

32 Many African governments have realised this and come to make use of the fact that a special status such as 'Least Developed Country' (LDC) or 'Highly Indebted Poor Country' (HIPC) can be beneficial to a creative regime. However, this topic would leave the core argument of this book.

propaganda for the idea of the fundamental equality of foreign cultures, shows its willingness to engage in dialogue, and condemns tutelary and dependency relations and cultural imperialism." (Gronemeyer 1992:66)

Structural oscillations: comprehension

It appears that the development sector is founded on structural oscillations in its management of heterogeneity. At first, *difference* must be evoked, thereby marking the otherness of receivers. Frequently, this ascription of otherness is experienced as pejorative by the target groups involved. These same target groups are then subjected to notions of *diversity* in order to conduct accountable project work with them. Interculturalism is propagated and favourable practical relationships are nurtured. When this stage is reached, universalistic approaches provide the basis from which funds, ideas and personnel can be transferred for the benefit of the receiver. The commitment of Western donors' or taxpayers' money is only justifiable for transparent, predictable projects and accountable procedures, and consequently formal-rational organisation techniques are applied. The most accountable ideas and goals are usually provided by donors themselves while receivers contribute their energy and political will.

Yet, at the same time it is acknowledged that all countries, cultures and societies have both the right and the obligation to devise their own solutions to development, while donors only assist where necessary. At this point a strong operative relativism may become mandatory in order to legitimise the act of cooperation. Aside from these relational matters a blatant issue of organisational legitimacy in donor agencies comes into focus: as long as poor parts of the world remain underdeveloped, only the development sector itself has the means and access to maintain relationships with those areas and societies. Inasmuch as whole continents rely on a status of underdevelopment, they function as undisputed 'resourceful areas' for beneficiaries from both the industrialised countries' aid industry and many of the poor countries' political powers. For the poor recipients (the 'counterparts' in the target countries) this arrangement carries the benefit of special treatment, which is far removed from the harsh realities of economic and political competition realities faced by those countries and actors that are not sustained by foreign resources on a basis of grants and donations. On the downside they are caught at the end of an asymmetrical web in which others benefit more from their situation than they do themselves.

6.3 Four Types of Transboundary Cooperations

Building on the comparative assessments of Chapter 4, four generalised archetypes of Transboundary Cooperations were derived from the empirical material. In the following step I will present these four transboundary types through a description of their most characteristic features. The types identified were (1) donor agencies, (2) multinational corporations, (3) small-medium enterprises and (4) diaspora businesses. It is likely that even more may be found which were not part of this study and therefore outside the current focus.[33]

Donor agencies – official development aid
Within the transnational fields that link poor and rich states, national donor agencies might be regarded as the 'kings of development'. They are highly institutionalised, thus guided by the upkeep and enhancement of their symbolic legitimation. The actual integration of their operative branches into the social environments of target countries is often rather limited. Nevertheless, individual experts are commonly confronted directly with the demand of striking a balance between their own organisation's self-centredness and the real-life challenges advanced by the host setting.

Difference and diversity: A practical main concern of donor agencies is the assignment of public resources and manpower to the interests of foreign countries. The primary legitimation for the complex that drives these activities is derived from a differentiation of the world into unequal parts, building on the notion of difference. In the words of two development researchers these actors employ

"the social construction of underdevelopment. Development experts and development sociologists have the power to determine what should be considered as underdevelopment. We assume that experts construct and create underdevelopment taking trends into consideration and then try to eliminate the phenomenon. Knowledge about underdevelopment is developed in the universities and the think tanks but also in the practice of development cooperation. This happens within the context of an 'epistemic culture' that makes it possible to create knowledge about development and underdevelopment as a specifically constructed fragment of a practically oriented science." (Evers/Gerke 2005:4)

---

33 Currently, as one example, the impact of Chinese protagonists on the African continent is widely discussed. For several reasons, this was not a central part of the research project.

However, donor agencies have gained experience and competences that enable them to act under extremely heterogeneous and ambiguous conditions in locations that are avoided by most other international actors. This is the positive aspect of their structural focus on difference.

Operative universalism and operative relativism: At the foundation of development lies the assumption that there is something of value that can be transferred from developed to underdeveloped parts of the world. This approach relies on the notion that ideas and methods that are successful in one context (country, society, target group) will be successful in another context as well. In order to mitigate the negative effects of a direct transfer from rich to poor, contemporary practice in development aid stresses the autonomy of the receiver. Participatory planning of development projects demands continuous dialogue with partners (e.g. the indigenous population) even if this is hard to achieve. The contrasts between local habits and the globalised world of experts are subsequently assuaged, often in the form of embellished project reports and symbolic achievements (cf Evers/Gerke 2005:12).

Institutionalisation and local embeddedness: Organisational institutionalisation is typically quite strong as activities are mainly legitimised on the basis of symbolical values. Despite the fact that many development actors in practical terms are deeply engaged in local affairs, their internal success measurements usually are not.

Multinational corporation – local subsidiaries

The term 'multinational enterprise' encompasses a huge variation of companies with different policies, markets and activities. Among the existing organisational forms, the subsidiaries of MNCs that apply local resources (at least partially) to produce consumer goods for markets in their host countries, such as the brewery from case 2, form a notable transnational business. They behave as an important local economic actor in the country in which they operate, owning local assets, employing domestic staff and using local resources, while simultaneously retaining their transnational advantages. The market strategy for such a subsidiary is frequently founded when catering to customers of the host country, and not their country of origin for export. Foreign capital, management and resources thus aim at generating profits within the host country itself.

Local assimilation and transterritorial enclave: The intriguing point about firms such as the brewery from case 2 is their reliance on local markets for both consumers and increasingly also for supplies and skilled manpower. In earlier decades it was common for Western companies in 'tropical', 'exotic' and 'underdeveloped' countries to behave as if they were acting in an entirely isolated sphere.

Almost every necessity was imported, most provisions and supplies were not available in the host country, and all experienced staff was foreign. Additionally, the local surroundings were difficult, if not hostile, for the maintenance of a technical-commercial facility. Nowadays, a subsidiary producing for the domestic market faces conflicting demands between local adaptation and a focus on internal strategies aimed at maintaining the MNC's private standards. Local adaptation in this context implies being dependant on local consumers and supplies, political support and the host society as a whole. The orientation at internal benchmarks enhances the corporation's efficiency in technical and administrative terms because it increases its overall control over its own processes and activities. Oftentimes, the level of know-how and the quality of resources within such firms is higher than that which can be found in poor host countries. This, however, is achieved at the cost of reducing its local adaptation to a degree where it in a certain sense can virtually lose the connection.

Diversity: It is acknowledged in the management of multinational corporations that there is great variation and plurality among the people they work with and the places they operate in across the world. In order to enable enterprises to achieve economies of scale, their operations across heterogeneous locations therefore have to rely on effective management of diversity. In an ideal world of diversity management, the variety of the world is grasped by a flexible and efficient management concept. All possible incidents of 'otherness' must be reduced to a predefined core of rationality and a shared sense of the company's operation. This kind of diversity, with a shared understanding of formal-rational values, functions as a precondition for multinational business organisations and corporate controlling. Thus what is 'normal' is defined by the corporation, not by the country in which it is operating.

Operative universalism: The strategies of multinational enterprises are essentially universalistic and build on the basic assumption that a global scale of operations can be achieved through rationalism and the principles of modern organisation. As is sufficiently proven, such an approach often leads to enhanced effectiveness and predictability. MNCs tend to judge all places and people from one centralised and standardised frame of reference in which feasibility, commercial benchmarks and technical aspects are emphasised. Corporate strategy consists of streamlined operations, global resource flows, complex rules of decision-making and, importantly, central accounting and controlling. The major benefit for the corporate centre lies in its ability to replicate effective processes across many countries while remaining in control of the entire company. Due to this standardised centralisation, subsidiaries are less ready to become assimilated into the local environment, making them less able to adapt to specific contexts without contradicting their corporate standards at the same time. In terms of the organisational culture, this operative universalism attempts to establish the same degree of familiarity and knowledge across subsidiaries worldwide. MNCs wish all countries to be markets governed by the rule of law; they usually have little interest in overly asymmetric conditions that go beyond the scope of calculability. They appreciate comparative advantages, but not operative relativism, something that is too different altogether.

Small-medium enterprises

Indigenous as well as foreign owned SMEs in African countries are perhaps the least obvious players in the field of Transboundary Cooperations. Rooted in a continually undifferentiated African private sector, their numbers, while limited, are most likely expanding. The primary goal of SMEs is to generate profits and secure the livelihood of their owners and employees. They are usually not bound to any organisational or institutional structures beyond their own immediate scope.

Technical-commercial orientation and local assimilation: Actors in this category are most sensitive to 'country risks'. In comparison to NGOs and development agencies they rely on commercial sustainability as well as their own earnings in risky economies. In contrast to multinationals they do not possess a transnational foundation of corporate resources and 'political muscle'; though SMEs with transnational connections are in a position to engage in specialised activities tailored to specific opportunities arising from local situations. Their ability to do so rests on the exploitation of transboundary resources in order to gain leverage over purely local competitors and weakly connected foreigners. Local entrepreneurs with strong connections to resourceful foreign partners are in a particularly flexible position.

"Local private sector investors that benefit from more intimate knowledge of local markets and customs are better able to protect themselves from some of the risks faced by the international community. These investors will often be prepared to become involved in [...] schemes that international investors would not contemplate." (World Bank/Public-Private Infrastructure Advisory Facility, 2005:14)

Diaspora commerce

The Indian traders from case 7 provided the background for the final transboundary type. Commercial activities of this kind exist worldwide and are certainly not limited to individuals and businesses of Indian origin. The following descriptions might therefore also apply to other groups exhibiting the patterns of diaspora commerce.

Local embeddedness and transterritorial enclave: The economic strategies of the Indian diaspora in Rwanda, as elsewhere, are very *glocal* in their foundations and objectives. Only a selective assimilation to the local setting takes place, while the social and cultural orientations of this group largely remain disconnected from the host country. Such actors and their operations feature several key elements of transterritorial enclaves even when their businesses are often directly linked to local markets.

Difference: Regardless of the places in which these diaspora networks choose to settle, their affiliations are rooted in kinship and ethnic belonging, which clearly signify who is part of the group and who is not. They live according to an essential distinction of the local social world that is categorised as an in-group (the diaspora members) and an out-group (the rest of the world). Other populations, including those of the host country, are at best appreciated but not to an extent that these 'others' could exercise any influence over the in-group's values, orientations and social boundaries. 'Others' are either regarded as 'different' and out-of-bounds, or at best interesting but not particularly relevant for matters of importance. Arranging the social universe in this manner greatly stabilises the, generally, sensible arrangements of settlement, livelihood and commerce in the host country and among family members. One of the foremost effects of diaspora culture is its ability to produce and maintain social identity and to preserve the collective significance of a geographical and symbolic origin. Yet, this means of identity production always involves a separation from 'others'. Such an effective, if somewhat rigid, form of social self-control enables the facilitation of trust and cooperation among members who are accordingly shielded from outer interference. Their principal mode of social organisation follows an understanding of 'general difference' in terms of the in-group living in a sphere of outsiders. "[T]he limits of diaspora lie precisely in its own assumed boundedness, its inevitable tendency to stress its internal coherence and unity, logically set apart from 'others'." (Ang 2003:142)

Diaspora formations conclusively transgress geographic boundaries on behalf of a globally dispersed 'people' but almost paradoxically this transgression can only be achieved by drawing a frame around the diaspora themselves. It is therefore important to recognise the duality of the diaspora identity: it can be the site of both support and exclusion, emancipation and confinement, solidarity and division.

Operative universalism: The lifestyles and businesses of well-established diaspora actors reflect the nature of their objectives and strategies: the objective is a reproduction of their socio-cultural and economic universe abroad in much the same way it would appear in their country of origin. Indian ways of life and social conduct are typically kept alive and are valued highly abroad. On the commercial front, a similar business model is frequently replicated across as many places or countries as possible, using the same suppliers, the same ideas and the same social network. From this point of view most parts of the world are seen in a comparable manner: individual opportunities are identified while humanistic or political ideas mean little in terms of orientations and strategies.[34] Spreading belief or ideology to others is a low priority, for the most part, while the pursuit of individual gain, family life and acquisition of social status within the in-group itself is regarded as paramount. These universalistic commercial strategies of replication are nevertheless commonly embedded in business models intended to garner profits from mercantile arbitrage or exclusive market access. These strategies take into account that well-connected traders will enter new markets with overpriced goods or benefit from their abilities to interact with local authorities in an informal fashion.

6.4 DIFFERENT KINDS OF TRANSBOUNDARY CAPITALISM IN AFRICA

When we say that we want to compare the cooperation patterns of transnational businesses with those from development aid, at first it is essential to be aware of the types of business we want to look at. Within the capitalist mode of production (cf Wolf 1997) it can be helpful to distinguish between different archetypes of doing business which render the outcome of capitalism different. With respect to the contemporary situation on the African continent, I work with two major differentiations: (1) locally productive vs. extractive enterprises, and (2) ethnic capitalism vs. universalistic capitalism. In the following I am going to differentiate

---

34 This may not be uncommon for transnational groups of actors, but in Africa it gains comparative relevance. Most Western foreigners deeply aspire to personally contribute to the well-being of Africa, whereas none of the encountered Indians displayed any such moral arguments.

between these forms of profit generation in the context of Transboundary Cooperations.[35]

Locally productive vs. extractive enterprises in Africa

Multinationals in the natural resource and mining business often cosy up to whichever regime is in power in order to protect their investment. At the same time enterprises producing consumer goods for export frequently move to whichever country offers the best deal on labour costs, moving on when the local situation deteriorates. And those companies who produce for the domestic market by using domestic resources have to come to terms with the local environment as a whole and become accepted members of the domestic economy much like any local competitor. Factors that must be taken into consideration include marketing, manpower, political stability and buying power. Those *locally productive* enterprises are foreign companies with investments in a host country that manufacture their products on the spot and sell them to domestic customers. Foreign management and capital in combination with international know-how are committed to subsidiaries responsible for the local production. The ranks of qualified personnel are increasingly filled with locals and a portion of supplies are typically obtained from the host country. Production factors of mixed origin are brought together to generate added local value, while a net profit is repatriated to the enterprise's head office in its home country (or any suitable tax haven). To effectively maintain such an arrangement the company has to integrate the interests of a mixed group of stakeholders: suppliers, foreign management and shareholders, local staff, customers and government as well as the domestic society in general. It cannot prosper without a base of goodwill from these interest groups. As a result, the foreign enterprise has to respect and to master the forces of the local market.

In contrast, the strategies of *extractive enterprises* are ruled by capitalism as well, but of a different sort: most commonly, extractive businesses gather mineral resources or other valuable materials to be taken away for commercialisation elsewhere, in resource markets in industrialised countries, for instance. These companies exploit deposits of raw materials or agronomical resources all over the world yet generally do not directly generate local productivity in the sense of value creation. In order to benefit from such activities the local powers are required to take away a compensation from the foreign enterprise. This can take place in the form of taxes, rents, fees, licenses, commissions, bribes, shares or any other form that suits the local power. Unfortunately, extractive enterprises do not depend on the

---

35 Even though the different manifestations of the capitalist mode are interdependent and cannot be fully separated from each other, here I'm concentrating on the effects of different capitalist approaches on the local context.

establishment of a productive local economy nor do they rely on the well-being of a local population that purchases their products. Their overall aim usually is the conduction of the extractive business with as little interaction with the local society as possible. The efficiency of such business models increase when they are able to separate themselves as much as possible from the surrounding context.

In the worst case all they require is a local authority that legalises the extraction of resources and guarantees their technical and physical security. For the well-known example of Nigeria's Oil industry, Obi (2001) described a situation where the people of the Niger delta were brutalised for decades by the Nigerian army and excluded from the benefits from the oil taken out of the lands they inhabited. They turned on the firms that pumped the oil and in return provided most of the government's tax revenue. Shell, the biggest long-term foreign investor, now has already spent large sums of money on mending ties with the locals. In his case study Obi writes on the emergence of mutually opposing transboundary formations in the Niger delta which are related to the local population with international support from civil rights and environmental groups, and the oil corporations with Nigerian central government, respectively. He states that these formations battle each other on all possible levels, which makes this a genuine *glocal* struggle. Wood (2004) and Frynas (2004) highlight another example of a West-African petro-state, Equatorial Guinea, where the governmental strategies are tailored towards profiteering from oil extraction while public legitimation and responsibility are extremely weak. Under such conditions foreign companies face strong incentives to adapt to the shadowy practices of those who wield local power. It should be noted that even if extractive enterprises are not productively engaged in the domestic economy and sometimes also participate in intransparent deals they nevertheless are aimed at technical optimisation and effective connections to the world markets.[36]

These extractive business models are very different from multinational enterprises that act as producers of consumer goods (such as the brewery from case 2). In my understanding, a mere exploitation of natural resources is not a value-generating factor combination in the classic sense of capitalist production. In extractive businesses of this kind, the factor combination is either realised elsewhere or

---

36 Alongside the large, formalised multinationals another type of extractive actor exists, who is limited to the context of developing countries. These are the shadowy profiteers of local crisis and international asymmetry, the warlords and rebel armies that cooperate with international merchants and corrupt authorities. Such transboundary formations are able to capitalise on the abundance of natural resources in conflict zones and the asymmetrical structure of the world economy. They would largely disappear as soon as effective regulative institutions were put into place.

not at all when a simple extraction of wealth only supplies private bank accounts. Extractive businesses do not have to sell products on the domestic market, and consequently the local situation is regarded as an external effect which must be minimised for optimal operation. The relevance of corporate social responsibility is increasingly stressed in this context and is also increasingly monitored.[37] It seems easier to target Western-based firms than third-world governments in terms of an improvement in transparency standards. But, and this is a crucial point, these measures are considered costs rather than opportunities for extractive capitalism. A domestic producer of consumer goods, on the contrary, has to customise the output of all its activities according to the situation and the demands of the local market. In this case the overall condition in the host country plays a significant role. Locally productive businesses should not only be interested in political stability. They are also driven to care for the host society's institutional development and the population's wealth and well-being out of their own business interest. From this point of view, the total amount of foreign investment allocated to a developing country matters little as long as most of it belongs to the primary resources sector.[38]

Ethnic capitalism and universalistic capitalism

Another aspect concerning the nature of transnational business is related to the question of heterogeneity and inclusiveness. From this perspective it is important to distinguish between two kinds of 'universality' in transnational capitalism. The 'real universal' type in my terminology is represented by the ideal type of the modern and rational enterprise. These are the multinational corporations and financial investors of our time who engage in every market that fits in their strategy. They seek to enhance their internal diversity in order to cope with diverse markets and environments drawing boundaries only with regard to commercial interests. These rationalistic enterprises uniformly assess all places, people and activities with the same measurements of risk and benefit. Optimally, they do not principally

---

37 Western companies are now increasingly driven to adopt transparency and compliance frameworks in order to limit irresponsible behavior in the extractive industries.

38 All these considerations are relevant for corporate activities in poor and developing countries. In industrial societies the well-being of the population is taken for granted such that the political priorities of large corporations might be quite different. Whereas in Africa an MNC may boast of its material contribution to society, in the West the very same company might scream for an improvement in its condition (less taxes, harder work, less constraints). Interestingly, the conditions in Africa are generally much worse and operations much harder to maintain than in the West, while corporate management in the West is often in a better position to enforce claims supporting their business.

prefer specific target countries or employees of a particular origin. Human variation and social heterogeneity are approached with the notion of diversity, as long as business runs. This is an idealised picture of the 'colourless capitalism' that knows no race, culture or tradition. Although this model remains rather abstract it has at least been partially realised in quite a number of business organisations. Major MNCs seek to enhance their internal diversity while at the same time increasingly treating all markets according to the same performance criteria; for them the world is measured against a universal mode of effectiveness. It should be noted that such an approach to international business is not (or no longer?) tied to Western actors, as managers of almost any origin are nowadays capable of forming highly effective transnational enterprises.

However, in a grossly simplified way it can be assumed that a substantial proportion of worldwide capitalist enterprises, investments, trades and firms are managed by visions and intentions that are different from the above described ideal type of the colourless capitalism. There exists a capitalist form that builds on a segregative social order, according to which profit is universal but people and places are not. What I would call 'ethnic capitalism' is a continuation of social heterogeneity in the world of enterprises and investments. According to Light and Karageorgis (1994), the classic approaches of understanding capitalism mostly worked with the assumption that ethnically discriminating forces within a society had only negative effects on economic prosperity. Minority groups were generally expected to face inevitable hindrances in their pursuit of economic prosperity, while economic success was expected to reduce ethnic boundaries and facilitate assimilation.

Under certain circumstances, however, certain advantages may be accessed by entrepreneurs who are part of an ethnic minority. Shared cultural values and social bonds within diaspora groups and well-organised ethnic communities reproduce networks of solidarity and exclusivity. Group members reject their assimilation into host societies as much as they reject the opening of their ethnic groups to outsiders. Here, capitalism indeed knows difference, and distinctions are made among people on the basis of their origin. Trust, cooperation and the general possibility of becoming part of a profitable business network in ethnically organised capitalism is not only a matter of success, but also one of belonging. For many Indian and Chinese businesses, for example, the model of ethnic capitalism forms the basis of their activities. Actors may interact differently with fellow Indians or Chinese than with Africans or Europeans. (For further reference on Indian and Chinese economic activities in Africa, cf Broadman, 2007, Goldstein/Pinaud/Reisen, 2006, and on South-South trade, Kaukab, 2006, for Chinese activities across Africa: Van Dijk 2009). Although ethnically based inclusion-exclusion practices cannot effectively take hold in highly competitive sectors of the world markets, they continue in kinship-based business networks rooted in and economically based migration, at the frontiers of commercial expansion unstable emerging markets or post-conflict or crisis economies (cf Hummel and Menzel 2001). Ethnisation of economic relations is an issue that contradicts the expectation of a socially dissolving force in capitalism. Capital itself is not allocated according transparent market forces but rather to genealogically affiliated individuals. It circulates between family members, businesses, countries or residence and industry sectors and always remains in the control of an in-group (Gambe/Hummel/Menzel 2001).

From above considerations follows the conclusion that regarding enterprises as actors of transnational capitalism is not sufficient to explain their interactions with African environments. The question regarding capitalist actors should be whether they generate local productivity or merely extract local wealth. Additionally, their impact on the forms of social inclusion and exclusion should be assessed. Capitalism always creates social inclusion and exclusion itself. The question is whether this is predefined through ethnic or other primordial belonging or comes about as a side effect of material accumulation in the productive process itself.

6.5 COMPARING DEVELOPMENT AID AND PRIVATE BUSINESS

What remains is to return to the question how development aid and private business as two major forms of cooperation between Africa and the West are to be compared. What are the main differences and similarities? What conclusions can be drawn from the observations?

To approach these questions first I will draw upon the distinctions among different kinds of transnational capitalism that were made in the previous chapter. It is imperative to know what kind of private business we want to compare with development aid. We remember from Chapter 6.4 that not all forms of profit-oriented Transboundary Cooperations are equally beneficial for their host society. Consequently, in order to compare the principles of development aid and private business, the operative mode of foreign aid should juxtaposed with the operative mode of the most productive forms of transnational capitalism. In the following a theoretical conclusion is drawn about the impact and effectiveness of these types of Transboundary Cooperations in respect to the committed resources and possible outcomes.

Development aid and private business – How are they perceived?

The situation of highly institutionalised and locally almost decoupled Transboundary Cooperations bears implications of great importance for the texture of African – European cooperation. When it comes to dealing with actors and individual expatriates from industrialised countries, parts of the African societies have already become specialised in their responses to the needs and benefits that the expats bring with them. What we can see is that Sub-Saharan actors are responding to the characteristic behaviour of those structures in a way that benefits them most and seems to make the most sense to them. This way of dealing with external actors can, and does, contradict the original intentions of the external actors, as was shown in the empirical material. One possible reason for this could be the tendency of Western organisations in African locations to settle themselves down into enclave-like micro-worlds.

The problem of Western 'institutionalised enclaves' in African countries

On an organisational scale the 'institutionalised enclaves' have become a commonly regarded embodiment of Western civilisation on the continent. It is related to this wider context that the Rwandan discourses on foreign assistance and the presence of Western expatriates differ grossly from the common Western discourses on the same subject. More often than not a typical development agency, implicitly acting as a representative of Western civilisation, reinforces an image of Western societies that does not have much in common with the inner values we would widely assume to be of central importance for ourselves. My interpretation is that many counterparts in the host country accepted these practices unquestioningly, assuming them to represent the general reality of Western thinking. That being said, the African counterparts themselves have the freedom to react to the situation in several ways. In the best case the donor project has connected up with suitable local partners and cooperates well. Other possible reactions represent indifference or even helplessness and confusion, and occasionally even radical forms of covered exploitation of the donors by the local counterparts.

The risk of bottom-up exploitation emerges from the effects of organisational institutionalisation. Meyer and Rowan mention that legitimation in formal organisations is achieved through an arrangement of already known elements, a feature that facilitates trust, but also supports unscrupulous practices.

"[T]he building blocks for organizations come to be littered around the societal landscape; it takes only a little entrepreneurial energy to assemble them into a structure. And because these building blocks are considered proper, adequate, rational, and necessary, organizations must incorporate them to avoid illegitimacy." (1991:45)

It is usually not too difficult to establish a formally acceptable and capable local agency that is able to gain the trust of foreign organisations, thus becoming a recipient of donor resources. Therefore, while operations may run smoothly on the symbolic level, in practice a gross disparity exists between the donors' goals and the activities on the ground.

It is to be expected that quite often foreign aid is not only of moderate effectiveness due to the high complexity of its subject, but also a victim of fraud. In this context, a Rwandan entrepreneur related his experience with a fake NGO: *"Back that time [in the post-war period] a friend came along because he urgently needed to borrow my office in a couple of days. He was running his own NGO and the white lady from the foreign organisation donating the funds came on visit. She had to do the controlling. So, me... yes, I had to give the office of my company to him and we removed everything that belonged to me. Then he brought huge numbers of folders and everything else that you need to run an NGO... everything he brought. It was perfect, the folders had labels on them with the correct names of departments and projects and all the bureaucracy. But the folders were mostly empty except some. He exactly knew the ones he was going to need. Me, I had to mimic his aide in my own office! When the lady asked for a certain paper or receipt, he told me which folder I had to bring to him. He opened them... all the folders, reports and papers the lady wanted to see were perfect, nothing was missing. The invoices were there, accounts, bills. After she went away the office was set to normal again... A total fake... the friend now has a big house and became wealthy from this business... But me I work too hard here and can't afford such a house. What do I get... from my honest work? That guy perhaps did the right thing."*

Even when assuming that this is an extreme example, supervising renegade local partners is difficult for Western donors. The aforementioned Rwandan businessman's account highlights a general weakness of institutionalised organisations' ability to achieve sincere, meaningful contact with members of targeted societies. It is difficult for them to ascertain whether their proposed activities are actually effective as planned. Even more difficult, however, is the detection of fraud, disinterest or even simple incompetence. While individual expatriates frequently encounter these problems in the course of their work, anticipating them within the formal logic of transnational cooperation structures proves much more problematic. Agencies that are structured as institutionalised enclaves have the capacity, and resulting weakness, of being able to shield themselves against the consequences of negative input. They rely primarily on institutionalised trust, symbolism and good faith while their operative success is measured through evaluations, reports and disbursements rather than financial or material output. In the long run, it is unavoidable that they engage (mostly local) individuals or even organisations who are capable of appearing like an ideal partner but are merely capable of mimetic symbolism. The use of specific rhetoric "most easily reinforces the belief that [the foreigners, R.P.] understand what Africa needs" (Chabal/Daloz 1999:117).

Promoting relativism or universalism?

Africa has long been neglected by most international businesses simply because it did not qualify for the application of universalistic business principles common in industrial countries (in terms of politico-economic structures, market demand and buying power). Yet, there have always been transnational enterprises working in African economies. We have seen that not all of them are built on the same structural foundation (extractive vs. locally productive, universalistic vs. ethnic/exclusive capitalism). Many belong to the category of extractive businesses, which exploit asymmetrical international relationships.

Locally productive enterprises also do exist, and they constitute a special type of Transboundary Cooperations which can be found among the ranks of large transnational corporations as well. The brewery from case 2, an example from my own fieldwork, possessed the ability to apply its universalistic strategy in Rwanda, a country previously not associated with extensive economic opportunity but rather with 'otherness' from an international viewpoint. The brewery combines the necessity of generating commercial returns with an adherence to the technical requirements with the facilitation of the economic, social and institutional environments of its host country. Its long-term operations are a magnet of predictability, formal stability and, after some adaptations, also a source of local business linkages. All this happens to its own benefit. The unique combination of universalistic and responsive characteristics in such enterprises renders them particularly active agents of socio-economic transformation in African societies. In my opinion the notion of positive 'spillover effects' (cf Gilroy 2005) emanating from such glocal centres of action are valid indeed. What must be noted, nevertheless, is the limitation of those beneficial enterprise set-ups on the aforementioned combination of factors (Chapter 6.4): using local resources, targeting local markets, conducting local production, investing foreign capital, applying international expertise/standards/quality and professional management. Although companies in possession of these features are undoubtedly intricate, they are highly valuable transboundary actors. They thus embody one of the most noteworthy forms of transnational capitalism, with beneficial side effects on both the local economy and the institutional environment.

How should private business and development aid be compared?

The above being said an important note seems to be required at this place. Even though the possible outcomes of different types of capitalism are discussed and the benefits of certain types of transboundary capitalism are laid out in detail (especially in Chapter 6.4, but also in other places throughout the book) it is not my goal to promote the idea of capitalism over all other forms of transnational exchange. The question was to research how development aid can be compared to private business. Our first assessment revealed that private business is conducted according to several different modes which relate differently to the local context. It turned out that local actors in developing societies seem to benefit most only from locally productive transnational enterprises. The comparison further revealed that it is hard for typical development organisations to top such locally productive transnational enterprises in several aspects that are typically seen as important for aid effectiveness. Even though development aid can address highly relevant topics and gain deep and sometimes almost unfiltered access to actors in a developing society, these activities often times do not work 'productively'. The reason for this might be found in the purely institutional legitimation of foreign aid which leads to intense but are rather symbolical forms of cooperation (where development aid is linked to hard performance indicators these indicators themselves are again based on purely institutional legitimation). Productive cooperations would ideally use personnel and resources as available in the participating contexts and apply a non-contradictive pattern that could positively integrate the life-worlds of the people involved. It becomes clear that cooperation modes that keep up human distinctions in the form of structural difference cannot reach such a level.

7. Conclusion

The act of cooperation across the boundaries of social spaces has proven to be a noteworthy issue. The discourse on foreign development aid in Africa and the phenomenon of a new dynamic in the private sector on this continent stimulated my interest in research on Transboundary Cooperations. I wanted to see how the ways of thinking and working in these two fields are actually connected to a 'real' local setting. Although the effects of globalisation are reflected by an ever-increasing density of linkages between places, people and countries everywhere, I felt a particular curiosity about the way foreign organisations and companies are operating on behalf of these interests (development aid and private business) in Rwanda, as this country seemed to possess an international attractiveness far beyond its size. The country provides a notably dense environment of research subjects: international, trans-local and bilateral actors, relief and help organisations, new and old local structures, some established international companies and a diverse set of prospective entrepreneurs. Beyond these considerations I also suspected a potential relevance of the topic for greater parts of Sub-Saharan Africa, and in some regards also for developing countries on other continents.

A retrospective

One of the main themes that implicitly surfaced in each of the case studies was the issue of maintaining an effective organisation in a setting that spans the boundaries of social spaces. Building on Rottenburg (2002, 2009), this issue can often be framed in quite a practical question: how do we apply universal procedures and (assumed) universal principles that constitute the field of rational organisation when allowing for the notion of contextual differences? On both the operative and the epistemic level, not all Transboundary Cooperations follow the same principles when addressing these challenges, as we have seen. In addition, we have also seen that it is not at all self-evident to what extent universal principles of effectiveness are understood as being really universal and relevant in their respective context (remember the distinction between operative relativism and operative universalism, but also the preferences of donor agencies or ethnic networks, for example). In the introduction I proposed a principal route for the research which was paraphrased in three initial questions:

First question: In which way are the objectives and purposes of foreign activities in African countries influenced by the fact they are taking place in Africa? In the course of Chapter 2 the meaning of this question was practically re-formulated as: How do actors deal with the significance of sociocultural heterogeneity in transnational relations rooted in an African context? Speaking about Transboundary Cooperations here implies an analysis of their heterogeneity management. Its relevance for the different types of Transboundary Cooperations was found to be an essential part of the research. Some conceptions of heterogeneity can work for some types of Transboundary Cooperations while they do not function for others. The way social, cultural and economic divergences are perceived and enacted necessarily leads to specific outcomes in transnational activities. In this sense it is of significance that the activities were located in Africa, but the exact significance is deeply connected to the organisational substructure of the actors and operations (Chapters 2, 3, 5 and 6).

Second question: How do different kinds of foreign activities in African countries tend to behave in terms of their organisational structure, goals, resources and internal control? For a typification I relied on the assessment of the empirical data through a mixed set of organisation theories and the notions of organisations, institutions and actors as the backbone of the analytic concept (Chapter 2 and Appendix 8.2). Businesses behave differently from development organisations in what they see as an appropriate work result mostly because of the differences in their local embeddedness and the importance given to influences of symbolic institutionalisation (Chapters 5.1, 5.2 and 6.1). Independent agencies and actors behave differently from those belonging to transnational organisations or corporations. Whereas in the Multinational Corporation control was increasingly managed in a manner similar to what is customary in the West as this best fits its goals (Chapter 4.2), the operations of other transboundary actors were more suited to the local environment. Ethnic networks such as the Indian entrepreneurs in East Africa isolate themselves from their environment by means that are locally appropriate (Chapter 4.7). Development agencies are sometimes overburdened by the handling of a complex requirement. They more often than not have to operate according to structurally inconsistent rules of action (Chapter 4.1, 4.6, 5.2 and structural oscillations in Chapter 6.2). Small and medium enterprises with a transboundary character, both domestic and international, are possibly faced with the most immediate experience of indigenous conditions in ways that affect organisational effectiveness. They act as players in the local market and, as deliverers of commercial goods or services, are bound to stand for the effectiveness of their technical outputs in a truly challenging environment (Chapters 4.3, 4.4, 4.5 and 4.7).

Third question: In which kinds of local settings do Transboundary Cooperations operate? Transboundary Cooperations were conceived as formalised organisational activities across the boundaries of social spaces with a purpose rooted in civil society and the private sector. Their centre of activity is located in the host country while control and resources may originate elsewhere but are locally redefined. They primarily operate in settings that are easily accessible for foreign actors or that are the outcome of the foreign activity itself. In this sense Transboundary Cooperations often contribute to the emergence of genuinely 'glocal' settings. Transnational actors of large and small scale are willing and able to engage in post-conflict and 'least developed countries' and they have a certain leverage in respect to the local environment to do so. Yet, there was no evidence in my research to suggest that indigenous actors had been crowded out or superseded by more powerful transboundary ones. Rather, and as an aspect of the glocal character of the transboundary settings, the transboundary organisations were to be seen as a nucleus that fostered transactions which otherwise would not have taken place. They added something to the domestic field. At the same time they enabled global discourses to get 'real', to touch the ground. And here also lies one of the biggest assets that developing countries have in face of the international community and the seekers of global markets: global formations wield great power, but only when they are granted the possibility to become local as well. In this sense poor countries are partly doing good business by virtually selling access to their local environment to the carriers of global discourses. This is the more so when a Transboundary Cooperation works on the basis of an operative asymmetry (importantly, many development aid schemes also consist of asymmetric elements).

It is beneficial for observers and practitioners in the field to develop an awareness of the 'organisational subconsciousness' of Transboundary Cooperations in which they are involved. Understanding its own premises will greatly help any individual involved in a Transboundary Cooperation to also better comprehend the cooperation's own structural impact on its situation. It is not always 'the Africans' who are hard to get by. Often greater parts of the reactions of the local counterparts are induced by the organisational structure of the cooperation itself. The same set of individuals could interact in ways totally different when subjected to a different cooperation structure. This is where the transboundary types come in.

In addition to these suggestions for organisational self-reflection, some general findings of a more practical nature should be noted as well:

- The actor most dependent on the success of a Transboundary Cooperation must provide the personal, organisational and technical means for that operation in addition to facilitating all the steps of adaptation and translation. In many typical project schemes this position is assumed by a key foreign actor.
- In situations where domestic stakeholders have a lot to gain individually from the continuation of professionalised operations they may also perform the role of central operative proponents. In the brewery (case 2), for example, these individuals were the Rwandan cadres who secured the successful local adaptation of corporate issues.
- In non-profit environments it was commonly the European/Western individuals who showed the most direct commitment to the success of a specific cooperation project. They were personally strongly involved, often full time, as the execution of the activity is the formal and emotional reason for their presence (conducting a particular project work) while time and resources are limited for them.
- Indigenous observers more often than not implicitly regard the operative cores of Transboundary Cooperations (organisations or companies) as constantly provisioned with financial and other resources from abroad. This is a liability particularly for foreign operated local enterprises because they run the risk of being perceived richer than they actually are. The underlying cause of this phenomenon is most likely rooted in the continuous and seemingly effortless availability of financial resources for the majority of the country's foreign humanitarian organisations.

Who gains?

This headline's question is not merely rhetorical. Transboundary Cooperations are arenas of the convergent and divergent interests of multiple stakeholders who follow their own strategies and are guided by private perceptions.[39] The activities and inactivities of many foreign organisations in Rwanda before and during the outbreak of the genocidal violence in 1994 can be regarded as a telling example of why and how objectives, organisation structures and activity patterns of trans-

---

39 Bierschenk (1988) and Hüsken (2006:256) have commented on the field of development aid as being situated in arenas structured by the specific interests of different groups. The notion of Transboundary Cooperations adds that the interests are connected to the deep organisational structures and their applied goals and values.

boundary actors matter. Many foreign experts as well as the international community in general were vaguely aware of the totalitarian drive in Rwandan society at that time. They were mostly taken by surprise by the start and rapid eruption of the mass killings despite the political situation becoming ever more critical over an extended period. During that period the majority of international organisations and aid managers attempted to continue as normal as long as possible before genocide and war brought their work to an end (Uvin 1998). How could an international community of field experts be taken by surprise by these events? How could they to a certain extent even be duped about the devastating nature of the totalitarian regime and the popular mass movement? A profound change went through the whole society that they did not notice although it was exactly their job to do something for the betterment of the Rwandan people in mutual cooperation and partnership. Should the international organisations have reflected the critical situation earlier? Could they have observed or performed something beneficial or constructive before it was too late? In other words, how much has the international diplomatic and development scene really shared the same life-world, the 'real Rwanda', with the Rwandans? How much is the world of one's cooperation partner actually part of one's own work plan? I pose these questions not as yet another accusation of human failure aimed at the people involved at that time. The attentive reader will have taken note of the 'local embeddedness' issue here, or more specifically, of the 'institutionalised enclaves' I mentioned in Chapter 6. In a certain way the options available for certain types of Transboundary Cooperations are set in a narrow corridor, predefined by their own organisational and institutional substructure. In part, what a given organisation can see and what it cannot is a structural matter (which, however, does not alleviate the individual responsibility of everyone involved).

Cooperation – What about difference?

Connecting actors, organisations and institutions effectively across the boundaries of social spaces is not a self-evident exercise. I propose that the question of conceptualising difference and managing its implications must prevail in all serious approaches. Concerning the subject of this book, regardless of how it might be conceptualised, in many regards the notion of cultural, social and economic divergences between Africa and the West seems to be indisputable. But I also believe that this situation does *not* hinder the introduction of institutions that make sense in respect to inclusive and productive Transboundary Cooperations. In this book we have examined various types of transnational activities in local Rwandan settings. The question of what is really necessary or appropriate in an African country such as Rwanda seems problematic to answer from abroad. At best, Transboundary activities are legitimated locally in order to overcome this handicap. While these activities should be inclusive, they also must be productive according to the highest international standards. Yet, such a perfect form of cooperation seems hard to achieve and the average Transboundary Cooperation somehow arranges itself with the given constraints. Typically we either stress technical efficiency, demanding that 'the local' adapts to a certain degree of self-erasement. Or we take note of the local specifically in order to gain legitimation from taking it into account, thereby putting at risk the efficient transfer of knowledge and technology. A theoretically ideal form might be found in locally productive transnational cooperations catering for local societies.

Transnational private business and development aid in Africa

A fundamental part of dispensing foreign aid is the realisation of a collaborative incorporation of indigenous knowledge and local cultures. Mutual 'cooperation' is an integral component in the legitimation of development aid. Donors legitimate both their activities and foreign influence by claiming to promote recipients' interests by means of strengthening local structures. If we are honest, however, development aid concerns altering other people's culture in the name of a noble cause.

In the case of foreign business, the operative goal lies in generating private profit. Achieving favourable conditions, however, often involves minimising local impact on business. Enterprises that cater for the local market must cope with adapting to domestic conditions while simultaneously maintaining their own standards. In severely poor or post-conflict countries achieving this balance presents a greater challenge than in regions that are more industrially advanced. Nevertheless, successful foreign enterprises largely alter the culture they are part of. These impulses for change can have genuinely positive effects on local development, as long as business is conducted in a legitimate and productive manner. Today, profit oriented European enterprises in Africa are frequently confronted with institutional landscapes that seem to have specialised primarily in interactions with institutionalised European actors from the aid sector. Both foreign businesses and aid agencies are often regarded in an identical way by host communities and local stakeholders. While aid organisations are always externally funded and provisioned, the enterprises have to earn their money themselves, even in the local economy, and cannot simply apply for a new round of funds when a project gets stuck. The fact that enterprises and aid organisations operate with totally different goals is sometimes forgotten in an environment saturated with foreign activity and aid disbursements. At this point I would like to return to the subject of multinational corporations. These large enterprises actively disperse their own management standards throughout the world while simultaneously adopting technical norms (like ISO) and social codes of interaction (e.g. professionalisation, trends from management literature, changing social and cultural expectations). Combined, multinational corporations compose "one of the most complex forms of organisation currently in existence" (Ghosal/Westney 1993:2, after Gilroy 2005:106f), and they seek to uphold this dedicated mode of complexity in the face of greatly diverse host societies. Large enterprises are increasingly able to shape the operative environment of their local subsidiaries in accordance with their own complex, if predictable, patterns of behaviour. Yet they also require exterior environments that are adaptive to their highly structured working style. If the local situation guarantees a suitable degree of compliance with the corporate logic, *diversity* management can and will be accomplished by MNCs. Thus, a global net of integration can be sustained among highly diverse local conditions. This has powerful effects on the local social environment to which MNCs attempt to adapt or in which they seek to elevate local conduct and standards. But *difference* in all its stimulating or problematic forms will gradually be discontinued.

They propose raising or changing health and social policies according to international norms, monitoring technical efficiency and safety and, most importantly, streamlining local administrative and financial capabilities according to global standards. This is typically a positive side effect of multinationals in countries with low levels of institutional and political differentiation, provided that the standards being transferred are sustainable and productive. The *Economist* once wrote about multinationals:

"They listen: even the World Economic Forum has invited representatives of 15 NGOs to put their case. They try: they set guidelines for dealing with environmental safety and sexual harassment in countries where no such words exist in the local tongue. Their corporate morality is a great deal better than that of the average government: most would kick out a chairman who behaved like Bill Clinton or Helmut Kohl. They are at least as accountable (to their shareholders and the law) and a good deal more transparent than the average NGO." (The Economist, January 29, 2000)

It must be noted, however, that these beneficial elements can only become established where foreign enterprises operate on a *locally productive* basis (as opposed to merely extractive or exploitative). Although few in number on the African continent, these companies have a substantial influence on national tax revenues, labour markets for skilled workers and can act as institutional-structural catalysts for host societies. The everyday work and life in such corporations has no representative character for the biggest parts of the African economy, and even less for the general society. Nevertheless, they potentially may become factors of development and stability to a much greater extent than their own size and turnover would suggest. As a concluding remark I would add that in economically and institutionally highly developed societies the leverage of Multinational Corporations on societal development greatly diminishes and many of the above stated benefits of this organisation type can as well be achieved by smaller and less integrated enterprises.

Throughout the aid sector, efficiency upgrades have also been achieved. Aid effectiveness assessments and impact observations are extensively applied in order to monitor and enhance the performance of projects. Yet, in spite of any formal efficiency criteria, it might be the case that the value of development cooperation cannot readily be measured by the same criteria that are applied to enterprises. As I tried to demonstrate, the different types of Transboundary Cooperations between the West, South Asia and Africa might lead to different structures of cooperation and exchange on a very practical level. The way in which the people involved perceive and act within a cooperation is interwoven with the epistemology embedded in the organisation structures of the cooperation itself. It is therefore not self-evident that any boundary crossing cooperation automatically leads to cooperative outcomes or a shared understanding. As we have seen in the case of development aid organisations, the maintenance of a formal cooperation can work as a goal in itself, even when the technical results or the emergence of shared understanding in fact remains low.

At the end of this study, I would conclude that the quality of the Transboundary Cooperations between Europe and Africa can still largely be improved. A search for better approaches should be included in the routines, especially those of bilateral actors.

Bayart, the political scientist, mentioned that the community of European actors and the Western world should admit their far-reaching ignorance of the ways in which African societies work and how their inhabitants seek to organise their affairs. Conclusively, development as a whole might just as well be left to Africans themselves (Bayart/Jolys/Osmanovic 2003:410). The goals of development, such as basic human rights and individual freedom, must be recognized and secured by populations instead of implemented by projects.

Until today, however, large parts of many African economies are directed at subsistence or at rent extraction. Both modes help to maintain the livelihood of the social core community, such as kin groups, but cannot generate surplus. Development aid in many cases merely provides additional means for sustaining this unproductive constellation even longer. Surplus is not only to be understood in material terms, it equally manifests itself in the emergence of supportive institutions and societal strength. For Transboundary Cooperations this implies that they should be more productive in their outcomes. They should not be focussed on what the actors involved expect to see in the 'other'. Instead the focus should be directed at the global potential which nowadays is available everywhere on the planet. Prosperity might come after productivity, but not without it. This is going to happen as soon as more profits can be made, and more wealth can be achieved, by productive approaches than by means of rent extraction.

The African continent is emerging on a new path of dynamic development, and with it the ways in which transnational actors cooperate on behalf of interests on this continent will also greatly evolve. Throughout this book we have considered the relevance of cooperations across boundaries and cultures, touched on the epistemology of the culturally strange and unaccountable. Building on this we explained the meaning of differences and diversities and applied these insights to the observation of organisations. We looked at a selection of case studies, applied our analytical tools and could identify several types of Transboundary Cooperations. Assessments of the underlying principles and effectiveness of transnational enterprises and development aid were made. The ideal form of a Transboundary Cooperation did not emerge from the empirical material thus far but potentials were discussed.

It should finally be mentioned that a good Transboundary Cooperation must indeed support the exchange of knowledge and understanding and at the same time leaves free space for the recognition of the unexpected that may emerge from the 'other'. By this, I would assume, the elements that are necessary to inspire local productivity and meaningful exchange are brought together.

8. Appendix

8.1 THE INSTITUTIONALISATION TEST

During this study a lot has been said about institutionalisation processes in organisations. The term 'institutionalisation' was introduced in the context of sociological Neo-Institutionalism and then developed into a practically relevant working concept in Chapter 5.2 to assess the case studies along the dimension of 'institutionalisation vs. technical orientation' (Chapter 5.2).

For readers interested in applying this concept to their own organisations, a brief outline of an institutionalisation test is presented here. This test should be taken as a rough guideline on how to introduce the idea of institutionalised organisations into one's own qualitative fieldwork or advisory activity. It is a slightly modified version of Kühl's approach, published in his previously quoted article on organisational fashions in the development sector (2004:236-240). The theoretical background of sociological Neo-Insititutionalisation is further exemplified in Chapter 8.2.

A heuristical test of the intensity of organisational institutionalisation

To determine whether and to what extent a given organisation is subjected to institutionalisation processes, this powerful approach begins with a basic question related to the nature of the organisation's primary mission: is an organisation dominated by *goals* or *values*? Goals provide a directive guidance for action while values signify that a cause is legitimate. Values have an integrative effect but are more diffuse while goals have steering abilities. Kühl identifies a strong orientation on abstract values in development organisations. Guidance by clear goals points to the importance of technical environments while guidance by values indicates the relevance of institutional legitimation. Thus, the more an organisation is controlled by abstract values instead of clear-cut goals, the stronger it may be subjected to institutionalisation effects. Five simple tests help to verify these orientations empirically:

(1) The accordance test

Important values applied in organisations usually concern major issues of societal relevance. The nature of such values is 'good', and so is the mission to pursue their promulgation. Thus, one of their characteristics is the difficulty to be against them. The person who argues against such a value carries the burden of explanation and moral justification. When a concept has been established as a value it does not mean that criticism becomes impossible, but criticism usually takes a specific structure. The first form of legitimate criticism is never directed against the goal itself but laments that it has previously been reached in the wrong way. A second form of criticism aims at mentioning that the concept has not yet delivered the expected results. A third form of internally legitimate criticism is directed against too high a degree of abstractness. Criticism against value guided activities of organisations asks only *how* things are done or defined. It never asks *if* they should be done at all. Intended or not, this form of criticism safeguards an organisational concept against *fundamental* critics. Example: When a project acknowledgedly fails that was conducted under the title of 'capacity development' this can only be attributed to errors in the concept, project design or execution, but the general idea remains untouched because 'capacity development' is one of the currently important values in development aid.

(2) The tautology test

Organisational and institutional values take the form of circular constructions which easily become tautological. Kühl presents a simple test procedure, building on Gälweiler (1986:89ff). Tautological explanations are at hand when something is recommended where the negation of that recommendation would lead to an alternative that self-evidently is out of question. As an example, the typical recommendation of management literature to proactively react to changes and surprises (Covery 1990, after Kühl 2004:238) reveals its tautological nature through its negation: not much speaks in favour of letting oneself be surprised by changes in business. The same management author is equally correct in suggesting attending to the most important things first. It is obviously not helpful to take care of most the important things at the end. As an example from the development sector, the concept of 'capacity development' is defined by major donor agencies as the ability of individuals, institutions and organisations to solve problems and to reach the development goals of their countries in an efficient, participative and sustainable way. But, who can seriously argue in favour of not reaching development goals?

Who would like to demand inefficient short-term development policies which rejects participation? (Kühl 2004:238). Organisations operating with such values possess a built-in autodefence against result-oriented critics. They need it to work under highly ambiguous conditions.

(3) The tool test

The function of goals in organisations is to correctly guide the allocation of means and resources. They have to be measurable and to enable the discussion as to which instrument will be most effective in a given situation. Due to their inherent abstractness, values, on the contrary, are not capable of providing guidance for the selection of operative means and instruments. Often no instruments are developed that can be applied to the execution or implementation of values. Example: capacity development as an ambiguous value of development aid gives no specific guidance as to how it can be reached. This leads to the situation that almost all practices and instruments already present in the development sector can be seen as supportive to it. The result is that the organisational realisation of values is quasi-automatic but rather symbolic, and all the conducted activities appear to have been supportive to it.

(4) The evaluation test

Unlike goals, values cannot be directly evaluated. They don't function as concrete guidelines because they have no directive qualities. Compliance with them cannot be measured, this remains open to individual or political judgement. In development organisations a gap has to be closed between the need to present a proof of short and medium-term effects and the resolve to stand up for a concept that will only show results over the very long term and where the results cannot be easily tracked back to single actors. Here the focus on values serves as an umbrella to cover these conflicting demands.

(5) The hierarchy of values test

Another way to identify values as steering factors in organisations is their reluctance to fit into a priority order (hierarchy of importance). Or, if they do fit into a priority order they tend to lose their character as a value. It is obvious that such defined value hierarchies wouldn't be rational for institutionalised organisations because they would lead to a fixed set of preferences independent of the concrete situation at hand. This is not what these organisations seek, as they aim at manoeuvring with all values at once according to the situation. The effect is that on the level of words and terms a symbiosis of the different values is acknowledged that is not always easy to achieve in practice. According to these abstract beliefs, for example, human rights, environmental protection, economic dynamism, aid for the poorest and a rational use of tax money are not only combinable but also mutually supportive and strengthening. But as practice shows, in situations of practical decision making in development cooperation values are often conflictive. The result is an 'elastic value opportunism'. It may be rational in one situation to promote peace at the expense of freedom, and in another situation to promote freedom while sacrificing peace. Equally in development aid, it has shown to be rational at one time, e.g. to promote a quick construction of roads after an only vague consultation of the population while at another time, however, one might establish a participative and time consuming programme under the label of capacity development (Kühl 2004:236-240).

8.2 THEORIES FOR ORGANISATION FIELD RESEARCH

Organisation research as a scientific field is notorious for its plurality of different and partially competing theories. Each of them points to a particular set of crucial issues while possibly neglecting others. With the many different issues in mind that are brought up by empirical fieldwork it thus turned out to be unlikely that a single 'school' or 'stream' of organisation theory would sufficiently handle every relevant aspect of Transboundary Cooperations.

The general meaning and the central importance of the terms *actor, institution and organisation* were previously explained in Chapter 2.3. What now follows is an introduction to a selection of organisation theory that provided a relevant input to the general concept or the assessment of the case studies. A closer look reveals incompatibilities between theories and research agendas. Even though viewpoints might be at odds among different schools of organisation research, this ought not to prevent their combination and adaptation for my specific purposes. A similar suggestion is made by Preisendörfer 2005, while in a similar sense Chabal/Daloz (1999, 2006) propose a theoretical syncretism, and for the field of organisational analysis, Bea and Göbel (1999) highlight the fact that no single organisation theory will ever cover all relevant aspects. In the remainder of this section a brief account of three most important approaches is given: a) New Institutional Economics, b) Sociological Neo-Institutionalism, and c) Actor-Centred Institutionalism.

a) Trust, cooperation and transaction costs: New Institutional Economics

Matters of trust and cooperation are basic factors in organisations, and especially in transnational cooperation (and even more so in African low trust societies).

The concept of individual rationalism is prominently included in the New Institutional Economics (NIE) and its approach to trust and cooperation. This set of theories combines an economical view on rational agency with a wider institutionalist framework. The most comprehensive and also best known part of NIE is formed by 'Transaction Cost Economics'. This sub-stream is mainly concerned with the question of why social and economic transactions of some types are predominantly executed through markets while others are handled within organisations. It also attempts to explain under which conditions which institutional arrangements might be empirically expected (Preisendörfer 2005:42ff).

Institutional arrangements: this term refers to the broader set of institutions (rules of the game) within which people and organisations operate. Three forms are usually identified: markets, hybrid contracts and organisations/hierarchies (Williamson 1985). The settings 'market' and 'organisation/hierarchy' are opposite extremes in a continuum. Markets aim at maximising externalities, while hybrid contracts are semi-organised and range from bilateral coordination to franchises and joint ventures (many African SMEs tend towards hybrid forms instead of organisations in a strict sense, see case 4). Organisations with their inherent hierarchical structures concentrate on processes with greater coordination complexity and would be too expensive otherwise.

In the handling of ambiguous interactions among non-equal participants, markets are rather inefficient as transaction complexities are too high to be handled on the spot. It can thus be stated that Transboundary Cooperations are not among the most suitable candidates for market arrangements. Organisations are in many cases better suited to meeting the specific conditions in place when it becomes necessary to integrate the global heterogeneity *within* one's own operations, and when transactions are related to translation. Hence the empirical focus on organisations. I did not encounter a workable 'market'-like Transboundary Cooperation at the time of research. Further challenges arise in African environments due to a comparatively low maturity of market structures which drives larger corporate actors to higher degrees of organisational self-reliance (see the brewery in case 2, where many things were organised internally).

b) Symbolism and legitimation: Sociological Neo-Institutionalism

Organisations are not only determined through choices based on material maximisation and technical rationality. A common starting point for organisation research within the framework of Neo-Institutionalism is the observation that activities of organisations are shaped to a great extent through 'myths of rationality' (Meyer/Rowan 1991[40]). Actors often have to accept contradictions between technical demands and physically measurable realities on the one hand and the evaluative, symbolic and representational demands of institutional environments on the other. In this respect a common interest of organisations is the maintenance of a high legitimation in accordance with professional standards and accepted procedures. Neo-Institutionalism points out that an established track record for doing things in a professional way cannot be seen as a factual equivalent of excellent work results, but it provides institutional legitimation for the actor. Note that actors would find it extremely more difficult to derive their institutional legitimation from effective work results alone. A common example for a strong institutional orientation is the practice of hospitals treating patients according to established medical procedures. The evaluation of hospital effectiveness does not much depend on the question how many of these patients are actually *cured*, but rather on whether the patients have been *treated correctly* according to the established medical procedures. Similarly, donor agencies in development aid carry out programmes and projects according to the directions of development policy and in line with the practices of project management. In the end the question is not so much whether a factual reduction of poverty has actually occurred in the target population, or, more directly, what the project's outcome was in the banal terms of life's daily struggle, but rather whether the necessary number of targeted people were involved and necessary cooperation partners participated. We see that institutional legitimation is achieved when the right things are done correctly and reflected appropriately by the social environment. Although in organisations such as development agencies or hospitals the actors build their work on technical procedures and are driven by the intention to achieve palpable results, their professional success actually depends on their performance in the fields of the 'ambiguous'. Neither 'health' nor 'development' are exactly measurable. The organisations are thus dependant on their institutional environments for a legitimation of their activities. In this sense, acceptance and legitimation comes from adherence to the symbolical rules of the game, and not from apparently factual achievements.

---

40 Note: All references to Meyer and Rowan's article from 1977 are made to the reprint in Powell/DiMaggio (1991).

Elements of symbolic legitimation applied by successful organisations tend to become imitated by followers who incorporate them into their own set-ups. In this way many aspects of organisational life are becoming more alike worldwide, and many elements of organisational behaviour increasingly resemble each other all over the world – not just because they are good or effective (which they might or might not be), but rather because a sense of 'correctness' is attached to them. These mimetic-institutional influences on organisations can be extremely powerful. It is also not uncommon that they reach an extent where they have the adverse effect of replacing inner-organisational learning and innovation with a habit of symbolic reference to external sources of legitimation.

On the theoretical side, Neo-Institutionalism directly opposes scientific positions that mostly focus on rational actors, as the approach of New Institutional-Economics does, even though both streams share the focus on institutions. The aim of Neo-Institutionalism is to surpass the limits of a focus on individual rationality as a main driving force in organisations. Instead it concentrates on the handling of ambiguity through institutions (DiMaggio/Powell 1991a:3ff). Detailed introductions can be found in DiMaggio/Powell (1991a), Preisendörfer (2005: 145ff), Walgenbach (1999) and others. Von Oppen and Rottenburg (1995) applied a Neo-Institutionalist approach in their work on African organisational anthropology. The following paragraphs give an outline of aspects of Sociological Neo-Institutionalism that are relevant to this research work.

Influence of institutional environments: Organisations adopt new elements because they are externally legitimated, and not because of their immediate efficiency. The compliance of organisations with institutionalised rules and expectations may be more important than inner effectiveness (Walgenbach 1999:330).

Organisational legitimation: The reduction of uncertainty and the enhancement of their survivability are seen as the primary goals of organisations. An organisation and its management gain legitimation through the compliance to institutionally acknowledged rules and the incorporation of symbolic practices (cf Meyer/Rowan 1991, DiMaggio/Powell 1991:75). Dettmar (1995) observed such legitimation processes in German-Nigerian joint ventures. Such practices of external legitimation can lead to an abandonment of intentional and internally reflected action in favour of merely copying what comes from outside (policies based on buzzwords, management fashions, etc.). Quite often such adaptations enhance the predictability of organisational behaviour which in turn enhances legitimation. An ideally legitimated organisation is completely covered by unquestionable standards, fulfilled expectations and adhered rules. All its goals and values appear important and all practices are positively sanctioned.

Legitimacy vs. efficiency: Highly institutionalised organisations often attempt to reach a state of complete legitimation. This can become a goal in itself, and possibly even contradict the goal of practical effectiveness. Almost everyone knows examples of departments and administrations whose output is negligible because they are so busy meeting regulation targets. As a result, new elements such as technical innovations, management methods or policies may become incorporated even when they have potentially negative impacts on technical efficiency. This happens when their implementation is expected by relevant institutional environments.

Diffusion and isomorphism: One central result of institutionalisation is the tendency of organisations to develop increasing similarities among each other. They tend to model themselves on similar organisations that are endowed with the appearance of a higher legitimation or seen as more successful. "The ubiquity of certain kinds of structural arrangements can more likely be credited to the universality of mimetic processes than to any concrete evidence that the adopted models enhance efficiency" (DiMaggio/Powell 1991:70). The underlying diffusion processes are driven by enforced rules, professional standards or outright imitation. As a general effect from these pursuits of institutional legitimation, organisations tend towards structural isomorphism.

In a nutshell, to secure organisational legitimacy and survival, organisations often do things "independent of the immediate efficacy" (Meyer/Rowan 1991:41). This means that they aim at conformity with institutionalised rules and accept conflicts with technical efficiency. The hypothetical opposite, a pure orientation on technical efficiency can be associated with high costs in terms of legitimation and rule conformity. Thus, being efficient is not enough when there is a lack of institutional legitimation.[41]

c) Actor Centred Institutionalism

Mayntz/Scharpf (1995) and Scharpf (1997) presented an approach to analysing actors and organisations. They take into account how the outcome of decisions and interactions among rationally operating actors is influenced by different types of actor constellations and institutional contexts. Political and organisational decisions depend as much on structural and institutional factors as on the actual decision problem. This means that the same issue might lead to a different outcome

---

41 This contradiction is a frequent element in the plot of action films with a rude but efficient police agent as the main protagonist. The agent breaks the rules of 'good policemanship' and thereby becomes an efficient hunter of criminals. His boss gets angry and demands compliance to the rules at first but is happy in the end because the criminals have been wiped out.

when negotiated under a different actor constellation, even when the same actors would be present.

What makes this model interesting here is the insight that the ways in which Transboundary Cooperations operate are not only formed by their task and purpose, but also through the underlying actor constellations and institutional backgrounds. This is actually one of the primary staring points for the present work on Transboundary Cooperations.

When we apply the latter to the Rwandan scene we can see that the local situation and the transcultural context pose some specific demands on foreign actors. However, the organisation's own set up and its own (!) institutional constellation determine how it deals with this and what outcome is derived at the end. It is a central proposition of my work to demonstrate that the concrete settings of Transboundary Cooperations have to be taken into account and that a general recourse to 'African conditions' or intercultural relations does not lead to sufficient explanations.

Institutional analysis and the rule of declining abstraction: What can be explained on the institutional level does not need to be explained on the level of independent actors. In many cases institutional information is sufficient to provide satisfying explanations and is therefore pragmatically useful to lower the degree of abstraction incrementally only where necessary. Although institutionalised rules are variable in time and space, they provide a stable form for the spaces that are guided by them. They are therefore a main source of regularities in organisational behaviour.

Actors as determining subjects: Actors make decisions and conduct activities. Institutions are sets of rules which guide the actor's choices. Individual humans are the principal actor type, while corporate actors and organisations are social entities consisting of individual actors but with additional characteristics.

8.3 FIELDWORK AND QUALITATIVE METHODOLOGY

The empirical data was gathered by means of anthropological fieldwork. It was generated in a sequence of field intervals with a total of nine months, covering a period of five years. Reflecting the comparative interest, the research design includes a variety of scenarios which led to seven case studies. In total the empirical material provided a grand picture of the field of interest, highlighting different facets much better than one stationary long-term study in one single organisation could (for multi-sited ethnography; Nadai/Maeder 2005, Marcus 1995).

As a means of access to the 'field' I mostly relied on personal contacts, mutual understandings and formal as well as informal research agreements. Such an approach proved to be a pragmatic way of dealing with sensitive topics under ambiguous conditions which often take place in hierarchical and competitive environments. What made the topic sensitive was the concern with personal attitudes, business relationships, administrative and political backgrounds. Obtaining such personal information was not a goal in itself but rather the precondition for seeing the anthropologically relevant aspects of the situation. The field data therefore could mostly not be obtained in a formal way. Aspects reaching into the privacy of individuals or organisations were excluded from the analytical work and are, as mentioned, not the target of a comparative organisation study. In regard of this privacy issue, Chapman (2001) gives helpful explanations on conducting ethnography in business studies and on the worthwhile effort of a qualitative approach to research on such occasions. When relying on highly personalised access to field data, ethnography, when carried out according to scientific standards, is not to be mistaken for detective work.

"The task of cultural understanding [...] involves observing what occurs between people in the intersubjective realm. These exchanges take place in the clear light of public interactions; they do not entail the mysteries of empathy or require extraordinary capacities for going inside people's heads, or worse, their souls." (Rosaldo 1999:30)

Doing fieldwork and the interpretative paradigm in social research

The grand ambition of anthropology is to take the actor's point of view into account and build its models and analyses to a greater extent from this 'internal' perspective. From a methodological point of view, social anthropology largely belongs to the category of qualitative-interpretative sciences. The social scientist is, by the act of research itself, a participant in the social scene that is to be researched, and thus never a truly independent observer.

Interpretative research is usually inductive and open, thus without a strictly formulated hypothesis that has to be verified. Instead, the researcher works on one or several case studies to develop his assumptions step by step. Quite often the best questions emerge from the proceedings of research and not all of them are necessarily to be asked right at the beginning. With growing understanding the researcher's vision becomes increasingly precise.

Characteristics of anthropological field research

According to Olivier de Sardan, anthropological fieldwork is characterised as an intermediary zone between epistemology and methodology (1995:74). This may to a large extent be due to the need of working with ideas and concepts that are constantly under-determined and without final statistical approval. An ethnographer's open approach to the field makes the discovery of new and unintended aspects more likely than research paradigms working with preformulated hypotheses. "Ethnographers are not interested in testing hypotheses, but in understanding a group of people." (Mouly/Sankaran 1995:34) It is clear that ethnographic field research is not about statistical validity, and consequently this is not regarded as one of its core qualifications. But, on the other hand, the practice of field anthropology is not just a matter of 'feeling', as it incorporates distinctive scientific competencies and standards. And

"opposed to journalists, novelists, makers of documentaries or other commentators, an ethnographer always follows an established paradigm of data generation and analysis embedded in an epistemological concept [...], his undertakings are therefore theoretically informed. [...] Where a view from within is provided, it has to be accompanied by a perceptual concept if it has to be called ethnography." (Mouly/Sankaran 1995:37, building their considerations on Sanday 1979)

Grounded theory

The steps between the explorative phase of fieldwork and the final formulation of analytical statements demand a strategy for data analysis and theory construction. This purpose was met by the grounded theory approach. My individual application of this concept is based on Wester's book (1995), which is a modified adaptation of the original publications by Glaser/Strauss (1967), Glaser (1978) and others. Grounded theory aims at a systematic development of qualitative theory, which derives its elements solely from field data. This makes it an inductive method directed at the content derived from the research subject itself, in opposition to formal theories based on axioms and predefined rules.

Data interpretation and theory construction in grounded theory always retain a preliminary character, and in the process of fieldwork each iteration of additional cycles of research and re-interpretation contributes to a deeper understanding of the subject. Glaser and Strauss demand this procedure to be repeated until a state of saturation is reached, which means that no additional data is found through which the researcher may discover new aspects of his subject. When additional input repeatedly leads to the same conclusions the researcher becomes empirically confident that his conceptual understanding of the subject is saturated. The whole process is iterative, or cyclic, and follows a pattern of 'reflection' >> 'observation' >> 'analysis' >> 'reflection' (Wester 1995:126). The goal is the achievement of a theoretically supported terminology based upon categories that emerged out of the original qualitative data.

However, one liability central to this process is the difficulty of generalisation and the fact that the research candidates (cases) of a survey are mostly not selected at random. A statistical generalisation is therefore not possible (Wester 1995:203). Nevertheless, despite a potential lack of formal generalisation, grounded theory leads to results which are highly *adequate* descriptions and explanations of their research subjects. Instead of comparing many objects according to a pre-formulated frame of reference it delivers a way of obtaining insights that have a strong fit with the observed subject. This is a way of conducting valid social science in heterogeneous settings.

Collection and treatment of field data

When fieldwork covers issues that are not merely 'cultural' in the sense of folklore but also touch organisations, administrations, work environments and business affairs, the availability of willing conversation partners and informants is not always self-evident. As an example, even a director in a bigger company who personally promised his support would not do anything that involved written documents. In such constellations an informal 'low-profile' strategy let the researcher blend into the environment, easing the situation and facilitating personal interaction. This informal approach turned out to be a methodical advantage and opened very fruitful possibilities for conversations and personal contacts of mutual benefit. Chapman made similar experiences: "Even managers who felt that it would be hard for them to find the time, have allowed the interviews to run on for several hours, and have given the appearance of enjoying them" (2001:26). In sum, the advantages of a low-profile, individual field access became evident in almost every research setting.

In several cases, participant observation lead to insights that are normally not intended for the public domain (anything between personal life situations and strategic business relationships). This fact brought with it the challenge of including data from such fieldwork where possible while securing the anonymity and confidence of involved persons and events. In addition to the anonymised quotes excluding various passages from the notes could not be avoided, nor could 'softening' them in such a way that they lost their 'edge' and became more general. Each quotation is identified by a short characterisation of the informant and transcribed closely to the oral original. Previously published examples for the use of anonymised field data include Hüsken's (2006) ethnographic study of German development experts and Mouly/Sankaran's (1995) fieldwork in the "conflictive setting" of a government agency where they even invented alternate names of departments and personnel. In his profound analysis of bilateral development practice, Rottenburg (2002, 2009) faced a similar challenge and fictionalised a whole ethnography.[42]

Qualitative analysis – analytic induction

Interpretation and presentation of qualitative data has to take into account the needs of a scientific readership and consequently has to relate to established terminologies and conventions. But it also has to pay respect to the constitution of an informant's own assumptions about the topic. This point may get lost when translating observations and statements into one's own conceptual framework, even though the practice of ethnographic fieldwork has a high probability of fulfilling both requirements. "Ethnography is a tool of thought through which people [...] can come to know the depth of differences separating them, grasp the precise nature of these differences, and construct a public vocabulary through which they can seriously talk to one another." (Rosaldo 1999:33)

For the act of qualitative analysis itself, an adapted version of the 'analytic induction' procedure turned out to be appropriate. It was introduced by Znanecki (1934), adopted by Denzin (1978:192f) and Wester (1995:152ff). As an analytic tool, it helps to search for patterns in qualitative data in the last phases of research when grounded theory has already produced certain conceptual categories and terms. It works as a test for a limited number of field hypotheses (Wester 1995:152). The analysis itself is an iterative process in which all available data from selected cases are confronted with a field hypothesis. Every positive match of the hypothesis and a specific characteristic of a research case contributes to a 'theory under construction'. The final theory is developed by a continuously renewed definition of the analytical item through a cyclic confrontation of the 'theory under construction' with negative cases which do not confirm the current hypothesis. The following steps illustrate the procedure:

1. Global definition of analytical item (e.g. "local assimilation"), derived from grounded theory.
2. Formulation of field hypothesis.

---

42 Rottenburg's act of fictionalisation was severely criticised by Kienzler (2005) for the seemingly correct reasons of scientific clarity and transparency. Yet, in my opinion, the analytical and normative value of the publication remains definitely undisputed. It is more to the point than many seemingly true accounts on similar subjects.

3. Examination of empirical case to check if hypothesis covers the case.
4. If not, analytical items will be re-defined with the aim to either exclude the case or to re-formulate the hypothesis. Excluding cases indicates that a hypothesis is at least less general, if not wrong.
5. In some cases, certain confirmation of the hypothesis is often available. Discovery of negative cases falsifies the explanation and therefore demands its re-formulation.
6. The procedure of case research, re-definition of analytical items and re-formulation of the hypothesis will be continued until the analytical items/hypotheses conform to the empirical descriptions. In this process every negative case demands re-formulation and re-definition of the hypothesis.

To sum up, analytic induction is a search strategy that filters out the most adequate analytic explanation for the empirical material on the basis of what is currently known about it (Wester 1995:155).

The setting in Rwanda – illustrating quotes

To round up this chapter I present various quotes from Rwandan interview partners, characterising the overall situation in the country during the time of the research. Disclaimer: The situation in the country is subject to constant change and the comments about the situation at large might possibly be considered one-sided, under-complex and already outdated. Nevertheless I decided to include some accidental statements for purely illustrative purposes:

In one situation a German expatriate complained about the numerous delays during a work-related travel caused by her Rwandan colleagues. One of them commented: *"I don't always need to be exactly on time. I'm not a minister."* (Ministers and high-ranking officials were known for their renowned and notorious punctuality which they displayed as a sign for the new direction that Rwanda was about to take.)

Concerning anti-corruption rules:
"People from the Congo have to adapt here. When your car gets stopped by the police and you say 'Hello Chef' and you attempt to shake the officer's hands to give him a banknote, you can run into serious trouble" [Rwandan immigrant from the DRC].

Discussion with an internationally experienced Rwandan businessman. He vehemently criticised a group of development experts for what he saw as naff and unsound talk about the Rwandan government. He emphasised the increasing stability of the rule of law. Businessman: *"Rwanda is so strict! ... Soon, Rwanda will not be an African country anymore [because laws are universally applied, and regulations effective and respected]."* Anthropologist [trying to provoke him]: „*But in the really big business and in big politics, doesn't it somehow seem to be different?"* Businessman: *"In the big business it's sometimes African again, because they have to survive."*

Concerning the professionalisation of public administrations:
"Foreigners permanently complain that the new mayors are all from [certain groups], but I have to say nowadays at least the posts are given to competent people, and that is also important" [Expatriate director of an aid agency].

Talk with a university teacher, watching the early evening traffic jam in Kigali city. Anthropologist: *"So many cars, incredible";* Teacher: *"Yes."* Anthropologist: *"I remember some years ago, there was much less traffic. Good to see people moving now."* Informant: „*Yes, the cars became many."* Anthropologist: *"Hmm."* Informant: *"I wonder where they've got that money from. Maybe from the Congo... but not from here."* Anthropologist: *"You think Rwandan money could not buy so many cars, or what?"* Informant: *"Not at all, where? You don't get enough money when you work only in Rwanda like normal."*

9. References

Ackermann, Andreas (2004): Das Eigene und das Fremde: Hybridität, Vielfalt und Kulturtransfers. In: Jaeger, Friedrich/Rüsen, Jörn (eds.): Handbuch der Kulturwissenschaften. Themen und Tendenzen, Band 3. Stuttgart, Weimar: J. B. Metzler. [The own and the strange: hybridity, plurality and culture transfers].

AfricaFocus Bulletin (2011): Africa: Economic Outlook. 15 January 2011. In: AllAfrica.com, http://allafrica.com/stories/printable/201101171176.html.

African Union (2005): Review of the Millennium Declaration and the Millennium Development Goals (MDGs): An African Common Position, produced by the African Union, in collaboration with the African Development Bank, UN Economic Commission for Africa, NEPAD, and UNDP.

African Union (2005b): Ministerial Statement, Thirty-Eighth Session of the Economic Commission on Africa / Conference of African Ministers of Finance, Planning and Economic Development, Abuja, Nigeria, 15 May.

Ang, Ien (2003): Together-in-Difference: Beyond Diaspora, into Hybridity. In: Asian Studies Review 27(2), p. 141-154.

Auty, Rick (2003): Towards a Resource-Driven Model of Governance: Application to Lower-Income Transition Economies. ZEF-Discussion Papers on Development Policy No. 60, Center for Development Research, Bonn, February 2003.

Axelrod, Robert (1984): The Evolution of Cooperation. New York.

Bachmann-Medick, Doris (2007): Cultural Turns. Neuorientierungen in den Kulturwissenschaften. 2. Auflage Reinbek bei Hamburg. [Cultural turns. New orientations in the cultural sciences].

Barlett, C.A./S. Ghoshal (1987): Managing Across Borders: New Organizational Responses. In: Sloan Management Review 2, p. 43-53.

Barlett, C.A./S. Ghoshal (1988): Organizing for Worldwide Effectiveness. In: California Management Review 31, p. 54-74.

Bayart, Jean-Francois (1993): The State in Africa: The Politics of the Belly. New York: Longman Publishing.
Bayart, Jean-Francois (2000): Africa in the world: a history of extraversion. In: African Affairs (2000), 99, p. 217-67.
Bayart, Jean-Francois (2004): Commentary: Towards a New Start for Africa and Europe. In: African Affairs, 103/412, p. 453-458.
Bayart, Jean-FrancoisJolys, Odile/Osmanovic, Armin (2003): Afrikas Dynamik und Europas Politik, und wo bleibt die deutsche Afrikawissenschaft? An interview. In: Afrika spectrum 38 (2003) 3, p. 409-413. [Africa's dynamics and Europe's politics, and where is German African studies got?].
Blenford, Adam (2007): China in Africa: Developing ties. In: BBC News, 26 November 2007. http://news.bbc.co.uk/2/hi/africa/7086777.stm (08 September 2009).
Bea, Franz Xaver/Göbel, Elisabeth (1999): Organisation. Stuttgart: UTB Lucius & Lucius.
Beck, Kurt (1991): Entwicklungshilfe als Beute. Über die lokale Aneignung von Entwicklungsmaßnahmen im Sudan. In: Orient. Deutsche Zeitschrift für Politik und Wirtschaft des Orients, 31, p. 583-601. [Development aid as booty].
Beyer, Jürgen (2001): "One best way" oder Varietät? Strategien und Organisationsstrukturen von Großunternehmen im Prozess der Internationalisierung, in: Soziale Welt 52/1, p. 7-28. [One best way or variety? - Strategies and organisation structures of large enterprises in the process of internationalsiation].
Beyer, Jürgen (2001a): "One best way" oder Varietät? Strategischer und organisatorischer Wandel von Großunternehmen im Prozess der Internationalisierung. MPIfG Discussion Paper 01 / 2, Mai 2001.
Bharati, A. (1972): The Asians in East Africa. Chicago: Nelson-Hall Company.
Biallas, Axel/Knauer, Jan (2006): Von Bandung zum Ölgeschäft: Indien und Inder in Afrika. In: GIGA-focus, Nummer 1, Januar 2006. German Institute for Global and Area Studies, Institut für Afrika-Kunde. [From Bandung to oil business: India and Indians in Africa].
Bierschenk, Thomas (1988): Development Projects as Arenas of Negotiation for Strategic Groups. A Case Study from Benin. In: Sociologia Ruralis 27, 2/3, p. 146 160.
Bierschenk, Thomas/Chauveau, Jean-Pierre/Olivier de Sardan, Jean-Pierre (2000): Courtiers en développement. Les villages africains en quête de projets. Paris, Karthala; Mayence, APAD.
Blume, Georg/Grill, Bartholomäus (2008): Afrikas neue Freunde. In: Die Zeit, 10 January 2008. [Africa's new friends].

Boiral, Oliver (2003): ISO 9000: Outside the Iron Cage. Organization Science Vol. 14,No. 6, November–December 2003, p. 720–737.

Bräutigam, Deborah (2003): Close Encounters: Chinese Business Networks as Industrial Catalysts in Sub-Saharan Africa. In: African Affairs (2003), 102, p. 447–467.

Broadman, Harry G. (2007): Africa's Silk Road: China and India's New Economic Frontier. Washington. The World Bank.

Burrel, G./Morgan, G. (1979): Sociological Paradigms and Organizational Theory. London.

Business Times (2005): Power shortages slow down hair salon business. Business Times Kigali, April 18-19, 2005.

Business Times (2005): Rwacom is losing 30% of its products. Business Times Kigali, April 18-19, 2005.

Callaghy, Thomas/Ronald Kassimir/Robert Latham (eds.)(2001): Intervention and Transnationalism in Africa. Global-Local Networks of Power. Cambrige University Press: Cambridge, New York.

Campbell, Christian (ed.)(2006): Legal Aspects of Doing Business in Africa 2006. Yorkhill Law Publishing

Cannon, Patrick (2005): Intervention and Transnationalism in Africa. Global-Local Networks of Power, book review. In: Journal of Third World Studies, Spring 2005.

Chabal, Patrick/Daloz, Jean-Pascal (1999): Africa Works. The Political Instrumentalization of Disorder. Bloomington: International African Institute in association with James Currey and Indiana University Press.

Chabal, Patrick/Daloz, Jean-Pascal (2006): Culture Troubles. Politics and the Interpretation of Meaning. Chicago: The University of Chicago Press.

Chapman, Malcolm (2001): Anthropology and business studies: Some Considerations of Method. In: Gellner, David und Eric Hirsch (eds.): Inside Organizations. Anthropologists at Work. Oxford, New York. p. 19-34.

Chowdhury, Shyamal K. (2002): Attaining Universal Access: Public-Private Partnership and Business-NGO Partnership, ZEF – Discussion Papers On Development Policy No. 48, Center for development Research, Bonn.

Christie, P./R. Lessem/L. Mbigi (eds.)(1994): African Management. Randburg.

Clark, John F. (Ed.): The African Stakes of the Congo War. Kampala: Fountain Publishers.

Cohen, Robin (2008): Global diasporas: an introduction. Second edition. London and New York: Routledge.

Colson, E. (1967): The Social Organisation of the Gwembe Tonga. Manchester, M. Univ. Press.

Corey, Allison/Joireman, Sandra F. (2004): Retributive justice. The gacaca courts in Rwanda. In: African Affairs, Vol 103, No. 410, p. 73-89.

Covery, Stephen R. (1990): The 7 Habits of Highly Effective People. Franklin Covey.

Davis, Natalie Zemon (1999): Religion and Capitalism Once Again? Jewish Merchant Culture in the Seventeenth Century. In: Sherry B. Ortner (ed.): The Fate of "Culture". Geertz and Beyond. Berkeley: University of California Press, p. 56-85.

Denzin, N.K. (1978): The Research Act. Chicago: Aldine.

Dettmar, Erika (1995): Segregation und soziokulturelle Integration in Joint Ventures. Das Beispiel Nigeria. In: Oppen, Achim von/Richard Rottenburg (eds.): Organisationswandel in Afrika: Kollektive Praxis und kulturelle Aneignung. Berlin. p. 79-106. [Segregation and sociocultural integration in joint ventures. The example of Nigeria].

Dhaliwal, Amarpal (1995): Gender at Work: The Renegotiation of Middle-class Womanhood in a South Asian-Owned Business. In Reviewing Asian America, edited by Wendy L. Ng et al., p. 75-85. Pullman: Washington State University Press.

DiMaggio, Paul J./Powell, Walter W. (1991): The Iron Cage Revisited: Institutional Isomorphism and Collective Rationality in Organizational Fields. In: ibid. (eds.): The New Institutionalism in Organizational Analysis. Chicago-London: University of ChicagoPress, p. 63-82.

DiMaggio, Paul J./Powell, Walter W. (1991a): Introduction. In: Powell, Walter W./DiMaggio, Paul J. (1991): The New Institutionalism in Organizational Analysis. Chicago: University of Chicago Press, p. 1-38.

Doevenspeck, Martin (2007): Lake Kivu's methane gas: natural risk, or source of energy and political security? In: Afrika Spectrum 42 (2007) 1, p. 91-106.

Drechsel, Paul (1999): Paradoxien interkultureller Beziehungen. In: (ibid. et al.)(eds.): Interkulturalität. Grundprobleme der Kulturbegegnung. Mainzer Universitätsgespräche, Sommersemester 1998. Mainz: Johannes Gutenberg-Universität, p. 173-212. [Paradoxes of intercultural relations].

Drechsel, Paul/Schmidt, Bettina (1995): Südafrika. Chancen für eine pluralistische Gesellschaftsordnung. Opladen: Westdeutscher Verlag. [South Africa. Chances for a pluralistic society].

East African Business Week (2006): Small Power Firms Target Lucrative Gap, Kampala, June 19, 2006.

Easterly, William/Levine, Ross (1997): Africa's Growth Tragedy: Policies and Ethnic Divisions. Quarterly Journal of Economics, 112 (4), p. 1203-1250.

ECA (2005). The Millennium Development Goals in Africa: Progress and Challenges, Addis Ababa: ECA.

Emmighaus, A. (1868): Allgemeine Gewerkslehre. Berlin. [General teaching knowledge on crafts and trades].

Eriksen, Thomas Hylland (2006): Diversity Versus Difference: Neo-liberalism in the Minority-Debate. In: Rottenburg, Richard/Schnepel, Burkhard/Shimada, Shingo (eds.) The Making and Unmaking of Differences. Anthropological, Sociological and Philosophical Perspectives. Bielefeld: transcript Verlag, p. 13-25.

Evers, Hans-Dieter/Gerke, Solvay (2005): Knowledge is Power: Experts as Strategic Group. ZEF Working Paper 8a (Center for Development Research, Bonn).

Evers, Hans-Dieter/Schrader, Heiko (eds.) (1993): The moral economy of trade. Ethnicity and developing markets. London and New York: Routhledge.

Falzon, Mark-Anthony (2003): Bombay, Our Cultural Heart: Rethinking relations between homeland and diaspora. In: Ethnic and Racial Studies 26(4), p. 662-683.

Fornäs, Johan (1995): Cultural Theory and Late Modernity. London: Sage.

Forstater, M./MacDonald, J./Raynard, P. (2002): Business and Poverty: Bridging the gap. Resource Centre for the Social Dimensions of Business Practice.

Fox, Richard/King, Barbara (2002) (eds.): Anthropology beyond Culture. Oxford: Berg Publishers.

Frankfurter Rundschau (2005): Hopfen und Malz nicht verloren. 11 March 2005. [Hops and malt not wasted].

Frankfurter Rundschau (2009): Waffen und Hilfe im selben Flugzeug. 12 may 2009. [Arms and aid in the same airplane].

Frynas, Jedrzej George (2004): The Oil Boom in Equatorial Guinea. In: African Affairs, 103/413, p. 527–546.

Fukuyama, Francis (1995): Trust: The Social Virtues and the Creation of Prosperity. New York: Free Press.

Gabriel, Manfred (ed.)(2004): Paradigmen der akteurszentrierten Soziologie. Wiesbaden: VS. [Paradigms of actor centred sociology].

Gallon, Peter-Thomas (1991): Mythos oder Methode bei der Planung von Partizipation: Die verklärte 'Fokololna'-Tradition und 'Soziale Integration' in einem madegassischen Dorf. In: Africa Spectrum 26, 2, 1991, p. 181-197. [Myth or method in the planning of participation: the misty-eyed 'Fokolona' tradition and 'social integration' in a madegassian village].

Gälweiler, Alois (1986): Unternehmensplanung. Grundlagen und Praxis. Campus: Frankfurt/ Main. [Enterprise planning. Foundations and practices].

Gambe, Anabelle/Hummel, Hartwig/Menzel, Ulrich (2001): "Greater China"? Zur Ethnisierung des chinesischen Unternehmertums in Südostasien. In: Hummel, Hartwig/Menzel, Ulrich (eds.): Die Ethnisierung internationaler Wirtschaftsbeziehungen und daraus resultierender Konflikte. Münster: Lit-Verlag. ["Greater China"? On the ethnisation of Chinese entrepreneurship in South-East Asia].

Gambetta, Diego (2000) 'Can We Trust Trust?' In Gambetta, Diego (ed.) Trust: Making and Breaking Cooperative Relations, electronic edition, Department of Sociology, University of Oxford, chapter 13, p. 213-237.

Ghai, Dharam P./Ghai, Yash P. (eds.)(1970): Portrait of a minority. Asians in East Africa. Nairobi: Oxford University Press.

Ghosal, S./Westney, D.E. (1993)(eds.): Organization Theory and the Multinational Corporation. New York: St. Martin's Press.

Gilroy, Michael (2005): The Changing View of Multinational Enterprises and Africa. In: Michael Gilroy/Thomas Gries/Willem A. Naudé (eds.): Multinational Enterprises, Foreign Direct Investment and Growth in Africa. South African Perspectives. Heidelberg: Physica/Springer, p.101-154.

Glaser, B.G. (1978): Theoretical Sensitivity. Advances in the Methodology of Grounded Theory. Mill Valley: Sociology Press.

Glaser, B.G./A.L. Strauss (1967): The Discovery of Grounded Theory. Chicago: Aldine.

Goldstein, A./Pinaud, N./Reisen, H. (2006): The Rise of China and India: What's in it for Africa? Policy Insight No.19.

Gregory, Shaun (2000): The French Military in Africa: past and present. In: African Affairs (2000) 99, p. 435-448.

Gries, Thomas/Naudé, Willem A. (2005): On Global Economic Growth and the Challenge Facing Africa. In: Michael Gilroy/Thomas Gries/Willem A. Naudé (eds.): Multinational Enterprises, Foreign Direct Investment and Growth in Africa. South African Perspectives. Heidelberg: Physica/Springer, p. 7-36.

Gronemeyer, Marianne (1992): Helping. In: Wolfgang Sachs (ed): The Development Dictionary. A guide to Knowledge as Power. Johannesburg: Witwatersrand University Press, p. 53-69.

GTZ (2005): Erfolgreiche Zusammenarbeit – nachhaltige Wirkungen. Projektergebnisse der GTZ und ihrer Partner. Neunte Querschnittsanalyse. http://www.gtz.de/de/dokumente/de-gtz-wirkungsbeobachtung.pdf. [Successful cooperation – sustainable effects. Project results of the GTZ and its partners].

Gudeman, Stephen (1986): Economics as Culture: Models and Metaphors of Livelihood. London: Routhledge and Kegan Paul.

Hansen, Klaus P. (2000): Kultur und Kulturwissenschaft. Eine Einführung, 2. Auflage, Tübingen. [Culture and culture science].

Hedlund, G./D. Rolander (1990): Action in Heterarchies - New Approaches to Managing the MNC. In: C.A. Barlett/Y. Doz/G. Hedlund (eds.): Managing the Global Firm. London, New York: Routhledge, p. 15-46.

Heidenreich, Georg (1995): Die Schreiner von Kanungu. Aspekte der Sozialordnung in ugandischen Handwerksunternehmen. In: Von Oppen, Achim/ Rottenburg, Richard (eds.): Organisationswandel in Afrika: Kollektive Praxis und kulturelle Aneignung. Berlin: Das Arabische Buch, p. 53-66. [The carpenters of Kanungu. Aspects of social order in Ugandan artisan enterprises].

Hoffjan, Andreas/Weide, Gonn (2006): Management Control Systems in German Multinationals – Balancing Global Standardisation and Local Customisation. Presentation held at IFSAM 8th World Congress, September 28-30, 2006.

Hummel, Hartwig/Menzel, Ulrich (eds.)(2001): Die Ethnisierung internationaler Wirtschaftsbeziehungen und daraus resultierende Konflikte. Münster: Lit-Verlag. [The ethnisation of international economic relations and resulting conflicts].

Hüsken, Thomas (2004): Georg Elwert und die Berliner Schule der skeptischen Sozialanthropologie. In: Eckert, Julia (ed.): Anthropologie der Konflikte. Georg Elwerts konflikttheoretische Thesen in der Diskussion. Bielefeld: transcript Verlag, p. 315-330. [Georg Elwert and the Berlin school of sceptical social antrhopology].

Hüsken, Thomas (2006): Der Stamm der Experten. Rhetorik und Praxis des Interkulturellen Managements in der deutschen Entwicklungszusammenarbeit. Bielefeld: Transcript. [A tribe of experts. Rhetoric and practice of intercultural management in German development assistance].

Hyden, Göran (1980): Beyond Ujamaa in Tanzania. Underdevelopment and the Uncaptured Peasantry. London: Heineman.

International Monetary Fund (2012): Regional economic outlook. Sub-Saharan Africa. World economic and financial surveys. Washington, D.C.

InWEnT (2006): Business and the Millenium Development Goals: The Business Challenge Africa. Background Paper to the 11th International Business Forum 8 – 10 October. Bonn: InWEnt.

Jennings, Michael (2002): 'Almost an Oxfam in itself'. Oxfam, Ujamaa and Development in Tanzania. In: African Affairs 101, p. 509-530.

Jungraithmayr, Hermann (2002): Eine Welt aufschließen. Reflexionen zur Feldforschung. In: Storch, Anne/Leger/Rudolf (eds.): Die afrikanistische Feldforschung. Frankfurter Afrikanistische Blätter 14 (2002), Köln: Rüdiger Köppe Verlag, p. 9-15. [Opening up a world. Reflections about fieldwork].

Kallscheuer, Otto (2005): Der Vatikan als Global Player. In: Aus Politik und Zeitgeschichte, 7/2005, p. 7-14. [The Vatican as a global player].
Kappel, Robert et al. (eds.) (2003): Klein- und Mittelunternehmen in Entwicklungsländern. Die Herausforderungen der Globalisierung. Hamburg, Schriften des Deutschen Übersee-Instituts, No. 58. [Small and medium enterprises in developing countries. Challenges of globalisation].
Kaschuba, Wolfgang (1995): Kulturalismus: Vom Verschwinden des Sozialen im gesellschaftlichen Diskurs. In: Zeitschrift für Volkskunde, 91. Jhg., p. 27-46. [Culturalism: on the disappearance of the 'social' in societal discourse].
Kassimir (2001): Producing Local Politics: Governance, Representation and Non-State Organizations in Africa. In: In: Callaghy, Thomas/Kassimir, Ronald/Latham, Robert (eds.): Intervention and Transnationalism in Africa. Global-Local Networks of Power. Cambrige University Press: Cambridge, New York.
Kassimir, Ronald (2007): If you are part of the solution, you are likely part of the problem: Transboundary Formations in Africa. In: Tiyambe Zeleza, Paul (ed.): The Study of Africa; Volume 2: Global and Transnational Engagements, London: Zed Press and Dakar: Codesria.
Kassimir, Ronald/Latham, Robert (2001): Conclusion - Toward a new research agenda. In: Callaghy, Thomas/Kassimir, Ronald/Latham, Robert (eds.): Intervention and Transnationalism in Africa. Global-Local Networks of Power. Cambrige University Press: Cambridge, New York, p. 267-78.
Kaukab, Rashid (2006): Perspectives and Potential for South-South Trade.
Kienzler, Hanna (2005): Book Review: Weit hergeholte Fakten. Eine Parabel der Entwicklungshilfe. In: Anthropological Theory September 2005 5 (4), p. 304-307.
Kocka, Jürgen (2000): Management in der Industrialisierung. Die Entstehung und Entwicklung des klassischen Musters. In: Schreyögg, Georg (ed.): Funktionswandel im Management: Wege jenseits der Ordnung. 3. Berliner Colloquium der Gottlieb Daimler- und Carl Benz-Stiftung, Berlin 2000, p. 33-51. [Management during industrialisation. The emergence and development of the classical pattern].
Köhler, Benedikt (2004): Strukturen, Strategien und Integrationsformen transnationaler Konzerne. In: Soziale Welt 55 (2004), p. 29-50. [Structures and forms of integration of transnational corporations].
Kühl, Stefan (2004): Moden in der Entwicklungszusammenarbeit. Capacity Building und Capacity Development als neue Leitbilder von Entwicklungshilfeorganisationen. In: Soziale Welt 55 (2004), p. 231-262. [Fashions in development cooperation. Capacity building and capacity development as new concepts for development organisations].

Kuper, Hilda (1969): 'Strangers' in plural societies: Asians in South Africa and Uganda. In: Kuper, L /Smith, M.G. (eds.): Case studies in African pluralism. California: University of California Press.

Latham, Robert (2001): Identifying the contours of transboundary political life. In: Callaghy, Thomas/Ronald Kassimir/Robert Latham (eds.): Intervention and Transnationalism in Africa. Global-Local Networks of Power. Cambridge University Press: Cambrige, New York. p. 69-92.

Latham, Robert/Ronald Kassimir/Thomas Callaghy (2001): Introduction: transboundary formations, intervention, order, and authority. In: Callaghy, Thomas/Ronald Kassimir/Robert Latham (eds.): Intervention and Transnationalism in Africa. Global-Local Networks of Power. Cambridge University Press: Cambridge, New York, p. 1-22.

Leonard, David (1997): Professionalization. In: John Middelton et al.: Encyclopedia of Africa South of the Sahara, Volume 3, p. 508-509.

Lessem, R. (1996): From the Hunter to Rainmaker, the Southern African Businessphere. Randburg.

Lessem, Ronnie/Nussbaum, Barbara (1996): Sawubona Africa. Embracing the four worlds in South African management. Sandton: Zebra Press.

Lieten, Kristoffel (1999): Mondiale ondernemingen en scheefgroei: een vergeten vertoog. In: Hoebink, Paul/Haude, Detlev/Velden, Fons van der (eds.): Doorloopers en Breuklijnen. Van globalisering, emancipatie en verzet. Assen: Van Gorcum. p. 11-125. [Global companies and inequality: a forgotten issue].

Light, L./Karageorgis, G. (1994): The Ethnic Economy. In: N. J. Smelser, R. Swedberg (eds.): The Handbook of Economic Sociology. Princeton: Princeton Univ. Press, p. 467-671.

Lorenz, Andreas/Thielke, Thilo (2007): The Age of the Dragon. China's Concuest of Africa. In: Spiegel Online, May 30, 2007. http://www.spiegel.de/international/world/the-age-of-the-dragon-china-s-conquest-of-africa-a-484603.html

Lowi, Miriam R. (1993): Bridging the Divide: Transboundary Resource Disputes and the Case of West Bank Water. In: International Security, Vol. 18, No. 1 (Summer 1993), p. 113-138.

Luhmann, Niklas, 1988: Die Wirtschaft der Gesellschaft. Frankfurt a.M.: Suhrkamp. [The economy of society].

Mankekar, Purnima (2002): 'India Shopping': Indian Grocery Stores and Transnational Configurations of Belonging. In: Ethnos, vol. 67:1, 2002, p. 75 – 98.

Marcus, George E. (1986): Contemporary Problems of Ethnography in the Modern World system. In: Clifford, James/Marcus, George E.: Writing Culture. The Poetics and Politics of Ethnography. Berkeley/Los Angeles: University of California Press.

Marcus, George E. (1995): Ethnography in/of the World System: The Emergence of Multi-Sited Ethnography. In: Annual Review of Anthropology, 24, 1995, p. 95-117.

Mayntz, Renate/Scharpf, Fritz W. (1995): Der Ansatz des akteurbezogenen Institutionalismus. In: Mayntz, Renate /Scharpf, Fritz W. (eds.): Gesellschaftliche Selbstregelung und politische Steuerung. Frankfurt a.M.: Campus, p. 39–72. [The approach of actor centred institutionalism].

Mbigi, L. (1997): Ubuntu: the African Dream in Management. Randburg.

Meyer, John W/Brian Rowan (1991): Institutional Organizations: Formal Structure as Myth and Ceremony. In: Walter Powell/DiMaggio, Paul (Hrsg.): The New Institutionalism in Organizational Analysis. Chicago, London: The University of Chicago Press. p. 41-62. [Note: Meyer/Rowan (1991) is a reprint of the classical 1977 article in American Journal of Sociology, 83, p. 340-363.]

Meyer, Marshall/Zucker, Lynne (1989): Permanently Failing Organizations. Newbury Park: Sage.

Morris, H.S. (1968): The Indians in Uganda. A Study of caste and sect in a plural society. Chicago: University of Chicago Press.

Mouly, V. Suchitra/Sankaran, Jayram K. (1995): Organizational Ethnography. An Illustrative Applikation in the Study of Indian R&D Settings. New Delhi: Sage Publications.

Nadai, Eva/Maeder, Christoph (2005): Fuzzy Fields. Multi-Sited Ethnography in Sociological Research. In: Forum Qualitative Social Research, Volume 6, No. 3, Art. 28. September 2005.

Nixon, Ron (2007): Africa, offline: Waiting for the Web. In: New York Times, 22 July 2007. http://www.nytimes.com/2007/07/22/business/yourmoney/22rwanda.html, 08 August 2011.

Niedner-Kalthoff, Ulrike (2005): Ständige Vertretung. Ein Ethnographie diplomatischer Lebenswelten. Bielefeld: transcript Verlag. [Permanent representation: An ethnography of diplomatic life-worlds].

North, D. (1990). Institutions. Institutional Change and Economic Performance. Cambridge: Cambridge University Press.

Northrup, David (1995): Indentured Labor in the age of imperialism, 1834 -1922. Cambridge: Cambridge University Press.

NRI & PIO Division (2001): Report of the High Level committee on the Indian Diaspora. Ministry of External Affairs, New Delhi. http://indiandiaspora.nic.in/contents.htm, 21 November 2012.

Ntihabose, Moise Mugabo (2003): Svensk-kinyarwanda ordbok. (Göteborg africana informal series, no 2.) Compiled by Jouni Maho. Göteborg University:

Dept of Oriental and African Languages. [Swedish – Kinyarwanda dictionary].

Oberkircher, Volker (2006): Die deutsche Greencard aus der Sicht indischer IT-Experten. In: Brosius, Christiane/Goel, Urmila (eds.): masala.de. Menschen aus Südasien in Deutschland. Heidelberg: Draupadi-Verlag. [The German greencard from the virwpoint of Indian IT experts].

Obi, Cyril (2001): Global, state, and local intersections: power, authority, and conflict in the Niger Delta oil communities. In: Thomas Callaghy/Ronald Kassimir/Robert Latham (Hrsg.): Intervention and Transnationalism in Africa. Global-Local Networks of Power. Cambridge, p. 173-193.

OECD (2006): 2006 Survey on Monitoring the Paris Declaration. Country Chapter: Rwanda. www.oecd.org/dataoecd/32/32/38920147.pdf.

Olivier de Sardan, Jean-Pierre (1995): La politique du terrain. Enquete 1, p. 71-112.

Orrells, Daniel, Gurminder K. Bhambra, and Tessa Roynon (2011, eds.): African Athena. New Agendas. Oxford.

Pearson, Michael N. (1998): Port Cities and Intruders: The Swahili Coast, India, and Portugal in the Early Modern Era. Baltimore, Maryland.

Ponte, Stefano (2004): The politics of ownership: Tanzanian coffee policy in the age of liberal Reformism. In: African Affairs, 103/413, p. 615–633.

Porter, M. (1980) Competitive Strategy, Free Press, New York, 1980.

Portes, Alejandro/Guarnizo, Luis E./ Landholt, Patricia (1999): The study of transnationalism: pitfalls and promises of an emergent research field. In: Ethnic and Racial Studies 22, p. 217-237.

Pouliot, Robert (2006): Governance, Transparency, and Accountability in the Microfinance Investment Fund Industry. In: Mattäus-Maier, Ingrid/Pischke, J.D. Von (eds.): Microfinance Investment Funds. Leveraging Private Capital for Economic Growth and Poverty Reduction. Berlin: Springer & KFW Entwicklungsbank, p. 147-174.

Powell, Walter W./DiMaggio, Paul J. (1991): The New Institutionalism in Organizational Analysis. Chicago: University of Chicago Press.

Preisendörfer, Peter (2005): Organisationssoziologie. Grundlagen, Theorien und Problemstellungen. Wiesbaden: VS Verlag. [Organisation sociology. Foundations, theories and problems].

Rae, Douglas/Taylor, Michael (1970): The Analysis of Political Cleavages. New Haven: Yale University Press.

Reckwitz, Andreas (1997): Struktur: zur sozialwissenschaftlichen Analyse von Regeln und Regelmäßigkeiten. Opladen: Westdeutscher Verlag. [Structure: on the social science of the analysis of regularities and patterns].

Reis, Michele (2004): Theorizing Diaspora: Perspectives on "Classical" and "Contemporary" Diaspora. In: International Migration 42 (2), p. 41-56.
Rieder, Christoph (2005): Trust and Germany's Economy. Munich: GRIN Publishing GmbH.
Robertson, Roland (1998): Glokalisierung: Homogenität und Heterogenität in Raum und Zeit. In: Beck, Ulrich (ed.): Perspektiven der Weltgesellschaft. Frankfurt/M: Suhrkamp, p. 192-220. [Glocalisation: homogeneity in space and time].
Ronge, Marius (2001): The Role of Organization for Multinational Companies in China. Dissertation der Universität St. Gallen Nr. 2557, Hochschule für Wirtschafts-, Rechts-, und Sozialwissenschaften. Bamberg: Difo-Druck Gmbh.
Rosaldo, Renato JR (1999): A Note on Geertz as a Cultural Essayist. In: Sherry B. Orther (ed.): The Fate of "Culture". Geertz and Beyond. Berkeley: University of California Press, p. 30-34.
Rottenburg, Richard (2000): Accountability for development aid. In: Kalthoff, Herbert/Rottenburg, Richard/Wagener, Hans-Jürgen (eds.): Facts and figures. Economic representations and practices. Jahrbuch Ökonomie und Gesellschaft 16. Metropolis, p. 143-173.
Rottenburg, Richard (2002): Weit hergeholte Fakten. Eine Parabel der Entwicklungshilfe. Stuttgart: Lucius. [Far fetched facts. A parable of development aid].
Rottenburg, Richard (2005): Code-switching, or why a metacode is good to have. In: Czarniawska, Barbara/Sevon, Guje: Global ideas. How ideas, objects and practices travel in the global econcomy. Liber AB, p. 259-274.
Rottenburg, Richard (2006): Social Constructivism and the Enigma of Strangeness. In: Rottenburg, Richard/Schnepel, Burkhard/Shimada, Shingo (eds.) The Making and Unmaking of Differences. Anthropological, Sociological and Philosophical Perspectives. Bielefeld: transcript Verlag, p. 27-42.
Rottenburg, Richard (2006a): Untrivializing Difference. A Personal Introduction. In: Rottenburg, Richard/Schnepel, Burkhard/Shimada, Shingo (eds.): The Making and Unmaking of Differences. Anthropological, Sociological and Philosophical Perspectives. Bielefeld: transcript Verlag, p. 7-12.
Rottenburg, Richard (2009): Far-Fetched Facts. A Parable of Development Aid. Cambridge: MIT Press.
Rwanda Development Gateway (2005): Intercontinental boss sacked. 4th September 2005.
Sachs, Wolfgang (1992): One World. In: ibid: The Development Dictionary. A guide to Knowledge as Power. Johannesburg: Witwatersrand University Press, p. 102-115.

Sachs, Wolfgang (1992a): Introduction. In: ibd. (ed): The Development Dictionary. A guide to Knowledge as Power. Johannesburg: Witwatesrand University Press, Zed Books, p.1-5.

Sanday, P.R. (1979): The Ethnographic Paradigm(s). In: Administrative Science Quarterly, 24, p. 527-38.

Scharpf, Fritz W. (1997): Games Real Actors Play. Actor-Centered Institutionalism in Policy Research. Boulder, CO/ Oxford: Westview Press.

Scherer, Andreas Georg (1999): Kritik der Organisation oder Organisation der Kritik? – Wissenschaftstheoretische Bemerkungen zum kritischen Umgang mit Organisationstheorien. In: Alfred Kieser: Organisationstheorien. 3. Aufl. Stuttgart: Kohlhammer, p. 1-37. [Criticising organisations or organising cristicism? - Epismetological notes on a critical application of organisation theories].

Scheumann, Waltina/Neubert, Susanne (eds.)(2006): Transboundary Water Management in Africa. Challenges for Development Cooperation. Study for the research and consutancy project 'Cooperation on Africa's transboundary water resources' on behalf of the Ministry for Economic Cooperation and Development (BMZ). Bonn: Dt. Institut für Entwicklungspolitik (DIE).

Schmundt, Hilmar (2006): Internet in jede Hütte. In: Der Spiegel, 52/2006, p. 128-130. [Internet into every hut].

Schreyögg, Georg (1996): Organisation. Grundlagen moderner Organisationsgestaltung. Wiesbaden. [Organisation. Foundations of modern organisation design].

Schreyögg, Georg (2000): Funktionswandel im Management: Problemaufriß und Thesen. In: ibid. (ed.): Funktionswandel im Management: Wege jenseits der Ordnung, Berlin, p. 15-32.

Scott, J.C. (1976): The Moral Economy of the Peasant: Subsistence and Rebellion in South-East Asia. New Haven.

Scott, Richard (1995): Institutions and Organizations. Thousand Oaks, London.

Scott, Richard (2003): Organizations: Rational, Natural, and Open Systems. 5th edition. Upper Saddle River: Prentice-Hall.

Shearer, David (1998): Private Armies and Military Intervention. Adelphi Papers. Routledge.

Sorensen, Pernille (2000): Money is the True Friend. Economic Practice, Morality and Trust among the Iganga Maize Traders in Uganda. (Anthropology and Development; 4), Hamburg: Lit.

Sosoe, Lukas K. (2006): Critical Note. Is African Philosophy different? In: Rottenburg, Richard/Schnepel, Burkhard/Shimada, Shingo (eds.) The Making and

Unmaking of Differences. Anthropological, Sociological and Philosophical Perspectives. Bielefeld: transcript Verlag, p. 61-66.

Soyinka, Wole (2006): Die verlorenen Dialoge der Zivilisation. In: Blätter für deutsche und internationale Politik, 3/2006, p. 337-344. [The lost dialogues of civilisation].

Spies, Eva (2009): Das Dogma der Partizipation. Interkulturelle Kontakte im Kontext der Entwicklungszusammenarbeit in Niger. Mainzer Beiträge zur Afrikaforschung, Köln: Rüdiger Köppe Verlag. [The dogma of participation. Intercultural contacts in the context of development cooperation in Niger].

Taylor, Ian (2003): Conflict in Central Africa: Clandestine Networks & Regional/Global Configurations. In: Review of African Political Economy No. 95, p. 45-55.

The Economist (2000): The world's view of multinationals. The Economist, 29 January, 2000, p.19.

The Economist (2000a): Business in difficult places. Risky returns. The Economist, 20 May, 2000, p. 101-102.

The Economist (2007): Keep looking ahead. Rwanda. The Economist, January 13, 2007. p. 35-36.

The Economist (2012): Africa's Singapore? A country with a bloody history seeks prosperity by becoming business-friendly. The Economist, 25 Feb 25, 2012.

The Monitor (2007): Indians Aid Flood Victims. Kampala, November 2, 2007.

The Nation (2008): Rwanda: 'Hotel Rwanda' a Myth Created By Hollywood, Says New Book (book review). Nairobi, March 24, 2008.

The New Times (2008): Kagame woos German investors to Rwanda, April 26, 2008.

THISDAY (2007): Time for continent to insist in defining its own future. Opinion by Paul Kagame. THISDAY Tanzania, October 5, 2007.

Tölölyan, Kaching (1997): The Nation-State and its Others: In Lieu of a Preface. In: Diaspora 1, p. 3-7.

Trouillot, Michel-Rolph (2002): Adieu, Culture: A New Duty Arises. In: Fox, Richard/King, Barbara (eds.): Anthropology beyond Culture. Berg Publishers.

Turner, Thomas (2007): The Congo Wars: Conflict, Myth, and Reality. New York: Zed Books.

Turok, B. (1993): South Africa's skyscraper economy: growth or development, in Hallowes, D. (ed.), Hidden Face: Environment, Development and Justice: South Africa and the Global Context. Scottsville: Earthlife Africa.

Udehn, Lars (2002): The Changing Face of Methodological Individualism. In: Annual Review of Sociology, Jg. 28 (2002), p. 479–507.

UN Industrial Development Organisation (2002). Corporate Social Responsibility and Developing Country SMEs, Vienna: UNIDO.

Uvin, Peter (1998): Aiding Violence. The Development Business in Rwanda. West Hartfort: Kumarian Press.

Uvin, Peter (2001): Difficult choices in the new post-conflict agenda: the international community in Rwanda after the genocide. In: Third World Quarterly 22 (2001).

Van Dijk, Meine Pieter (ed.)(2009): The New Presence of China in Africa. Amsterdam: Amsterdam University Press.

Vlassenroot, Koen/ Raeymaekers, T. (2005): The Formation of Profit, Power and Protection. Conflict and Social Transformation in Eastern DR Congo. Occasional Papers from the Centre of African Studies, Copenhagen.

Von Oppen, Achim/ Rottenburg, Richard (eds.): Organisationswandel in Afrika: Kollektive Praxis und kulturelle A neignung. Berlin: Das Arabische Buch.

Wadhwani, Anita (1998): Working Overtime. India Currents. Dec. 98–Jan. 99, p. 44–46.

Walgenbach, Peter (1999): Institutionalistische Ansätze in der Organisationstheorie. In: Alfred Kieser (ed.): Organisationstheorien. 3. Aufl. Stuttgart: Kohlhammer, p. 319-345. [Institutionalist approaches in organisation theory].

Warnier, Jean-Pierre (1995): Around a plantation: the ethnography of business in Cameroon. In: Daniel Miller (ed.) (1995): Worlds Apart. Modernity through the prism of the local. Routhledge, London and New York, p. 91-109.

Wester, Fred (1987/1995): Strategieen voor kwalitatief onderzock. Bussum: Coutinho. [Qualitative research strategies].

Wild, Volker (1997): Profit not for profit's sake: history and business culture of African entrepreneurs in Zimbabwe. Harare: Baobab Books, Oxford: African Books Collective.

Williamson, Oliver (1985): The Economic Institutions of Capitalism. New York: Free Press.

Williamson, Oliver (1990): Die ökonomischen Institutionen des Kapitalismus. Tübingen.

Wittgenstein, Ludwig (1922/1988): Tractatus Logico-Philosophicus. London: Kegan Paul.

Wolf, Eric (1997): Europe and the people without history. Berkeley, London: University of California Press.

Wolff, Jürgen H. (2005): Entwicklungshilfe – Ein hilfreiches Gewerbe? Münster: LIT. [Development aid – a helpful trade?].

Wood, Geoffrey (2004): Business and politics in a criminal state: The case of Equatorial Guinea. In: African Affairs, 103/413, p. 547-567.

World Bank and International Finance Corporation (2006): Doing Business in 2006: Creating Jobs.Washington, D.C, World Bank and IFC.
World Bank and World Bank Institute (2005): Business Action for the MDGs: Private Sector Involvement as a Vital Factor in Achieving the Millennium Development Goals.
World Bank Institute (2006): Business and the Millennium Development Goals. Business & Development Discussion Papers, Paper No.4.
World Bank Institute, InWEnt, Instituto Ethos and The Global Compact (2005): Fighting Poverty: A Business Opportunity, Report of the 10th International Business Forum.
World Bank/Public-Private Infrastructure Advisory Facility (2005): Private Solutions for Infrastructure in Rwanda. A Country Framework Report. Washington: World Bank.
World Bank (2009): Global Economic Prospects 2009. New York.
World Bank (2011): Global Economic Prospects 2011. New York.
World Bank (2014): Global Economic Prospects 2014. New York.
World Bank and International Finance Corporation (2011): Doing Business: Making a Difference for Entrepreneurs 2011. Washington, D.C, World Bank and IFC.
World Bank and International Finance Corporation (2012): Doing Business in the East African Community 2012. Washington, D.C, World Bank and IFC.
Zachary, Pascal (2007): Startup: Rwanda. In: CNN Money.com/Business 2.0 Magazine, August 1, 2007. http://money.cnn.com/magazines/business2/business2_archive/2007/08/01/100138832/index.htm, 17 September 2008.
Zapf, Wolfgang (2004): Modernization Theory – in the Non-Western World. In: WeltTrends 44 (Herbst). 12. Jahrgang, 2004, p. 100-107.
Zevenbergen, Aernout (2002): Bye bye, bwana. Afscheid van de Ontwikkelingswerker. In: Internationale Samenwerking, number 10, October 2002, p. 32-37. [Bye bye bwana. Farewell to the development expert].
Ziltener, Patrick (2006): Die Gesellschaftliche Heterogenität der Länder Afrikas und Asiens und ihre Entwicklungsrelevanz. In: Zeitschrift für Soziologie, Jg. 35, Heft 4, August 2006, p. 286-304. [Societal Heterogeneity in Africa and Asia: a Comparative Analysis of Its Impact on Development].
Znaniecki, F. (1934): The Method of Sociology. New York: Farrar and Reinehart.

LIST OF ABBREVIATIONS

COMESA – Common Market for Eastern and Southern Africa
DR Congo/DRC – Democratic Republic of the Congo
EU – European Union
Expat – colloquial for 'expatriate', foreign individual
FDI – Foreign Direct Investment
FRW – Francs Rwandaises / Rwandan Francs
GAAS – Generally Accepted Accounting Standards
HIPC – Heavily Indebted Poor Countries
ICT – information and communications technologies
IMF – International Monetary Fund
IRIN – Integrated Regional Information Networks
ISO – International Organization for Standardization
IT – information technologies
LDC – least developed country
MDG – Millennium Development Goals
MNC – Multinational Corporation
MNE – Multinational Enterprise
MW – Megawatt
NGO – Non Governmental Organisation
NIE – New Institutional Economics
NRI – Non Residential Indian
ODA – Official Development Assistance
PIO – Person of Indian Origin
PPP – Public Private Partnership
PSP – private sector participation
ROI – return on investment
SME – Small and Medium Enterprises
TBC – Transboundary Cooperation
UN – United Nations
UNDP – United Nations Development Programme
UNIDO – United Nations Industrial Development Organization

LIST OF FIGURES

Diagram 1:
Relationships between institutionalisation and local assimilation | 182

LIST OF TABLES

Table 1:
Local assimilation vs. transterritorial enclaves | 153

Table 2:
Institutionalisation vs. technical orientation | 163

Table 3:
Key characteristics of 'diversity' and 'difference' | 169